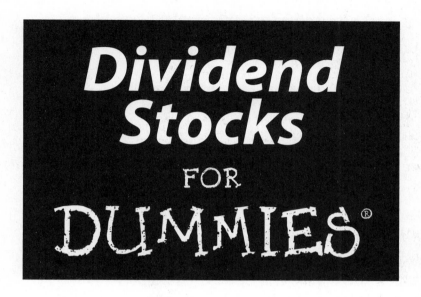

Dividend Stocks FOR DUMMIES®

by Lawrence Carrel

WILEY

Wiley Publishing, Inc.

Dividend Stocks For Dummies®

Published by
Wiley Publishing, Inc.
909 Third Avenue
New York, NY 10022
www.wiley.com

Copyright © 2010 by Wiley Publishing, Inc., Indianapolis, Indiana

Published by Wiley Publishing, Inc., Indianapolis, Indiana

Published simultaneously in Canada

For general information on our other products and services, please contact our Customer Care Department within the U.S. at 877-762-2974, outside the U.S. at 317-572-3993, or fax 317-572-4002.

For technical support, please visit www.wiley.com/techsupport.

Wiley also publishes its books in a variety of electronic formats. Some content that appears in print may not be available in electronic books.

Library of Congress Control Number: 2010924587

ISBN: 978-0-470-46601-8

Manufactured in the United States of America

10 9 8 7 6 5 4 3 2 1

WILEY

About the Author

Lawrence Carrel is a seasoned financial journalist and author of *ETFs for the Long Run: What They Are, How They Work, and Simple Strategies for Successful Long-Term Investing* (Wiley). He currently writes a blog of the same name at www.ETFsForTheLongRun.com.

After working as a newspaper reporter and editor, Carrel got in on the ground floor of the online publishing business when financial news entered the Internet age. As a founding staff member of The Wall Street Journal.com, he was one of the original writers of its *Cyber Investing* column and among the first to write about small stocks for the Web. Later at SmartMoney.com, his daily market commentary tracked the dot-com bubble and the crash of 2000. A year later, he created *SmartMoney*'s daily online hot stocks column, *The One-Day Wonder*. Over five years, he reported on nearly 1,200 different companies in almost every industry.

In 2006, Carrel originated SmartMoney.com's *Under the Radar* column, which looked for investments among small stocks, and the *ETF Focus* column just as the exchange-traded fund (ETF) industry began its era of explosive growth. In 2007, he took over the weekly ETF and mutual funds columns at TheStreet.com. While there, Carrel predicted the 2008 stock market decline in August 2007 and told readers to start shorting the market with ETFs. He was also the first to report on the connection between the subprime mortgage crisis and the plunge in municipal bonds. And a year before it happened, he was the first to focus on the possibility of money market funds "breaking the buck."

For three years, Carrel served as a daily contributor to *The Wall Street Journal This Morning* radio show and has been a guest commentator on MSNBC, CNN, and numerous other news networks. He has addressed the NASDAQ Stock Market as an ETF expert, and served as a founding featured journalist on The Investor Network, a social network for investors. In addition, his work has appeared in *The Wall Street Journal, Barron's Online,* Bankrate.com, *The Big Money, ETF Report, Financial Planning, Hard Assets Investor,* IndexUniverse.com, and *Structured Products*. In a break from financial journalism, Carrel worked as a contributing editor on the college humor compilation, *Lunacy: The Best of the Cornell Lunatic* (Lunatic Press). A native of Buffalo, New York, and a graduate of Cornell University, he lives in New York City with his two sons.

Dedication

To Judy Hayes, who believed in me when no one else did.

Author's Acknowledgments

Thanks to acquisitions editor Stacy Kennedy, who chose me to author this book, ironed out all the preliminary details to make the book possible, and exhibited incredible patience, faith, and understanding during the process. I'm extremely grateful to Joe Kraynak, a gifted editor and collaborator, who was instrumental in helping me complete this book; my wonderful agent, Marilyn Allen at Allen OShea Literary Agency, for getting me on this project; and Russell Wild, for recommending me to Marilyn.

Alissa Schwipps, my project editor, deserves a loud cheer for serving as a gifted editor — shuffling chapters back and forth, shepherding the text and graphics through production, making sure any technical issues were properly resolved, and serving as the unofficial quality control manager. Megan Knoll, copy editor, earns an award for ferreting out my typos and grammatical errors, making things clearer to understand, and fixing other language foe paws (or is it faux pas?), in addition to assisting Alissa as reader advocate. I also tip my hat to the production crew for doing such an outstanding job of transforming a loose collection of matchbook covers, napkins, scraps of paper, and illustrations into such an attractive bound book. Thanks to technical editor Noel Jameson for flagging technical errors in the manuscript and offering his advice from the world of dividend stock investing.

I want to thank the following people for giving their time to help me acquire the information necessary to write this book: Stuart Bell of WisdomTree Investments, Gary Bradshaw of Hodges Capital Management, John Buckingham of Al Frank Asset Management, Jennifer Connelly of JCPR, Anthony Corrao of Oppenheimer & Co., Lauren DeSanto of Morningstar, Jaime Doyle of SunStar, Mark Farber of Weiser LLP., Tom Forsha of Aston/ RiverRoad Dividend All Cap Value Fund, Dan Genter of RNC Genter Capital Management, Carol Grauman of JCPR, David Guarino of Standard & Poor's, Kathryn Hyatt of The Vanguard Group, Frank Ingarra of the Hennessey Funds, Rebecca Katz of The Vanguard Group, Naomi Kim of Dow Jones Indexes, Tony Kono of SunStar, Annette Larson of Morningstar, John R. Lieberman of Perelson Weiner LLP., Ivy McLemore of Invesco Aim, Melissa Murphy of SunStar, Vita Nelson of The MoneyPaper, Lisa Osofsky of Weiser LLP., Rebecca Patterson of Dow Jones Indexes, Josh Peters of Morningstar,

Steven M. Rogé of R. W. Rogé & Co., Bill Rogers of Mergent, Tom Roseen of ThomsonReuters, Henry Sanders of Aston/RiverRoad Dividend All Cap Value Fund, Jeremy Schwartz of WisdomTree Investments, Kevin Shacknofsky of Alpine Funds, Howard Silverblatt of Standard & Poor's, Jordan Smyth Jr. of Edgemoor Investment Advisors, Nadine Youssef of Morningstar, and William Zimmerman of Morgan, Lewis & Bockius.

I also want to thank my friends and family for their love and support: Kirsten Mogg, Judy Carrel, Jerome Carrel, Jackson Carrel, Janice Carrel, Marc Carrel, Theo Carrel, Darrin Greene, Nick Wade, Steven Fox for his legal help, and Greg Candela for the beer. I also owe an enormous amount of gratitude to Sterling Barrett and Joe Barello, who saved this project by procuring for me on short-notice a top-notch computer when both my desktop and laptop died a week before this book was due.

Publisher's Acknowledgments

We're proud of this book; please send us your comments at http://dummies.custhelp.com. For other comments, please contact our Customer Care Department within the U.S. at 877-762-2974, outside the U.S. at 317-572-3993, or fax 317-572-4002.

Some of the people who helped bring this book to market include the following:

Acquisitions, Editorial, and Media Development

Senior Project Editor: Alissa Schwipps

Contributor: Joe Kraynak

Acquisitions Editor: Stacy Kennedy

Copy Editor: Megan Knoll

Assistant Editor: Erin Calligan Mooney

Editorial Program Coordinator: Joe Niesen

Technical Editor: Noel Jameson

Senior Editorial Manager: Jennifer Ehrlich

Editorial Assistants: Rachelle Amick, Jennette ElNaggar

Senior Editorial Assistant: David Lutton

Cover Photos: © Steven Puetzer/Getty Images

Cartoons: Rich Tennant (www.the5thwave.com)

Composition Services

Project Coordinator: Kristie Rees

Layout and Graphics: Ashley Chamberlain

Proofreaders: Cara L. Buitron, Lindsay Littrell

Indexer: Sharon Shock

Publishing and Editorial for Consumer Dummies

    Diane Graves Steele, Vice President and Publisher, Consumer Dummies

    Kristin Ferguson-Wagstaffe, Product Development Director, Consumer Dummies

    Ensley Eikenburg, Associate Publisher, Travel

    Kelly Regan, Editorial Director, Travel

Publishing for Technology Dummies

    Andy Cummings, Vice President and Publisher, Dummies Technology/General User

Composition Services

    Debbie Stailey, Director of Composition Services

Contents at a Glance

Table of Contents

Introduction

*T*he purpose of the stock market is to enable companies to raise the capital they need to start or grow their businesses. Instead of borrowing money from a bank and paying interest on it, a company can sell shares of itself to investors. Over the years, the stock market has gone from being a respectable venue for investors to purchase partial ownership in companies to something more akin to a casino. Seduced by reports of individuals earning millions nearly overnight by investing in high-growth stocks, speculative investors poured money into many companies that offered nothing more than a promise of sales and profits, further inflating share prices. When the needle point of reality finally popped the bubble, the poor unfortunates who failed to cash out their chips early enough were blown away like dust.

Fortunately, the deflated bubble (along with some dividend-friendly tax legislation) brought many investors down to earth and back to the basics — investing in companies with a proven track record of earning profits and paying dividends. As they return to the fold, investors are beginning to realize what their parents, grandparents, and great-grandparents already knew — dividend investing offers a host of benefits that provide a safer and often more profitable way to invest in the stock market.

Dividend investing is nothing new. In fact, since 1602, when the Dutch East India Company became the first corporation to issue stock, dividends have been the primary way for investors to receive profits from their investments without dissolving the company or selling the investment. However, following a dividend-investment strategy is new to many modern investors who've been focused solely on growth investing. If you count yourself among this crowd or are just starting out and plan on investing in dividend stocks, you've come to the right place. *Dividend Stocks For Dummies* contains all you need to know to develop your strategy, find and evaluate potentially good dividend stocks, manage your portfolio, and avoid the most common and critical mistakes.

About This Book

I'd love to be able to hand you a list of stocks and send you off with instructions to buy each one, but investing doesn't work that way. Every investor is different. You have a unique personality, specific goals, and a tolerance for risk that's different from your neighbors next door or across the street. Every company is different, too, operating in a specific industry, offering unique products and services, and being managed to varying levels of success. As an investor, your goal is to pair yourself up with investment opportunities that are a suitable match. That's what this book is all about.

In *Dividend Stocks For Dummies,* I present the idea of dividend investing and lead you through a process of self-examination to determine the type of investor you are, identify your goals, and develop an overall strategy that can move you most efficiently (and safely) from point A to point B. I show you how to find promising candidates and how to then evaluate them by using time-tested criteria so that you choose the best stocks to meet your needs. I mention some historically well-performing stocks you may want to check out, show you various ways to buy and sell shares, and offer guidance on managing your portfolio after you've purchased some shares.

The best part about this reference book is that *you* decide where to start and what to read. I've written every chapter to stand on its own, so you can start at the beginning of the book or pick any chapter from the table of contents and dig in.

As you read, keep one important point in mind: Past performance of a stock is no guarantee of future returns. I know, I know — you've heard that one before. But it's worth repeating. What it boils down to is this: If I mention a company in this book that I think is a potentially good dividend stock, don't assume I'm telling you to buy it. You may want to look into it, but I'm not necessarily recommending it. After all, by the time you read this book, that stallion of a stock may be a bust. Whatever you invest your money in or spend your money on is entirely your choice. I provide some guidance in picking stocks that may be likely to outperform other stocks, but I provide no specific recommendations. Take all the credit for your good investment decisions, but take all the blame for bad ones, too.

Conventions Used in This Book

I use several conventions in this book to call your attention to certain items. For example:

- ✔ *Italics* highlight new, somewhat technical terms that I follow up with straightforward, easy-to-understand definitions.

- ✔ **Boldface** text indicates key words in bulleted and instructive steps numbered lists.

- ✔ Monofont highlights Web and e-mail addresses.

- ✔ When this book was printed, some Web addresses may have needed to break across two lines of text. If that happened, rest assured that we haven't put in any extra characters (such as hyphens) to indicate the break. So, when using one of these Web addresses, just type in exactly what you see in this book, pretending as though the line break doesn't exist.

What You're Not to Read

You can safely skip anything you see in a gray shaded box. We stuck this material in a box (actually called a *sidebar*) for the same reason that most people stick stuff in boxes — to get it out of the way, so you wouldn't trip over it. However, you may find the case studies and brief asides in the sidebars engaging, entertaining, and perhaps even mildly informative. You can also pass over text tagged with a Technical Stuff icon; it's technical or historical information that isn't vital to understanding the topic at hand.

Foolish Assumptions

While writing this book, I made a few foolish assumptions, mainly about you and how much you know about investing:

- You have a general understanding of investing and your investment options, including CDs (certificates of deposit), money market funds, stocks, bonds, mutual funds, real estate, and so on. If you don't, check out *Investing For Dummies,* 5th Edition, by Eric Tyson (Wiley).

- You grasp the basics of stock market investing. I provide a brief refresher in Chapter 2, but to develop a deeper understanding, check out *Stock Investing For Dummies,* 3rd Edition, by Paul Mladjenovic (Wiley).

- You realize that investing always carries some risk, that some risks are greater than others, and that *not* investing can also be risky.

- You have some money (capital) to invest. It doesn't need to be stuffed in your pocket or sitting in a bank account. It can be money you already have invested, perhaps sitting in an IRA or 401(k).

- You want a safer way to invest your hard-earned dollars, so you're interested in introducing or adding more dividend stocks to your portfolio.

How This Book Is Organized

Although I encourage you to read this book from cover to cover to maximize the return on your investment, *Dividend Stocks For Dummies* presents the information in easily digestible chunks so that you can skip to the chapter or section that grabs your attention or meets your current needs, master it, and then skip to another section or simply set the book aside for later reference.

To help you navigate, I divvy the 22 chapters that make up the book into six parts. The following sections provide a quick overview of what's covered in each part.

Part I: Introducing Dividend Investing Basics

Share prices grab headlines. Dividends don't. As a result, investors are often in the dark about dividend investing, even if they're well-schooled in picking stocks based on share price alone.

In this part, I bring you up to speed with a brief primer on dividend investing, explore dividend stocks in a little more detail, and then reveal over a half-dozen advantages that dividend stocks offer.

Part II: Selecting an Investment Approach and Picking Stocks

Picking stocks is like playing matchmaker for yourself. When you're looking for a date, you need to know who you are and what you're looking for before you start skimming the personal ads. In the same way, you need to know what type of investor you are and your overall investment strategy so that you can find a suitable match.

The first couple of chapters in this part show you how to perform an investor self-assessment, which includes gauging your tolerance for risk, so that you can determine what kind of investor you are and what situation you're in. Based on the results of this assessment, you can choose the investment approach that's likely to be best for you. Finally, in the last two chapters of the part, I show you how to identify stocks that pay dividends and then how to evaluate them to pick the best dividend-paying stocks of the bunch.

Part III: Exploring Income-Generating Industries

The stock market groups businesses by market sector, which can be a single industry or a combination of connected industries, including consumer staples, energy, transportation, technology, utilities, and health care. Companies in certain sectors are more likely to pay dividends than companies in other sectors. In addition, some companies within a sector are generally better income-generating (dividend-paying) companies than others.

The chapters in this part introduce you to the sectors that are better known for paying dividends. For each sector, I explain the types of companies included in the sector, why companies in the sector are more likely than companies in other sectors to pay dividends, and what to look for when considering companies in this sector. For each sector, I also provide a list of companies that have had a pretty good track record for paying dividends.

Part IV: Checking Out Dividend Investment Vehicles

Not so long ago in a land not very far away, the only way to invest in the stock market was to buy shares directly from the company or from other investors. Since then, some inventive souls have developed all sorts of ways to buy and sell shares. This part introduces you to the most common and effective methods as they relate specifically to dividend investing.

Here, you discover how to reinvest your dividends one drop at a time with dividend reinvestment plans (DRIPs), eliminate the middleman (or woman) with direct purchase programs (DPPs), diversify through mutual funds and exchange-traded funds (ETFs), and invest in foreign companies that pay dividends without having to exchange your dollars for euros or yen.

Part V: Managing Your Portfolio

Although other parts of this book address the intricacies of dividend investing, including analyzing specific companies, this part takes a step back to reveal big-picture tasks, including coming up with a solid strategy, examining various ways to buy and sell shares, and monitoring tax legislation so that you can keep more of your earnings.

Part VI: The Part of Tens

Every *For Dummies* book includes a Part of Tens, and I didn't want to be the first author to break rank, so I included one in this book, too. In this part, I cover the ten most prevalent myths and misconceptions about dividends and ten common dividend investing mistakes (along with suggestions on how to avoid them). As a bonus, the end of the book also includes an appendix of Dividend Acheivers.

Icons Used in This Book

Throughout this book, you can spot icons in the margins that call your attention to different types of information. Here are the icons I use and a brief description of each:

Everything in this book is important, but some of it's more important. When you see this icon, read the text next to it not once but two or three times to brand it on your brain cells.

Tips provide insider insight from behind the scenes. When you're looking for a better, faster, safer, and/or cheaper way to do something, check out these tips.

This icon appears when you need to be extra vigilant or seek professional help before moving forward.

Investing has its fair share of highly specialized language and concepts that typically flies above the heads of mere mortals. Whenever I explain something highly technical, I flag it with this icon so that you know what's coming.

Where to Go From Here

Dividend Stocks For Dummies is designed to appeal to a universal audience of intermediate and experienced investors at all stages of developing and managing their investment portfolios.

For the new dividend stock investor, I recommend you read the book from cover to cover starting with Chapter 1. More experienced divided stock investors who already know themselves and their goals and have an effective strategy in place to reach those goals may want to skip to Chapter 7, where I show you how to track down income-generating, dividend paying stocks, or Chapter 8, where I show you how to evaluate them.

Regardless of your experience, however, feel free to skip around and read whatever catches your interest. Each and every tidbit of knowledge and insight you acquire can only serve to make you a more astute investor.

Part I
Introducing Dividend Investing Basics

The 5th Wave   By Rich Tennant

"It's surprising considering his portfolio is so conservative."

In this part . . .

If you can't tell the difference between dividend stock and livestock, you've come to the right place. In this part, I lead you on the nickel tour of what dividend investing is all about, reveal the bare essentials of dividend stocks and how they differ from their non-dividend paying counterparts, and showcase the numerous advantages you can reap by investing in dividend stocks.

Chapter 1

Wrapping Your Brain Around Dividend Investing

In This Chapter

▶ Understanding dividend stocks and their benefits and risks

▶ Preparing to become a savvy dividend stock investor

▶ Knowing what to look for as you shop for dividend stocks

▶ Monitoring and adjusting the holdings in your portfolio

*I*nvesting is a lot like car shopping on a budget. When you're shopping for a car, you usually have at least a vague notion of how much car you can afford, and you want to get the most car for your money without getting stuck with a lemon. When you're shopping for investments, you want the biggest bang for your buck without exposing yourself to more risk than your strategy calls for. And you have plenty of choices of where to put your money — stocks, bonds, mutual funds, money market accounts, real estate, or even socking it away in the bank.

For many investors, dividend stocks offer the best of both worlds — a healthy balance of risk and return. Investors receive the benefits of both share price appreciation and the ability to realize profits through *dividends* (cash payments) without having to sell shares. (Later in this chapter, I list more of the many benefits of dividend stocks, and in Chapter 3, I explain them in greater detail.)

In this chapter, I pack the essentials of dividend investing into a nutshell, starting with the bare basics, such as defining what a dividend is, and taking you to the very end — managing your portfolio after you populate it with promising dividend stocks. Along the way, I reference other chapters in this book where you can find additional information and guidance on each topic.

Coming to Terms with Dividend Stocks

Dividend stocks are stocks that pay dividends — payments in cash (usually) or shares (sometimes) to stockholders. Through dividend payments, a company distributes a portion of its profits to its shareholders every quarter and pumps the remaining profits back into the company to fuel its continued growth.

The percentage of total profits a company pays in dividends to shareholders is called the *payout ratio*. For more about payout ratios and how to use the number in evaluating dividend stocks, check out Chapter 8.

In the following sections, I explain the purpose of dividends, reveal several potential advantages of investing in dividend stocks, and remind you that investing in anything always carries some risk.

Understanding why companies pay dividends

Successful companies are profitable companies. They earn money, and they can use that money in several ways:

- ✔ **Reinvest it:** Companies usually invest a good chunk of their profits, if not all of them, into growing the business.

- ✔ **Pay down debt:** If, in addition to selling shares, companies borrowed money to raise capital, they may use profits to pay down the debt, thereby reducing the expense of their interest payments.

- ✔ **Buy back shares:** Companies may use profits to buy back shares that they feel are undervalued, or for other reasons. In some cases, they initiate buybacks to artificially inflate the share price and improve investor confidence in the company.

- ✔ **Pay dividends:** Paying dividends is a form of *profit sharing* — spreading the wealth among the company's owners, the shareholders.

A company's dividend policy generally reflects the board of directors' and shareholders' preferences in how to use profits. Two schools of thought govern their decision:

- ✔ **Pro growth:** This school believes a company is better off reinvesting its profits or using profits to pay down debt or buy back shares. This strategy makes the company more valuable, and the share price rises accordingly. Shareholders benefit when they sell their shares for more than they paid for them.

✔ **Pro profit-sharing:** This philosophy stems from the belief that share-holders own the company and should share in its profits.

Other factors can also influence dividend policies. For example, the Jobs and Growth Tax Relief Reconciliation Act of 2003 (JGTRRA), which lowered the maximum tax rate on dividends from 39.6 percent to 15 percent, boosted dividend payments on the S&P 500. For more about how tax legislation can affect dividends, check out Chapters 3 and 20.

Appreciating the advantages of dividend investing

Receiving dividends is like collecting interest on money in a bank account. It's very nice, but not exciting. Betting on the rise and fall of share prices is much more exhilarating, especially when your share prices soar. Placing excitement to the side, however, dividend stocks offer several advantages over non-dividend stocks:

✔ **Passive income:** Dividends provide a steady flow of passive income, which you can choose to spend or reinvest. This attribute makes dividend stocks particularly attractive to retirees looking to score some supplemental income.

✔ **More stable companies:** Companies that pay dividends tend to be more mature and stable than companies that don't. Startups rarely pay dividends, because they plow back all the profits to fuel their growth. Only when the company has attained a sustainable level of success does its board of directors vote to pay dividends. In addition, the need to pay dividends tends to make the management more accountable to shareholders and less prone to taking foolish risks.

✔ **Reduced risk:** Because dividends give investors two ways to realize a return on their investment, they tend to have a lower risk-to-reward ratio, which you can see in less volatility in the share price. A stock with lower volatility sees smaller share price declines when the market falls. Low volatility may also temper share price appreciation on the way up.

✔ **Two ways to profit:** With dividend stocks, your return on investment (ROI) increases when share prices rise and when the company pays dividends. With non-dividend stocks, the only way you can earn a positive return is through share price appreciation — buying low and selling high.

✔ **Continued ownership while collecting profits:** One of the most frustrating aspects of owning shares in a company that doesn't pay dividends is that all profits are locked in your stock. The only way to access those profits is to sell shares. With dividend stocks, you retain ownership of the company while collecting a share of its profits.

- ✔ **Cash to buy more shares:** When you buy X number of shares of a company that doesn't pay dividends, you get X number of shares. If you want more shares, you have to reach into your purse or pocket to pay for them. With dividend stocks, you can purchase additional shares by reinvesting all or some of your dividends. You don't have to reach into your pocket a second or third time. In most cases, you can even enroll in special programs that automatically reinvest your dividends (check out Chapter 14 for details).

- ✔ **Hedge against inflation:** Even a modest inflation rate can take a chunk out of earnings. Earn a 10-percent return, subtract 3 percent for inflation, and you're down to 7 percent. Dividends may offset that loss. As companies charge more for their products (contributing to inflation), they also tend to earn more and pay higher dividends as a result.

- ✔ **Positive returns in bear markets:** In a bear market, when share prices are flat or dropping, companies that pay dividends typically continue paying dividends. These dividend payments can help offset any loss from a drop in share price and may even result in a positive return.

- ✔ **Potential boost from the baby boomers:** As more baby boomers reach retirement age and seek sources of supplemental income, they're likely to increase demand for dividend stocks, driving up the price. Nobody can predict with any certainty that this will happen, but it's something to remain aware of in the coming decades.

For more about the potential advantages that dividend stocks offer, see Chapter 3.

Acknowledging the risks

Investing, as well as not investing, exposes you to some degree of risk; there's no such thing as safe investing, only safer investing. You can lose money in any of the following ways:

- ✔ **Share prices can drop.** This situation is possible regardless of whether the company pays dividends. Worst-case scenario is that the company goes belly up before you have the chance to sell your shares.

- ✔ **Companies can trim or slash dividend payments at any time.** Companies are not legally required to pay dividends or increase the payments they make. Unlike bonds, where a failure to pay interest can put a company into default, a company can cut or eliminate a dividend whenever it wants. If you're counting on a stock to pay dividends, you may view a dividend cut or elimination as losing money.

  Most companies try their best to avoid these moves because cutting the dividend may cause shareholders to sell, lowering the share price.

✔ **Inflation can nibble away at your savings.** Not investing your money or investing in something that doesn't keep pace with inflation causes your investment capital to lose purchase power. With inflation at work, every dollar you scrimped and saved is worth less (but not worthless).

Potential risk is proportional to potential return. Locking your money up in an FDIC-insured bank that pays an interest rate higher than the rate of inflation is safe (at least the first $100,000 that the FDIC insures), but it's not going to make you rich. On the other hand, taking a gamble on a high-growth company can earn you handsome returns in a short period of time, but it's also a high-risk venture. The following section explores risk tolerance in greater depth and reveals various approaches to investing that can expose you to different levels of risk.

Dividends' worst year ever

No doubt about it. The years 2008 and 2009 were brutal for dividends, with the latter being the worst year for dividend investors ever, according to Standard & Poor's. Over those two years, the U.S. experienced the worst financial crisis since the Great Depression, and the stock market lost more than half its value. Dividend stocks weren't immune. The worst part for dividend investors was that two major income-producing sectors — financial services and real estate — were responsible for the housing bubble. In the ensuing crash, real estate values plummeted, sending many real estate companies and their lenders into a serious cash crunch. Many of the dividend-company advantages were violated as mature, stable, low-risk companies stopped following age-old rules and became leveraged to the hilt.

Amid a severe liquidity crisis, companies desperate to conserve cash slashed or eliminated dividend payouts. The dividend giants that succumbed included Dow Chemical (DOW), initiating its first cut since it started paying dividends in 1912; General Electric (GE), which lowered its dividend for the first time in 71 years; and Pfizer (PFE).

According to Standard & Poor's, out of the approximately 7,000 stocks that report dividends, 804 stocks cut their payouts in 2009, or 631 percent more than the 110 that cut their dividends in 2007. In addition, the cuts were very deep; investors lost $58 billion in income.

Among the dividend-paying companies in the S&P 500 Index, 68 companies lowered their dividend payouts; 10 eliminated dividends completely, compared to 8 dividend cuts and 4 eliminations during 2007. Together, these 78 companies cut dividend payouts by $51.6 billion, or 21 percent, from 2008 — the highest amount ever for the index. And 2008 wasn't a great year, either, with 40 cuts and 22 eliminations. Meanwhile, a little more than half as many companies increased their dividends compared with 2007, 151 versus 287. By the end of 2009, the S&P 500 had only 363 dividend paying companies.

The bright side is that those 363 stocks make up 73 percent of the index, constituting a large universe of dividend companies to choose from. Although being in the S&P 500 is no guarantee of stability, most S&P 500 stocks are stable, profitable companies. Begin your research by looking at the 151 companies that raised their dividends in 2009.

Prepping Yourself for the Journey Ahead

People often invest more time and effort planning for a weekend vacation than they do preparing to become an investor. They catch a commercial for one of those online brokerages that makes investing look so easy, transfer some of their savings to the brokerage or roll over their IRA (individual retirement account), and try to ride the waves of rising investment sentiment to the land of riches.

A more effective approach is to carefully prepare for the journey before taking the first step. The following sections serve as a checklist to make sure you have everything in place before you purchase your first dividend stock.

Gauging your risk tolerance

Every investor has a different comfort zone. The thrill-seekers crave risk. They want big returns and are willing to take big risks to get them. Riding the rollercoaster of the stock market doesn't bother them, as long as they have some hope they'll end up on top. On the other end of the spectrum are conservative investors willing to trade high returns for stability. Prior to investing in anything, you can benefit by determining whether you're more of a thrill-seeker, a conservative investor, or someone in between.

In Chapter 5, I offer several methods for gauging risk tolerance, but regardless of which method you choose, you should account for the following factors:

- **Age:** Younger investors can generally take bigger risks because they have less money to lose and more time to recover from lousy investment decisions.

- **Wealth:** "Never bet money you can't afford to lose" is good advice for both gamblers and investors. If you're relying on the money you're investing to pay your bills, send Johnny to college, or retire soon, you're probably better off playing it safe.

- **Personality:** Some people are naturally more risk-tolerant than others. If you tend to get worried sick over money, a low-risk approach is probably more suitable for you.

- **Goals:** In football, if your goal is to possess the ball longer than the other team, you generally play it safe and run the ball. If your goal is to score lots of touchdowns, you're more likely to take more risks and "air it out." The same holds true with investing. If your goal is to reap big rewards quickly, you may conclude that the risk is worth it. If your goal is to build wealth over a long period of time with less chance of losing your initial investment, a slow, steady approach is probably best.

For more about gauging and managing risk when investing in dividend stocks, see Chapter 5.

Only you can determine the right balance of risk and reward for you and your goals. You can obtain valuable guidance from a financial advisor, but how you choose to invest your money is entirely up to you (at least it should be).

Choosing the right approach

Tossing a bunch of ticker symbols into a hat and drawing out names of the companies you want to invest in is no way to pick a dividend stock. Better approaches are available, as presented in the following sections.

Value

The value approach is like shopping at garage sales. Investors hope to spot undervalued stocks — stocks with share prices that appear to be significantly lower than they're really worth. When hunting for values in dividend stocks, investors look for the following:

- **Strong earnings growth:** Companies that earn bigger profits with each passing year demonstrate they're growing and thriving. A shrinking profit usually means trouble — bad management decisions, increasing competition, or other factors chipping away at the company's success.

- **High yields:** *Yield* is the ratio of annual dividends per share to the share price. If shares are selling for $50 each and dividends are $2.50 per share (annually), the yield is $2.50/$50.00 = .05 or 5 percent. Stocks with higher yields deliver higher dividends per dollar invested. For example, a dividend stock with a yield of 5 percent generates a nickel for every dollar invested, whereas a yield of 25 percent generates a quarter per dollar.

- **Low price-to-earnings ratio (P/E):** *P/E* tells you how many dollars you're paying to receive a share of the company's profits. If a company earns an annual profit of $3.25 for each share of its common stock and the shares sell for $50, the P/E is $50/$3.25 = 15.39. In other words, you're paying $15.39 for every dollar of profit the company earns. The P/E ratio provides a barometer by which to compare a company's relative value to other companies and the market in general. (Head to Chapter 2 for more on common stock.)

A good P/E ratio is one that's lower than the P/E ratios of comparable companies. As a general rule, investors look for P/E ratios that are lower than the average for a particular index, such as the S&P 500 or the Dow Jones Industrial Average (DJIA). See Chapter 2 for more about these stock market indexes; Chapter 8 explores P/E ratios in greater depth.

- ✔ **Solid history of raising dividend payments:** Like strong earnings growth, covered earlier in this list, a solid history of raising dividend payments demonstrates that the company is thriving. Every year it has more wealth to share with investors.

- ✔ **Solid balance sheet:** A *balance sheet* is a net worth statement for a company, listing the cost of everything it owns and subtracting the cost of everything it owes. Ultimately, a healthy balance sheet shows that the company has enough assets to cover its liabilities and then some. The remainder is called *shareholder equity.* For more about balance sheets, flip to Chapter 8.

- ✔ **Sufficient free cash flow:** Ideally, a company's cash flow statement (as described in Chapter 8) shows that the company brings in enough actual cash each quarter to more than cover its expenses as well as the dividend distributions.

The quality of a good company that's rarely mentioned but is most important is management. Unfortunately, company insiders have the best insight into how effectively management is doing its job. You can draw many conclusions by inspecting quarterly reports and crunching the numbers, but a lot can happen between filings, so those documents take you only so far. One way to gain insight is to see whether the company insiders are buying shares of their own company. Another is to read about companies that interest you in various business publications, including *The Wall Street Journal, Forbes, Kiplinger,* and dozens of others.

Growth

The growth approach to investing in the stock market focuses on a company's prospects for generating future earnings. These companies are expected to see their revenues and profits grow at a pace faster than the rest of the market. As such, this approach tends to be more speculative than the value approach. Growth investors may pay more for shares than their past results or actual performance justifies.

With the growth approach, value isn't the key variable. Although P/E ratios remain important, growth investors are willing to pay a higher price for shares than value investors. Because growth investors look to share price appreciation for returns, they're more likely to focus their attention on companies that don't pay dividends. They want younger companies that reinvest their profits to accelerate the growth rates of future earnings and revenues. If the company continues to exhibit strong growth, the share price should move significantly higher. Growth investors are well advised to consider the following:

- ✔ **Revenue growth:** Although earnings (profits) can grow through cost cutting, revenue growth demonstrates the company's sales are increasing.

- ✔ **Projected growth:** Projected growth consists of analysts' estimates of the percentage the company's revenues will grow in a year. These projections always carry some uncertainty, but investors should still take them into consideration.

- ✔ **Profit margins:** If the company reports a profit, growth investors want to see profits and revenues growing on a steady basis. Profits not keeping pace with growing revenues may be a sign that the company's profit margin is suffering.

- ✔ **Realistic share price projection:** Generally speaking, growth investors consider investing in companies only if they have a realistic expectation that the share price will double no later than five years down the road. The key word here is "realistic." Investors must base projections on data rather than gut feelings.

Income

The goal of income investing is to obtain a steady and relatively secure income stream. When purchasing equities, focusing on income means buying stocks that pay dividends. Because most growth companies don't pay dividends, most income investors are basically value investors that not only want to buy at a good price but also look for a high yield and a solid history of rising dividend payments. The income investor looks for companies well equipped to not only continue paying dividends but also increase the cash amount of those dividend payments.

Collecting capital to fuel your investments

Before you can invest in anything, you need some cash. That's something I can't help you with — either you have it or you don't. Most investors gather investment capital the old fashioned way — they earn it. After paying their bills, investors save part of their remaining income in a bank account, a retirement account, stocks, bonds, or mutual funds. You can either allocate a specific amount of your weekly salary for investing or use some cash already lying around that you want to put to work in something that may offer higher returns.

Don't let that capital burn a hole in your pocket. You decide when, in what, and how much to invest, so spend some time shopping for the right stocks before buying. Rushing the process significantly increases the risk of losing money.

Teaming up with a seasoned pro

Although this book provides the information and guidance required to competently invest in dividend stocks, many people don't feel comfortable managing their investments by themselves. Some investors want an investment advisor to consult with and bounce ideas off of, and others want to understand the process but leave the actual details to the professional. This book should give you the tools to manage your portfolio by yourself. However, if you do decide to hire an investment advisor, I urge you to consult a qualified professional with a track record of *successfully* investing in the stock market for several years.

Experienced investment advisors can offer you a wealth of advice and information on most areas of financial planning, including taxes, insurance, and strategies that have been successful for them. They can also function as a sounding board when you need feedback on a stock you're thinking of buying or selling and help steer you clear of potential pitfalls.

If you don't want to pay a fee for an investment advisor's advice, consider joining an investment club where you can pool your capital to create a more diversified portfolio than you can on your own. You can also bounce ideas off fellow club members before making any investment decisions. The extra eyes and ears may have information about a company that convinces you to move forward or step back from a particular transaction. They also provide a good source of investment ideas you may not have previously considered.

Selecting First-Rate Dividend Stocks

A good dividend stock isn't just one that pays a high dividend. The strength and consistency of the dividend are very important, along with share price and the company's prospects for a rosy future. Before you can evaluate and select dividend stocks, however, you need to identify a few promising candidates.

In the following sections, I point you in the direction of dividend stocks, introduce you to the basics of evaluating them, suggest a few methods for reducing the potential risks, and mention some convenient ways to purchase shares.

Distinguishing dividend stocks from the rest of the pack in your research

Wherever you find stocks, you can find dividend stocks:

- ✔ Google Finance at `www.google.com/finance`
- ✔ Yahoo! Finance at `finance.yahoo.com`
- ✔ Various personal finance magazines and Web sites

> ✔ *The Wall Street Journal*
> ✔ *Financial Times*
> ✔ This book!

Many stock listings include both a dividend column and a dividend yield column. If the company hasn't paid a dividend, you see something like 0.00 or a hyphen (-). Some listings show only the previous and current share price and the single-day and year-to-date gain or loss. In that case, you need to dig deeper to find out whether the company pays dividends and the amount of the most recent payment. With most online stock listings, you simply click the ticker symbol for more information about the company. For more about tracking down dividend stocks, see Chapter 7.

You can also find leads on potentially good dividend stocks in this book, specifically in Parts III and IV. In Part III, I introduce you to sectors (industries) that have a strong history of paying dividends and highlight several companies in each sector that you may want to check out (the following section serves as a teaser for Part III). In Part IV, I reveal various investment vehicles that may expand your options.

Exploring sectors where dividend stocks hang out

Companies in certain industries, such as utilities and telecoms, are more likely to pay dividends than companies in other industries, including technology and biotech. The biggest reason for this tendency is that some industries have larger, more established companies, compared with industries that have a higher concentration of smaller, growth-oriented companies.

As you begin investing in dividend stocks, you may want to focus your efforts on the following sectors; you can find out more about these sectors in Part III.

> ✔ **Utilities:** Electricity, water, and natural gas (suppliers, not producers)
> ✔ **Energy:** Oil, natural gas (producers, not suppliers), and Master Limited Partnerships (MLPs)
> ✔ **Telecoms:** Carriers (U.S. and international) and wireless
> ✔ **Consumer staples:** Food/beverages, prescription drugs, household products, tobacco, and alcohol

Prior to the mortgage meltdown that started in 2007, real estate and financials would have been at the top of the list. As I'm writing this book, they're just at the top of the trash heap.

Crunching the numbers

Eeny, meeny, miny, moe is no way to pick dividend stocks. Savvy investors carefully inspect the company reports — balance sheet, income statement, and cash flow statement — and crunch the numbers to evaluate the company's performance, at least on paper. As you prepare to evaluate a company, research the following figures or calculate them yourself by using numbers from the company's quarterly report (Chapter 8 shows you how):

- ✔ **Current dividend per share (DPS):** The quarterly cash payment each investor receives for each share of company stock they own.

- ✔ **Indicated dividend:** The projected annual dividend for the next year, assuming the company pays the same dividend per share for each quarter of the next year.

- ✔ **Dividend yield:** A ratio that compares the amount the company pays out in dividends per share to its share price. You use yields to gauge a dividend's rate of return. Yields move inversely to share price — that is, yields go up when share prices go down (and vice versa).

- ✔ **Earnings per share (EPS):** The portion of a company's profit allocated to each share of stock. If XYZ Company sold 2 million shares of stock and earned a profit of $1 million, it earned 50 cents per share, or $1 million/2 million shares = $0.50. A company that earns $1 per share is twice as profitable as the one that earned 50 cents a share.

- ✔ **Price-to-earnings ratio (P/E):** The ratio of the share price to the annual earnings per share, which tells you how many dollars you need to invest to receive a dollar of the company's profits.

- ✔ **Payout ratio:** The percentage of a company's net profit it pays to shareholders in the form of dividends. The payout ratio indicates whether the company is sharing more of its profits with investors or reinvesting it in the company.

- ✔ **Net margin:** The ratio of net profits to net revenues, indicating the percentage of each dollar of sales that translates into a profit. High net margins typically indicate that a company has little competition and large demand for its products. This situation allows the company to charge a high price for its products or services.

- ✔ **Return on equity (ROE):** The ratio of a company's annual net profit to shareholder equity, ROE provides some indication of how effective a company is turning investor dollars into profits.

- ✔ **Quick ratio:** An indication of a company's liquidity or ability to meet its short-term financial obligations. The higher the ratio, the more likely it can afford to pay dividends moving forward.

✔ **Debt covering ratio:** An indication of whether a company has sufficient operating income to cover its current liabilities, including payments on debt.

✔ **Cash flow:** The difference in how much actual cash comes into the company during the quarter versus how much it pays out. A company can make a lot of sales in a quarter, but if clients don't pay their bills, no cash comes into the firm. A positive cash flow shows more cash enters the company than leaves it. Negative cash flow means the company is spending more cash than it actually brings in.

Don't evaluate a company based on one value. The numbers work collectively to paint a portrait of the company's current financial status. For additional guidance on interpreting these values, see Chapter 8.

Performing additional research and analysis

Numbers paint a fairly detailed portrait of a company's current financial status and can even be used to some degree to forecast the company's future performance. Numbers, however, provide no context. They may indicate potential problems or opportunities, but they don't reveal what's causing those problems or making those opportunities available. They provide little indication of the company's management philosophy or expertise; or outside factors, such as the state of the economy, what's going on in the sector, and what analysts and investors think about the company's future prospects.

To find out everything you need to know to make a wise decision, you have to do some research. Here are some suggestions to find out more information about the companies you're thinking of investing in:

✔ **Read the quarterly earnings reports of the companies you're thinking of investing in.** Every public company is legally obligated to file these reports with the U.S. Securities and Exchange Commission (SEC) — the federal regulator of Wall Street.

✔ **Research companies on the Internet.** You can usually find plenty of information on the company's Web site, in online financial publications, and on sites such as Yahoo! Finance and Google Finance. Use your favorite search engine to search for the company by name.

✔ **Check out the competition online, too.** Which company is leading the pack, and what is it doing that the others aren't?

✔ **Read reports written by stock analysts at investment banks.** These analysts spend a lot of time each quarter investigating whether companies are performing up to their own expectations.

✔ **Subscribe to and read financial publications online or off.** Sorry, but not everything is available for free on the Internet — you usually have to pay for the best information, whether you get it online or in print.

✔ **Check out what other investors have to say.** Many investors maintain blogs that provide useful insights and can give you some sense of investor sentiment.

Blogs may provide insight, but *never* base an investment decision on a blog or comment from an investor. These people may have an agenda that conflicts with yours. Some people talk up stocks on Internet chat boards and blogs to raise the share price on the stocks they own so that they can cash out.

Building and Managing Your Portfolio

When you evaluate individual companies, you're involved in what can best be described as identifying the best pieces for an investment puzzle. When you actually buy shares to assemble a portfolio, you shift to a more "big picture" perspective. Although you must micromanage the portfolio by keeping an eye on each investment, you also need to evaluate how each investment fits into your master plan and ultimate investment goals.

In the following sections, I highlight the key tasks required to effectively build and manage a dividend investment portfolio. In Part V, I provide additional details and guidance.

Settling on a stock-picking strategy

Every investor has a unique investment strategy for spinning straw into gold. Usually the best approach is a combination of several strategies to achieve the right balance of risk and return while efficiently and effectively reaching the investor's goal.

Any general in the military can tell you that strategies don't always unfold as planned on the battlefield, but not having a strategy in place is pure folly. Develop the best strategy possible, but keep in mind as you move forward, that you may need to adjust it.

The following are some semifamous strategies that investors have developed for picking dividend stocks for their portfolios (see Chapter 18 for details):

- **The Dogs of the Dow:** In 1991, Michael O'Higgins proposed an investment strategy called *The Dogs of the Dow* based on the fact that a dividend stock's yield rises whenever its share price drops. Proponents of this theory believe that the components of the Dow Jones Industrial Average with the highest dividend yields have the greatest potential for capital appreciation in the coming year.

- **The Geraldine Weiss Approach:** Geraldine Weiss, editor of *Investment Quality Trends* (www.iqtrends.com), is a leading expert on dividend investing who promotes buying high-yield blue-chip stocks. The overall strategy is to buy high and sell low — that is, buy when dividend yields are at the historic highs and sell when the dividend yields hit historic lows. Sticking with blue-chips helps avoid financially troubled companies.

- **Relative Dividend Yield:** Developed by money manager Anthony Spare, this approach rates stocks by comparing a company's dividend yield to that of the average yield of the S&P 500. In his book *Relative Dividend Yield: Common Stock Investing for Income and Appreciation,* 2nd Edition (Wiley), Spare recommends giving careful consideration to stocks with a dividend yield that's more than double the average on the S&P 500.

- **Dividend Achievers:** Dividend Achievers identifies companies that have an outstanding track record for increasing dividend payments every year. To make it on the U.S. Broad Dividend Achievers Index, U.S. companies must have at least ten consecutive years of increasing regular dividends, be listed on the NYSE or NASDAQ, and have a minimum average daily cash volume of $500,000.

Limiting your exposure to risk

In the world of investing, risk is an ever-present reality, but you can implement several strategies to limit your exposure:

- **Education and research:** Knowledge is power, and by reading this book, you're already engaged in the pursuit of the requisite insight and know-how.

- **Dollar cost averaging:** *Dollar cost averaging* is investing a fixed amount of money at regular intervals (such as monthly) toward the purchase of a particular investment. With dollar cost averaging, sometimes you pay more for the investment and sometimes less. This strategy reduces your chance of paying a premium for a large number of shares and then losing a huge amount of money when the price drops.

✔ **Diversification:** Don't put all of your golden goose eggs in one basket by investing heavily in any one company, sector, or type of investment. By diversifying your portfolio with stocks, bonds, and cash, you not only spread the wealth but also lower your risk profile.

✔ **Strategic timing:** No, I'm not recommending that you try to time the market. What I do recommend is that you match your investment strategy to your time frame. Be aware of how many years you have before you need this money. The less time you have, the more conservative your investments should be. As you get older, consider allocating a higher percentage of your portfolio to safer investments, such as bonds, to protect your capital.

Buying and selling shares

After dealing with all the preliminaries, including settling on an investment strategy and carefully researching individual stocks, you're almost ready to start trading. Almost, because you need to address one more preliminary — how you're going to go about buying and selling shares. You basically have four options:

✔ **Direct:** You may be able to purchase shares directly from the company. For more about direct purchase programs, see Chapter 14.

✔ **Broker:** Brokers buy and sell shares on commission. In other words, they execute trades on your behalf. A full-service broker charges more but may offer some valuable insight and advice. A discount broker merely processes your order. If you're a do-it-yourselfer, this route is the way to go.

✔ **Investment advisor:** A registered investment advisor is a step above a broker. An advisor can help you build and manage a portfolio to meet your financial goals, recommend stocks and other investments to consider, and meet with you regularly to make adjustments.

For additional details on buying and selling shares, including crucial information on placing limit and stop-loss orders, check out Chapter 19.

Reviewing your portfolio regularly

In the best of all possible worlds, you can build your portfolio and let it set sail without a care in the world. In the real world, you must continue to invest

at least some time and effort reviewing your portfolio and making adjustments. Monitoring dividend stocks consists of reevaluating them regularly,
using the same criteria you used to select them in the first place: dividend,
yield, price-to-earnings ratio, payout ratio, and so on. When you notice the
performance of one of the stocks in your portfolio slipping or have reason
to believe it will start slipping, you may need to replace it with a better pros-
pect. In addition, you probably want to make adjustments to your portfolio as
your goals change. At the very least, you should check your portfolio twice a
year to make sure your asset allocations match your strategy.

Don't fall asleep at the wheel. Companies, even large, well-established companies, can run aground. Remain vigilant and jump ship before that happens.

Staying on top of possible tax code changes

Tax legislation can make investing in dividend stocks more or less attractive. For many years, dividends were taxed as ordinary income — at a rate as
high as 39.6 percent. In other words, for every dollar in dividends, investors
had to fork over about 40 cents to Uncle Sam. In 1981, when the rate on long-
term capital gains was reduced to a maximum of 20 percent, many investors
shifted from dividend to growth stocks to give themselves a tax cut.

The Jobs and Growth Tax Relief Reconciliation Act of 2003 (JGTRRA) changed
all that. It dropped the tax rate on long-term capital gains and dividends to a
maximum of 15 percent, leveling the playing field.

Tax legislation can be a game changer, and Congress can change the rules at
any time. Remain vigilant to protect yourself from unfavorable tax legislation
and to take advantage of favorable legislation. Remember, the less you pay in
taxes, the more you get to keep and perhaps even reinvest. For more about
tax considerations, check out Chapter 20.

Checking Out Various Investment Vehicles

Investment vehicle is a fancy term used to describe an investment product
other than basic stocks or bonds. Sometimes it refers to a product, such as
a fund, which holds many different stocks or bonds. Other times, it refers to

a way to purchase stocks or bonds other than a straightforward purchase. Some examples are

- ✔ **Dividend reinvestment plans (DRIPs):** Many companies that pay dividends allow investors to enroll in DRIP programs, which automatically reinvest dividends to purchase additional shares. This strategy is usually a great way to compound returns.

- ✔ **Direct stock purchase plans (DSPs):** DSPs allow you to purchase shares directly from the company rather than through a broker, which can save you some money on commissions and fees. They're also called *direct purchase plans,* or DPPs.

- ✔ **Dividend-focused mutual funds:** The main benefit of a dividend-focused mutual fund is the same as that for any mutual fund — it provides an easy way to diversify your holdings. In exchange, you relinquish your control over picking individual stocks to the mutual fund manager.

- ✔ **Exchange-traded funds (ETFs):** An ETF is basically an index mutual fund that trades like a stock. Quite a few ETFs focus on dividend investing. You can find out more about ETFs in Chapter 16 and even more in my book *ETFs for the Long Run: What They Are, How They Work, and Simple Strategies for Successful Long-Term Investing* (Wiley).

- ✔ **Foreign dividends:** Some foreign companies pay dividends, too, and with foreign dividend investment vehicles, you don't even have to worry about trading in your yens, euros, and shekels for dollars.

In Part IV, you have the opportunity to explore these dividend investment vehicles in greater depth and gain insight into which ones may be best for your situation and investment strategy.

Chapter 2

Brushing Up on Dividend Details

In This Chapter

▶ Taking a look at stock market indexes

▶ Getting up to speed on dividend stock basics

▶ Understanding how dividends influence the stock market

▶ Raising your awareness of key dates affecting dividend payments

*A*s an investor, you may think you need to know only two facts about dividend stocks — that some companies pay dividends and some don't. However, knowing a few additional details about these stocks can make you a much savvier and more confident investor.

In this chapter, I cover the nuts and bolts of how dividends work and bring you quickly up to speed on the two main indexes that reflect the stock market's overall health. I explain a few key concepts, including yield, and explore factors that contribute to making one dividend stock a better choice than another. I also explain some key dates that affect when companies pay dividends, which may influence your decision of when to buy and sell shares.

Checking Out the Major Stock Market Indexes

People measure the health of the stock market by using various indexes. An *index* is sort of like a thermometer for a market. When business is good, the index tends to rise. When business is bad, it falls. Thousands of indexes measure every industrial sector in the United States and business performance in every country in the world. To take the temperature of the energy sector or the financial sector, you can find an index specifically for those industries. If you want an index of just dividend stocks, you can find that too.

Two major indexes measure the broad market — the Dow Jones Industrial Average (DJIA) and the Standard & Poor's 500 Index. These indexes are known as the stock market's *benchmarks*. They not only measure the health of the stock market but also provide a historical basis from which you can derive data, gain valuable perspective on what's going on in the markets, and draw conclusions. When the media say the stock market is up or down, they mean the Dow and the S&P 500 are up or down. When they say the market is mixed, they mean these two indexes are going in opposite directions. The indexes are important to you because most of the stocks on them pay dividends.

I reference these indexes throughout this book, so you should know what each index represents and how they differ. If I refer to one index more than another in a particular discussion, I do so only because the index I'm referring to provides more or better data to illustrate the point under discussion. In the section "Appreciating the Role Dividends Play in the Market" later in this chapter, I use these indexes to reveal the impact that dividends have had on the stock market over the past hundred years or so.

In addition to these two long-time barometers, the NASDAQ Composite Index has become a benchmark for the NASDAQ Stock Market. Most pertinent, I don't deal with the NASDAQ because the majority of its components don't pay dividends. Most are small, high-growth stocks, such as technology and biotechnology.

Dow Jones Industrial Average

Invented in 1896 to track just 12 companies, the Dow Jones Industrial Average is the oldest stock market index. It goes by a few nicknames, such as the Dow Industrials and the DJIA, but most people know it simply as the Dow. Today, the Dow consists of just 30 companies in the major industries in the United States.

Critics complain that the sample of 30 companies is too small to serve as an accurate measure of the stock market's performance and that its price weighting doesn't take into account the sizes of the companies in the index. However, the Dow has been measuring the stock market for more than 113 years, which gives it a lot of credibility.

Price weighting values companies based on their share price, not total market value. As its name says, the Dow is an average. So a company with a share price of $50 makes up five times more of the index than a company with a share price of just $10, even if the lower priced stock produces twice the profits or has more shares trading in the market.

Standard & Poor's 500

Better known, as the S&P 500 or just the S&P, the Standard & Poor's 500 Index holds 500 of the largest companies in the U.S., but not necessarily the top 500. Created in 1957, the S&P is considered a more representative index because it holds about one-tenth of all the publicly traded companies. More importantly, this tenth of the market's companies collectively represents about 75 percent of the stock market's total dollar value.

The index weights the companies based on their value in the market — a value measured by the company's *market capitalization*:

Market Capitalization = Share Price × Number of Outstanding Common Shares

For example, in early 2009, ExxonMobil was the largest company in the index, with a market capitalization of $338 billion. It held an index weighting of 4.86 percent. AT&T, the second-largest company, wasn't quite half the size of Exxon, with a market capitalization of just $148 billion, so its weighting of 2.14 percent was less than half of Exxon's weighting. Giving larger companies more influence over the index makes the S&P 500 a more accurate measuring tool for the broad market.

When I call the shares *outstanding,* I'm not referring to the strength of the company or any other positive characteristic. *Outstanding stock* tells you the number of shares the company has sold to investors and can now trade on the market.

Recognizing the Difference between Common and Preferred Stock

To raise capital, companies can issue two types of stocks: common and preferred. Each type or class of stock offers different rights, benefits, and restrictions, as I explain in the following sections.

Common stock

When people talk about stocks, they typically mean *common stock,* the most popular and widely-held type of equity. When I refer to *stock,* I mean common stock.

Compared to preferred stock (see the following section), common stock offers the following advantage and disadvantage:

- **Advantage:** Holders of common stock share in the company's profits through increasing dividends and a rising share price. Common shareholders elect the board of directors and vote on broad corporate issues such as mergers.

- **Disadvantage:** Shareholders receive the last claim on earnings and the company's assets. In other words, if the company goes bankrupt, you receive your payment after all the creditors and preferred stock holders get paid. In almost every bankruptcy, common shareholders get nothing.

Preferred stock

As its name implies, preferred stock holds advantages over common stock. However, its disadvantages actually outweigh its advantages in most cases.

Following are some of the advantages preferred stock offers shareholders:

- **Fixed dividends:** Dividend payments remain more stable, which can be an advantage in times when the company is having trouble making a dividend payment but a disadvantage when dividends rise. Often the yields are higher than common dividends and the corporation's bond interest rates.

- **Payment priority:** Holders of preferred stock are first in line to receive dividends. In other words, they receive their dividends before holders of common shares receive theirs. With *cumulative preferred stock,* if the company has unpaid and overdue debts to the preferred shareholders, all the unpaid preferred dividends must be distributed before the common shareholders receive a penny. If the firm is in serious trouble (little cash, no assets to sell for cash, and no ability to borrow to pay the dividend), the dividend may have to *accrue* (accumulate).

- **Greater claim to any of the company's assets:** In the event of a bankruptcy and ensuing liquidation, holders of preferred shares receive any money left over before holders of common shares receive any money. In liquidations, common shares often become worthless.

Preferred shares also carry some considerable disadvantages:

- **Fixed dividends:** Although a fixed dividend payment can be an advantage when the company fails to earn a profit, it also means the dividend payment doesn't rise when the company earns bigger profits. Fixed payments also make the shares interest-rate sensitive. If interest rates rise, the share price may fall in order to boost the yield. I explain how yield works later in this chapter.

✔ **Less share price appreciation:** Because the dividend is fixed, the price of preferred shares is based on the yield they offer. As a result, preferred shares actually trade more like a bond than a stock.

✔ **No voting rights:** Holders of preferred shares have less say than common stock holders in how the company is managed and who sits on the board of directors.

In short, holders of common stock assume more risk but stand to gain more when the company is profitable.

You can usually tell the difference between a company's common and preferred stock by glancing at the ticker symbol. The ticker symbol for preferred stock usually has a *P* at the end of it, but unlike common stock, ticker symbols can vary among systems; for example, Yahoo! Finance lists preferred stock with the company's ticker symbol followed by a hyphen, the letter *P,* and then the series letter (for example, J.P. Morgan preferred is JPM-PE), whereas Google Finance includes only the series letter (without the *P,* JPM-E).

Focusing on Company Fundamentals

You've probably heard a few success stories about investors tossing darts to choose the companies they invest in or kids assembling a portfolio that significantly outperforms the S&P 500. Stories like these may be entertaining, but they often send a dangerous message that picking good stocks is a random, hit-or-miss activity. On the contrary, consistently successful investors do their homework and crunch the numbers. They carefully inspect each company's *fundamentals,* including the following:

✔ **Revenue:** Total amount of money the company received from sales

✔ **Expenses:** Total amount of money the company spent to generate income

✔ **Net Profit:** Revenue minus expenses; also called *earnings*

✔ **Assets:** Cash value of everything the company owns

✔ **Liabilities:** Cash value of everything the company owes

✔ **Debt:** Total amount of money the company owes to lenders; a kind of liability

✔ **Cash flow:** Positive if the company brings in more actual cash than it paid out; negative if the company spent more cash than it brought in

In Chapter 8, I show you how to perform a fundamental analysis of a company based on the company's quarterly reports, including its balance sheet, income statement, and cash flow statement.

Fundamental analysis focuses on a company's financial metrics; *technical analysis* examines share price in an attempt to forecast future share prices based on the charting of historical trends and market conditions. I encourage you to give more credence to fundamentals and less to technicals.

Paying Tribute to Yields

One of the easiest and fastest ways to determine the relative value of a particular dividend stock is to look at its *yield* — the ratio of dividends per share to the share price. For example, if shares are selling for $25 each and dividends are $2.50 per share (annually), the yield is $2.50 ÷ $25 = .10 or 10 percent.

The yield is the magic number. Yield tells you the percentage rate of return you can expect from the dividend, making it very useful in comparing the returns you can expect from different investment options. However, yield isn't the sole factor in determining the comparative value of dividend stocks. When you sell your shares, whether the share price rose or fell, and by how much also contributes to the total return on your investment. For additional details on evaluating dividend stocks, check out Chapter 8.

Appreciating the Role Dividends Play in the Market

In the stock market, share prices command all the attention. You hear about how much the share price of General Electric or Ford or Google rose or fell. You hear analysts pitching their best guesses on whether a particular stock's value will rise or fall. What you rarely hear about are dividends, and that's unfortunate given the impact that dividends have had and continue to have on the market.

In the following sections, I shine the spotlight on dividends and their contributions to the overall value of the stock market's returns. Hopefully, you come away with a greater appreciation for the power of dividends. If you don't, you can read more about the benefits of dividends in Chapter 3.

Acknowledging dividends' contributions to returns

Total return measures a stock's total performance from both dividends and share price appreciation. If a stock starts the year at $50 and pays a $4 annual dividend, the dividend yield is 8 percent: $4 ÷ $50 = 8 percent. If the stock gained $6 to end the year at $56 (up from $50), it saw *capital appreciation* (increase in value based on its market price) of 12 percent:

$6 ÷ $50 = 12 percent

Add the dividend yield and capital appreciation together, and you get the total return of 20 percent. (Total return of an index over many years often includes the reinvestment of the dividends on an annual basis.) I explain how reinvesting dividends annually affects total return in Chapter 3.

From January 1926 to December 2008, the S&P 500 Index (and its predecessors) delivered an annualized total return of 9.69 percent per year. The shocking aspect of that is that over those 83 years, *price appreciation* (rising share prices) accounted for only 5.5 percentage points of that 9.69 percent. Dividends actually accounted for the remaining 4.19. In other words, dividend income comprised 43.27 percent of the S&P's returns:

4.19 percent ÷ 9.69 percent = 43.27 percent

The numbers from the Dow paint a similar picture. From January 1, 1930, (about two months after the crash of 1929) to December 31, 2008, the cumulative return on the Dow was 5,914.64 percent or 7.96 percent on an annualized basis. Price appreciation accounted for just 4.62 of that 7.96 percent points, and dividends accounted for the other 3.34. Looking at it another way, dividend income comprised about 41.96 percent of the Dow's total returns:

3.34 percent ÷ 7.96 percent = 41.96 percent

An *annual rate of return* is the return for a 12-month period, such as January 1 to December 31. An *annualized rate of return* is the rate of return for a period longer or shorter than one year. The number is either multiplied or divided to determine an equivalent return for a one-year period.

Dividends made up 43.27 percent of the S&P's total return and 41.96 percent of the Dow's total return. These numbers are pretty consistent and clearly indicate that if you forgo dividends, you give up more than 40 percent of the potential profits you can derive from the stock market.

Investment returns in the form of dividends take on even greater importance in a bear market. In bear markets, stocks can go for years without posting any significant capital gains, but companies often continue to pay dividends. Dividends may provide the only returns you receive when share prices drop or flatline.

To gain a clearer perspective, take a look at the Dow Jones Industrial Average over the 11-year period from January 1, 1999, to December 31, 2008. During this period, the stock market experienced some serious ups and downs — the rally of the technology bubble that peaked in early 2000, the ensuing crash that bottomed out in 2002, the rally of the housing bubble that lifted stocks to an all-time high in 2007, and then a plunge of more than 50 percent in 2008 through early 2009.

Figure 2-1 shows what would have happened if you had invested $100 in the Dow stocks on the last day of 1998. By the end of 2008, based on share price appreciation alone, that $100 would be worth $95.59, representing a return of –4.41 percent. Including dividends, however, the total return would be $117.95 — a nearly 18-percent profit on your investment and a 22.36-percentage point jump over price appreciation alone. And that doesn't even include reinvesting the dividends! (For more about compounding returns by reinvesting dividends, see Chapter 14.)

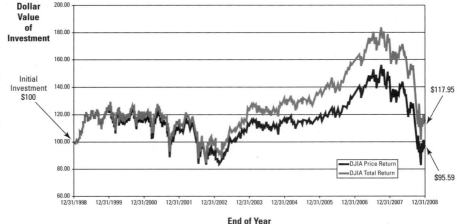

Figure 2-1: Dow return on share price versus return on share price plus dividends for 1998–2008.

Courtesy Dow Jones Indexes

Witnessing the positive effects of dividends on stock prices

In the midst of investor irrationality, dividends tend to calm the raging stock market seas by injecting some sanity into the marketplace in a couple of ways. First, they make managers more accountable to shareholders. Shares of growth companies can be particularly vulnerable to price fluctuations. Obsessed with growth and lacking the accountability to shareholders that dividends provide, managers often spend profits to acquire businesses that don't fit strategically with their main business. This disregard can send stock prices soaring when investors believe the acquisitions will increase profits, but disappointments can have the opposite effect, sending share prices to the cellar. Plummeting share prices sometimes give back more than 90 percent of their previous gains. Having to pay dividends encourages managers to be more sensible in their acquisitions and provides them with less cash to squander on poor decisions.

Second, dividend payments provide steadier returns to investors. Even when stock prices are in a freefall, shareholders can usually count on receiving their dividend payments. This dependability not only calms the nerves of potentially anxious shareholders but also gives them more capital to reinvest in the company or in other companies, which can help further in stabilizing the stock market.

Celebrating Important Dates in the Life of a Dividend

Dividends aren't paid like clockwork. Unlike other forms of income-generating investments, companies have no legal obligation to pay dividends. This fact means the company's board of directors must actively declare, every single quarter, whether it will pay a dividend.

Because dividend stocks, like all other stocks, can be traded on the open market, companies need some way to determine who (the buyer or the seller) gets the next dividend payment when shares are exchanged. You may assume that the person who owned the shares the longest during the quarter would get the dividend payment. After all, if you own the shares for 10 of the 12 weeks that comprise the quarter, you should have more right to the dividend payment than the investor who owned the shares for just the other 2 weeks, right? Well, not exactly.

When you buy and sell dividend stocks, dates determine who gets the dividend and who doesn't. To determine the rightful recipient of dividend payments, companies keep track of several dates in the life of a dividend share, including the date of declaration, trade date, settlement date, date of record, ex-dividend date, and the actual payment date. Because each dividend is a unique event, the company must specify the important dates for this payment. In the following sections, I explain in more detail how these dates are used to determine the rightful recipient of the dividend payment.

Date of declaration

The *date of declaration* is the date on which the company's board of directors announces its next quarterly dividend payment. The declaration typically begins with something like this:

> Chicago, IL — January 29, 2011 Carrel Industries, a provider of consumer products, today announced that its Board of Directors has declared a quarterly cash dividend on its common stock of 44.5 cents per share. The dividend is payable on February 27, 2011, to stockholders of record on February 13, 2011. Carrel Industries initiated quarterly cash dividend payments in the third quarter of fiscal year 2005 and has increased the dividend by 5 percent from the dividend level one year ago.

In this example, the date of declaration is January 29, 2011. The declaration also contains two more key dates: the *payment date* (February 27, 2011, in the example) and the *date of record* (February 13, 2011, in the example). I explain these two dates a little later in this chapter.

Trade date

Stock trading is a lot like buying or selling a house. You buy the house one day but you don't actually become the official owner until after the closing. With all stocks, the day you buy your shares is the *trade date*, but you don't actually take ownership of the shares until several days later on the settlement date, described in the following section.

Settlement date

The *settlement date* (also called the *closing date*) is the date on which the transaction becomes finalized — the buyer pays for the securities and becomes the official shareholder of record while the seller relinquishes her ownership status and collects the money. For equities, the settlement date is the trade date plus three business days (known as T + 3). The seller has three business days after the trade date to deliver the shares to the buyer.

Rarely do investors receive actual stock certificates to prove ownership, as they did in the good old days. Instead, companies keep electronic records of transactions to facilitate the process of trading shares. The person holding possession of the shares according to these company records is called the *shareholder of record.*

Date of record

The *date of record* is the cut-off date for dividend payment eligibility. In other words, to receive the next scheduled divided payment, your name needs to be on the company's books as the shareholder of record on or before the date of record. If you buy and close on shares before the date of record, you receive the dividends. If you buy before the date of record but settle after it, the seller receives the dividends because she's listed as the official owner on the date of record.

Ex-dividend date

Ex-dividend means "without dividend," so the ex-dividend date determines the payment of dividends on the purchase and sale of shares.

- ✔ **Purchase:** Buy shares before the ex-dividend date, and you qualify for the declared dividend. Buy shares on or after this date, and you're ineligible for the most recently declared dividend.

- ✔ **Sale:** Sell shares on or after the ex-dividend date, and you collect the declared dividend. Sell shares before this date, and you miss out on the payment.

The ex-dividend date is arguably the most important date to the dividend investor, but the press release rarely mentions it.

So where does this all-important ex-dividend date come from? After a company chooses the date of record, the stock exchanges or the National Association of Securities Dealers, Inc., sets the *ex-dividend date* two days prior to the date of record. This system creates a three-day period before the date of record during which anyone buying shares is ineligible to receive the declared dividend payment. Why three days? Because a trade on or after the ex-dividend date settles after the date of record.

Recapping the life of a quarterly dividend

The following table helps you keep track of what happens to your dividend on what date by breaking down the sample declaration in the nearby "Date of declaration" section. I've repeated the example here so you can more easily match up the dates.

Chicago, IL — January 29, 2011 Carrel Industries, a provider of consumer products, today announced that its Board of Directors has declared a quarterly cash dividend on its common stock of 44.5 cents per share. The dividend is payable on February 27, 2011, to stockholders of record on February 13, 2011. Carrel Industries initiated quarterly cash dividend payments in the third quarter of fiscal year 2005 and has increased the dividend by 5 percent from the dividend level one year ago.

Event	Sample Date	Comments
Date of declaration	Jan. 29, 2011	The date the company declares the quarterly dividend
Trade date	Before the ex-dividend date	The day you call your broker to buy the shares of stock
Settlement date	On or before the date of record	The day your stock purchase becomes finalized and you become the shareholder of record; can be as many as three business days after the trade date
Date of record	Feb. 13, 2011	The date by which you must be on the company's books of record to qualify for the dividend
Ex-dividend date	Feb 11, 2011	Starts the three-day period before the date of record during which, if you buy the stock, you don't qualify for the dividend
Payment date	Feb. 27, 2011	Hooray! The date the company issues and mails dividend checks to the shareholders of record as of the date of record

Because the dividend returns value to the shareholder, ex-dividend also means that the dividend is value removed from the stock's price, meaning the dividend stock typically trades lower on the ex-dividend date. So, if a company's shares close at $10 the day before the ex-dividend, and the dividend is 25 cents a share, on the morning of ex-dividend the stock opens up at $9.75.

Don't base your decision to buy or sell solely on whether you'll be eligible for the declared dividends. Consider both the share price and the yield to determine what's in your best interest.

Payment date

The *payment date* (also referred to as the *distribution date*) is many shareholders' favorite day — on this date, the company distributes dividends to shareholders. Most companies pay dividends after the end of each three-month fiscal quarter. When a company's fiscal year aligns with the calendar year, the fiscal quarters end on the following dates:

- ✔ **First quarter:** March 31
- ✔ **Second quarter:** June 30
- ✔ **Third quarter:** September 30
- ✔ **Fourth quarter:** December 31

A company's fiscal year may not align with the calendar year. For example, the calendar year runs from January 1 to December 31, but a company's fiscal year may run from August 1 to July 31 or October 1 to September 30.

Chapter 3

Grasping the Dividend Advantage

In This Chapter

▶ Exploring the potential benefits and drawbacks of dividend investing

▶ Knowing what factors typically signify a sound company

▶ Identifying early warning signs of a troubled company

▶ Recognizing factors that can influence dividend investing's fluctuating popularity

*W*henever you're in the market for anything — a house, a car, or even a tasty dessert — you weigh the advantages and disadvantages of your options. In the case of a car, you may compare price and features. Reliability or size and mileage may be more important to one buyer than another. The same is true for investments. You can put your money into all sorts of investments, such as stocks, bonds, mutual funds, real estate, and commodities; each investment carries its own potential risks and rewards, and each can play a unique role in an individual's investment strategy.

Because this book (and hence this chapter) focuses on dividend-paying stocks, I'm not about to discuss your overall investment strategy or the pros and cons of each type of investment vehicle. Eric Tyson's *Investing For Dummies,* 5th Edition (Wiley), is geared more toward investors who require this general guidance. Instead, this chapter focuses specifically on the advantages (and a few possible drawbacks) of dividend-paying stocks — stocks that not only change in value but also pay a portion of the company's profits to the shareholder — assuming, of course, the company is profitable. As an added bonus, I reveal some of the reasons why dividend stocks had fallen out of favor and are now staging a comeback.

Weighing the Pros and Cons of Investing in Dividend Stocks

Prior to investing in anything, savvy investors examine the risk/reward profile to determine whether they want to take a chance and roll the dice. Although dividend stocks are generally less risky than non-dividend stocks (for reasons I explain in the following section), they do carry some risk and may not hold sufficient promise of rewards for some investors. To make a well-informed decision of whether dividend stocks are right for you, evaluate the pros and cons, as described in the following sections.

This is your money, so don't let anyone, including me, tell you how to invest it. As the investor, you need to determine whether the pros outweigh the cons or vice versa. As I explain in the later section "Understanding the Rise and Fall of Dividend Stocks' Popularity," dividend stocks can become a more- or less-attractive option as conditions change.

Exploring the pros

As you may have guessed, I have a strong preference for stocks that pay dividends over those that don't, and for good reason. In the following sections, I describe the many benefits of investing in dividend stocks.

Gaining two ways to win

With dividend stocks, you have two ways to win: when the share value rises and when the company cuts you a dividend check, paying you a portion of its profits. If the share price rises by 4 percent, and the company pays a 3-percent dividend, you pocket a 7-percent profit, minus taxes, of course. (Or you can reinvest your dividends to buy more shares — see "Compounding returns via reinvesting" later in this section.)

In addition to providing two ways to win, the share-price-plus-dividend advantage allows you to hedge your bet. If share prices fall by 4 percent and the company pays a 3-percent dividend, you lose only 1 percent of your investment. Of course, companies can always choose to slash dividends, so you're not completely safe, but you're often safer than if you're relying solely on rising share prices to score a profit.

Securing a steady stream of income

Investors often talk about the beauty of passive income. Instead of having to work to earn a buck, you put your money to work for you. Dividend stocks enable this dream to come true. You buy shares, and as long as the company is profitable and paying dividends, you have a steady source of income without having to lift a finger.

With most other investments, you don't realize a profit until you sell. Before you tell a broker to sell, any profit is a *paper profit* — you can see it on a statement, but you can't spend it or stick it in your piggy bank. If your investment drops in value, that profit can go "poof!" Just ask anyone who held shares of Enron before news of its scandal broke.

Dividend stocks are different. Companies pay out the dividends in cold, hard cash. These aren't paper profits that can disappear in a bear market. Dividends are money in your pocket, and after they're paid they can't be taken from you.

Companies typically pay dividends on a regular basis — usually every fiscal quarter (three months).

Achieving profits and ownership

If your stocks don't pay dividends, the only way you can wring cash out of your investment is by selling your shares. Unfortunately, selling shares means relinquishing your ownership in the company — something you may not want to do if you think the company will grow and the share prices will rise. With dividends, you receive a return on your investment while holding onto the shares for potential capital appreciation.

Compounding returns via reinvesting

Compounding is one of the most powerful forces in the world of investing. It's like the old riddle: How much wheat do you end up with if you place one grain of wheat on a checkerboard square and then double the amount each time you move to the next of the 64 squares? Answer: Enough grain to bury India 50 feet deep! That's a little exaggerated in terms of investing, but compounding returns follows the same principle.

Suppose two investors, Party Pete and Frugal Frank, each own 100 shares of company ABC Inc. at $20 a share, a $2,000 investment. Each receives a dividend of $2 per share — a 10-percent yield that gives them $200 at the end of the first year (100 shares times $2). Party Pete uses the $200 to take his wife out for a fun night of dinner and theater. Frugal Frank uses his $200 to buy 10 new shares of ABC Inc. Now Frank owns 110 shares.

Note: Most stocks pay quarterly dividends, but to make this example easy to understand, I'm assuming one dividend payment of $2 a year rather than four quarterly payments of 50 cents.

The next year the dividend remains at $2. Pete receives another $200 and again spends the money to have fun with his wife. Frank now receives $220 (110 shares times $2). He reinvests his dividends again. Now he can buy 11 new shares, giving him a total of 121 shares.

After the third year the dividend is still $2. Party Pete receives another $200 and uses it to go away for a weekend trip. Meanwhile, Frugal Frank now receives a payment of $242. He uses this money to buy 12 new shares, giving himself a total of 133 shares.

After the third dividend gets paid, the stock's price jumps to $25. Both Pete and Frank decide to sell all their shares. Who earned more? Frugal Frank, of course! Here's how the numbers break down:

On the initial investment of 100 shares bought at $20 each, both Pete and Frank made $500.

Sale Price	$25/share × 100 shares	=	$2,500
Subtract			
Initial Investment	$20/share × 100 shares	=	$2,000
Price Appreciation	$5/share × 100 shares	=	$500

To figure out each investor's total return you need to add in the dividends.

Because Pete didn't reinvest any of his $200 dividend but took it all in cash, he received a total of $600 in dividends. Together with his capital appreciation, he earned $1,100:

Price Appreciation ($500) + Dividends ($600) = Total Return $1,100.

Because Frank reinvested his dividends, each year he had more shares on which dividends were paid. For the three years, his dividends totaled $662. This means Frank earned $62, or 10 percent, more than Pete in dividends alone.

Dividends	$200 + $220 + $242	=	$662

Over the three years, Frank reinvested $660 of these dividends to buy 33 more shares at $20 each. When he sold these additional shares for $25, he received $825, for an additional profit of $165. This gave him a total return of $1,327

Price Appreciation ($500)

+ Dividends ($662)

+ Appreciation from shares bought with reinvested dividends ($165)

Party Pete's sale of his original 100 shares, for a $5 profit per share, gave him $500 in capital appreciation, for a 25-percent return from price alone: $500 ÷ $2,000 = .25. Add in the $600 in dividends ($200 in dividends a year for three years) and Party Pete's total return (dividends plus price appreciation) comes to $1,100, for a total rate of return of 55 percent: $1,100 ÷ $2,000 = .55.

Meanwhile, doing nothing but reinvesting his dividends, Frugal Frank earned $1,327, or 20.6 percent more profit than Party Pete. This gave Frugal Frank a total rate of return of 66.4 percent in just three years: $1,327 ÷ $2,000 = 0.664.

Hedging against inflation: Another way to WIN

In August 1974, then-president Gerald R. Ford encouraged his fellow Americans to Whip Inflation Now (WIN). Inflation was at about 11 percent back then, and just about everybody in the country was wearing a WIN button. One of the best ways to keep inflation from taking a bite out of your investment earnings is to invest in dividend-paying stocks. The big advantage dividends hold over other income generating investments is they have the potential to keep pace with inflation. As prices rise, profits also tend to rise, and companies can afford to raise their dividend payments.

Inflation takes a bite out of earnings. With inflation at a modest 3 percent, a 7-percent annual return on an investment (not bad) nets only a measly 4-percent annual gain.

When you account for inflation, stock appreciation from 1926 to 2008 is pretty dismal. Over that period, the S&P 500 earned an annualized total return of 9.69 percent per year. Of that percentage rise, dividends accounted for about 4.19 percent, and price appreciation accounted for 5.5 percent. Subtract 3 percent for inflation, and stock appreciation alone produced an annualized average return of only 2.5 percent.

The Dow is even worse. Of its annualized total return of 7.96 percent, dividends accounted for 3.34 percent, and share appreciation contributed 4.62 percent. Subtract 3 percent for inflation, and investors who counted solely on stock appreciation for earnings realized an annual return of only 1.62 percent.

Banking on the buy-and-hold advantage

Dividend investors tend to be more committed than non-dividend investors. They're in the market for the long haul and want to own shares in companies that deliver returns in good times and bad. As a result, dividend shares tend to out-perform non-dividend shares when the market heads south. Several factors contribute to this trend:

✔ When stock prices are falling, investors are under pressure to sell to either secure their gains or limit their losses. As more and more investors sell their shares, prices drop even more, often triggering a vicious cycle that drives share prices even lower.

✔ Investors typically sell their dividend stocks last. They hold onto those stocks longer because dividend stocks continue to give them a return on their investment.

✔ The fact that many dividend stock investors don't sell tempers any decline in the share price.

> ✔ Investors burned by the large losses from their high volatility stocks look for safer, more stable investments. They may move their money into dividend stocks to protect their gains (with a safer investment) or as a way to capture some returns in a bad environment for price appreciation. Greater investor demand can drive up the share price of dividend stocks even as the rest of the market stagnates. This situation creates a *profit circle:* Greater demand pushes a stock price higher, which creates greater demand, which pushes the price even higher.

Stocks that offer only capital appreciation through rising stock prices have little chance of providing a positive return when stock prices are falling. Thus, many investors sell these stocks sooner than dividend stocks.

Riding the possible baby boomer retirement surge

In the preceding sections, I discuss the classic advantages of investing in dividend stocks. However, another factor may contribute to the success and stability of dividend stocks: the graying of the baby boomers, those 77.3 million people born in the United States between 1946 and 1964. Beginning in the 1980s, this demographic has had a tremendous influence on the stock market and will continue to into the foreseeable future.

Lessons from the stock market crash of '87

Although low volatility stocks see much smaller gains than high volatility stocks during bull markets, low volatility provides its benefit on the downside with a less dramatic decline in share prices.

A study done by two professors of finance at Cornell University in the wake of the stock market crash of 1987 proves this fact. Professors Avner Arbel and Steven Carvell proved that the safest stocks in the market — those with high yields, low price-to-earnings ratios, low price-to-book ratios, and low betas — suffered the least in the crash. (*Beta* measures how well a stock follows the broader market. Low beta stocks seem to march to their own drummers.)

A follow-up study by the same professors showed that the stocks that fell the most had been recommended the most by stock analysts at investment banks because of predictions for the biggest earnings growth. Stocks with the lowest projected growth declined the least. The 25 stocks most recommended by Wall Street in the weeks before the crash tumbled 19.7 percent versus an 11-percent decline in the S&P 500.

High-yielding dividend stocks with yields of 3.8 percent or more did fall 16.71 percent during the crash. However, growth stocks with low or no yields got pummeled, plunging 31.79 percent. "It has always been a question whether dividend yield matters," Professor Carvell told the *New York Times* soon after the study's publication. "In this type of situation, it mattered."

This huge sea of workers has begun retiring. By 2030, the Congressional Budget Office expects the number of people in the United States ages 65 and older to approximately double, according to the office's November 2003 report "Baby Boomers' Retirement Prospects: An Overview."

In order to maintain their preretirement lifestyle in retirement, baby boomers will need to rely on their investments to supplement their income. This necessity will likely cause many to change their investment strategies from one primarily focused on growth to an income-based approach. Translation: Boomers face an increasing need to score supplemental income, and the smart ones who have money to invest are likely to consider dividend stocks as a prime source of that supplemental income. Traditionally, retirees tend to reposition their assets into more conservative portfolios that focus on income generation over capital appreciation through growth. Nobody has any reason to believe that this trend will change when the boomers retire. Assuming this scenario happens, both stock prices and dividends should rise accordingly.

Investigating the cons

Whenever you sign on the dotted line with a broker, mutual fund manager, or other intermediary, he usually presents you with a long disclaimer that basically boils down to a single statement: "Past results are no guarantee of future performance." In other words, yesterday's winner can be tomorrow's loser. Investing always carries some risk, and dividend stocks are no exception. A few dangers to be aware of:

✔ In general, dividend-paying companies see less price appreciation than growth stocks.

✔ Share prices can drop whether the stock pays dividends or not.

✔ Companies can slash or eliminate their dividend payments at any time for any reason. As a shareholder, you're at the end of the line when checks are cut.

✔ Tax rates on dividends can rise, making dividend stocks a less attractive option — for the company to pay and for you to receive. See "Understanding the Rise and Fall of Dividend Investing's Popularity" later in this chapter for details.

Not investing also carries risk. If you stuff your money in a mattress or bury it in a coffee can in the backyard, someone can steal it or mice, bugs, or inflation can eat away at it.

Gaining Confidence by Investing in Solid Companies

When you see that a company is doling out healthy dividends to shareholders, you know it has positive cash flow — more cash is flowing in than flowing out. The company can cover its bills, compensate its employees, pay its taxes, and still have some money left over to distribute to investors. Perhaps even more important, dividends typically are a sign that the company is fundamentally sound, which means it should exhibit the following qualities:

- ✔ Maturity
- ✔ Effective management
- ✔ Stability
- ✔ Earnings growth

In the following sections, I describe these qualities of fundamentally sound companies in greater detail and point out some of the early warning signs that crop up when a company or an entire sector starts experiencing problems.

Just because a company looks good on paper and is paying dividends doesn't guarantee it's healthy. Underlying issues may be chipping away at the company's foundation before signs of trouble appear. A company with negative cash flow from operations can hide its troubles by borrowing money, selling off assets, or issuing new stock. These moves are short-term fixes that the company can't sustain or hide for long. You can reduce your risk through careful research and diversification, but you can never eliminate it entirely. The guidance I provide in the following sections can assist you in identifying companies that operate on sound fundamentals. For additional guidance on assessing a company's strength, check out Chapter 8.

Maturity: Boring, but stable

As I mention in Chapter 1, dividend stocks evoke a mental image of Grandma's portfolio and, like Grandma, most of the companies that pay out dividends are what you'd probably call *mature*. They're settled in. They may have slowed down a bit in terms of growth, but they're rock-steady and highly dependable.

Companies proceed through various stages of life, just like people:

- **Infancy:** Startup companies typically have great prospects but require more money and attention to get up and running. During a company's infancy, it's probably spending more money than it's earning, but its low share price and potential for big profits are attractive to growth investors. Without an influx of sufficient cash to fuel their growth, companies at this stage risk becoming like malnourished children, and their growth can be stunted.

- **Childhood:** Assuming a company survives its infancy, it typically develops quickly. At the childhood stage, revenues often grow in leaps and bounds, too, but the risk factor for investing in the company remains high. After all, children are prone to having accidents and making mistakes.

- **Teenage:** During this stage (but not necessarily company age), companies can be as different as any two teenagers. Some are fairly mature. They earn enough to cover their expenses and perhaps even a little surplus. They make good choices. They're fairly independent. Other companies are accidents waiting to happen — irresponsible, misdirected, accident-prone, ready to take risks without carefully evaluating the situation, and constantly needing more and more capital just to stay afloat. Companies at this stage generally still have plenty of growth potential, but poorly managed companies have more potential for failure.

- **Adulthood:** Mature companies are like adults. They've done most of their growing already. Mature companies still raise profits, but typically at a slower rate. Although they may not see big year-over-year advances in share price and profits, their long experience has taught them effective, efficient ways to earn money consistently. You can always find exceptions, but a mature company is one that generally takes fewer outrageous risks to score big.

Strive to become a mature investor, too. The novice is often eager to scoop up shares of growth companies in their infancy or early childhood in the hopes the share price doubles or triples in a short period of time. In their irrational exuberance, these novice investors may fail to account for the risk factor — the more you stand to gain, the more you stand to lose (generally speaking). I'm not saying that investing in companies in their infancy is necessarily bad, but it's typically riskier than investing in an established company with a proven track record.

Good management

Dividends typically signify good corporate management. To pay out a dividend, a company must have cash on hand. Management can't fake it. It can (and sometimes does) fake paper profits by padding its sales and profits on reports, but it can't fake paying cash dividends to shareholders. Paying dividends over a long period of time makes a positive statement about the company's financial health. When you see a company paying dividends, you can expect to find confident managers in charge, exerting fiscal discipline, good corporate governance, and transparency in the company's earnings reports:

- **Management confidence:** Paying a dividend provides a clear signal about management's confidence in the company's ability to continue to post profits.

- **Fiscal discipline:** The decision to pay a dividend isn't entered into lightly. As soon as a company starts paying a dividend, shareholders come to expect it. Cutting or eliminating a dividend reflects very poorly on the managers and the company in the eyes of investors.

- **Corporate governance:** Dividends provide a form of corporate governance for shareholders. Corporate managers, by the nature of their positions, know more about a company's operations than do outside shareholders. Contemporary corporate scandals show that some managers make decisions to benefit themselves at the expense of the company and its true owners, the shareholders. Because companies can't fake dividends, payments provide a good benchmark for shareholders.

- **Earnings transparency:** In light of earnings-manipulation scandals, paying dividends validates the company's accounting process and increases the credibility of the earnings reported currently and in the past. Again, you can fake sales and earnings figures, but you can't fake cold, hard cash.

In addition, paying dividends subjects companies to certain checks and balances. Companies that pay out dividends need to be more judicious with how they spend shareholder money. They have less cash on hand to undertake corporate investments or acquisitions of other companies. Should a dividend-paying corporation decide to make a large investment or acquisition, it has to go to the capital markets, for either debt or equity, to fund the project. When companies seek outside money, investors and other interested outside parties scrutinize the plans and can often derail anything they deem foolish or overly risky. In other words, dividends make management more accountable to investors.

Public and private organizations sell either debt or equity to raise capital to fund their operations. The stock and bond markets, collectively known as the *capital markets,* are where capital is sold and traded.

Holding managers accountable

In a 2004 speech about corporate governance, Mark J. Warshawsky, assistant U.S. Treasury Secretary for Economic Policy, said that "investments made with retained earnings are usually subject to less scrutiny than those financed with outside equity or debt, reducing the pressure on corporate managers to undertake the most productive investments. Thus dividends increase corporate accountability vis-à-vis investors. And critically, when managers are required to go to the capital markets to finance investments or acquisitions they become subject to the objective discipline of the markets' assessment."

Economist Michael Jensen studied how managers at companies with substantial cash flow but few profitable investment opportunities often make investments in low-return projects or enter businesses outside the corporation's expertise. Often managers do make these investments to justify high compensation or promotions for themselves. These kinds of investments often lead to lower sales growth and profits, and subsequently suboptimal stock returns. However, paying out dividends limits management discretion, giving managers fewer opportunities to make unproductive decisions.

By investing in dividend stocks, you and your fellow shareholders have more power to keep corporate managers from gambling foolishly with what rightfully belongs to the shareholder.

Stability

Dividend companies typically provide for the necessities of life: food, water, electricity, gas, a place to live, and the all-important personal hygiene. As a result, the classic industries for dividends include:

- Utilities
- Real estate
- Energy
- Finance
- Telecommunications
- Consumer staples, such as food and clothing

Because people always purchase these products and services, even when times are tough, the industries that provide them are generally more stable. Less stable companies provide what consumers can live without — computers, cellphones, digital music players, restaurants, and anything travel related, such as hotels and airlines.

You're probably about to jump out of your seat and scream "Financials? Real estate? Stable? Not going out of business? Are you crazy?" Yes, I know that during the stock market bubble that peaked in 2007, financials broke the mold of stable companies and went bonkers themselves. I know that many ran their companies poorly and with little shareholder oversight even as they paid out dividends. And yes, I know that many financial institutions went bankrupt, losing lots of money for investors. But please stay seated.

Every rule has exceptions. Yes, many financials broke the rules, but the red flags were waving before the bubble burst, and attentive investors who knew the warning signs bailed out early (check out "Spotting early warning signs" later in this section). Overall, however, dividend companies are more stable than non-dividend companies. In fact, paying dividends is probably one factor that helped some financial companies survive the crash, assuming they didn't have to take money from the government.

Don't buy shares and then fall asleep at the wheel. Take nothing in the stock market for granted. It's always moving, so remain vigilant. In this chapter and throughout this book, especially in Chapter 8, I show you how to assess the health and growth potential of companies before purchasing shares. Use these same strategies to reevaluate your holdings regularly — I recommend at least annually, if not quarterly.

Strong earnings growth

Investors often think mature companies pay out a large portion of their profits as dividends because they can't find investments that offer good returns in their traditional businesses. Reality offers a more nuanced view. Take a look at General Electric (GE). You can't find a more mature company than GE or one that had increased dividend payments more consistently. Yet, the company has pumped a good portion of its earnings into growth and diversification, building and running 12 major business units in state-of-the-art technology, from jet aircraft engines to household appliances.

Spotting early warning signs

Companies that pay dividends are generally more stable than companies that don't, but they're not always more stable, as became obvious with the downfall of the financial sector in 2008. Until that time, financial companies, in general, had a long and strong reputation for paying sizeable dividends. The sector's demise serves as a reminder that there's no such thing as a safe sector or a safe stock. Even General Electric, which owns a huge financial unit that got hurt in the subprime mortgage debacle, was forced to cut its dividend in 2008 for the first time since the Great Depression.

Many people who bet big on the financial sector were skewered, but many attentive and knowledgeable investors moved their money before tragedy struck, because they spotted the early warning signs — indications of trouble below the surface that you can't see just by looking at annual reports, share prices, or dividends. When investing, you need to remain attentive and know what to look for, including the following signs of trouble:

- ✔ Problems in the company's main business
- ✔ Declining sales
- ✔ Falling profits
- ✔ Rising debt
- ✔ Negative cash flow
- ✔ Dividend cuts
- ✔ Declining health of the industry
- ✔ Negative news stories about the company or industry
- ✔ Investigations by regulators or the police
- ✔ Declining economic conditions
- ✔ Chief executive contracting a serious illness

Understanding the Rise and Fall of Dividend Stocks' Popularity

Throughout this chapter, I present dividend stocks as the next best thing to winning the lottery, but this scenario isn't always the case. For various reasons, dividend stocks become more or less attractive. For example, earlier in this chapter I discuss the likelihood that baby boomers, looking for a stable source of supplemental income, may significantly increase demand for dividend stocks. Other factors may also come into play to further strengthen or weaken demand.

In the following sections, I point out the key factors that may affect the popularity of dividend stocks so that you're aware of conditions that can increase or decrease the net return on your dividend investments.

We don't need your stinkin' dividends: Dividends fall out of favor

For most of the 20th century, dividends accounted for about half of the stock market's return — approximately 40 percent, to be precise. Yet, in the year 1999, dividends had fallen to account for only about 7 percent of the market's total returns. Why did investors turn their backs on this easy, relatively consistent money? A combination of factors over the last two decades of the 20th century led investors to treat dividends as second-class citizens:

- **Dividend-bashing tax laws:** A dramatic change in the tax laws sparked dividends' sudden fall from grace. In 1981, tax rates on long-term capital gains were cut to a maximum of 20 percent, and dividends continued to be taxed at an investor's tax rate for ordinary income, which ran as high as 70 percent! (*Long-term capital gains* are profits from the sale of investments held longer than one year.) Before the long-term capital gains tax cut, Standard & Poor's says 94 percent of the S&P 500's component stocks paid out more than 50 percent of their earnings in dividends. By 2002, only 70 percent of companies on the S&P 500 paid dividends. On average, the dividend payout ratio was slashed nearly in half to 30 percent of profits.

- **Double taxation:** Dividends are taxed twice, both at the corporate and individual levels — a practice known as *double taxation*. Coupled with changes in the tax code, this double taxation took an even bigger chunk out of dividends. Even older, mature companies, the kind that historically paid dividends, changed their dividend policies. With price appreciation receiving more tax benefits than dividends, companies decided to focus on increasing shareholder value through price appreciation.

- **Growing popularity of growth investing:** When dividend investors realized that taxes were taking a good chunk out of their earnings, many changed strategies. Do the math, and you quickly realize that paying 20 percent on long-term capital gains beats paying nearly 40 percent on dividend income. The changes in the tax code sparked a rush into investments with the potential for huge price appreciation. Most of these investment dollars moved into small, growth-oriented companies that didn't pay dividends. This capital infusion was a major factor in the bull markets of the 1980s and the 1990s.

- **Growth company boom:** During the bull market, the number of new companies entering the stock market soared. The U.S. economy was firing on all cylinders. With astronomical growth in the high tech industries of computer technology, telecommunications, and the Internet, the U.S. stock market's value grew by nearly 1,000 percent. With price gains like this, investors weren't interested in waiting around 20 years to see results they could achieve in less than 12 months.

✔ **Share buybacks:** Companies cut dividends and used the excess capital to buy back their shares on the open market, thus lowering the number of shares available for purchase. This reduction isn't necessarily a negative for share holders. Share buybacks send a message to the market that management believes the stock is under-priced. Buybacks boost a stock's price by creating more demand for shares. Buybacks can also boost the earnings per share, as explained in the nearby sidebar.

The terms *profit, net profit, net income,* and *earnings per share* all refer to the amount of money that remains after the company pays off all its expenses, including taxes. Companies pay out dividends after they determine their net income.

Boosting earnings per share with buybacks

When companies buy back shares, investors stand to benefit in two ways:

✔ The law of supply and demand raises the stock price.

✔ Earnings per share rise because the companies' profit is distributed to fewer shares.

Investors generally understand the law of supply and demand and how it plays out on the stock market, but many have trouble understanding why a corporate buyback increases the earnings per share.

Strictly speaking, earnings per share describes the amount of profit allocated to each share of stock. Here's how it works: When a company earns a *net profit* (profit minus all expenses and taxes), it distributes that profit equally to all the shareholders. If, for example, a company earns a net profit of $4 million and has 2 million shares, each share receives $2 ($4 million divided by 2 million shares). However, if the company buys back 1 million shares, leaving just 1 million shares outstanding, the earnings per share jumps to $4 (the same $4 million profit now divided by only 1 million shares).

Most of the time, a rise in earnings per share means an equal increase in total profits. Because measuring earnings per share makes comparing companies easier than comparing total profits, most investors use earnings per share rather than total profit in their research. If they see rising earnings per share, they automatically assume the company increased profits. Rising profits increase investor interest in the stock, which pushes the stock's price higher. But the buyback can be misleading in that it falsely gives the impression that profits are rising when they're not; you just get a bigger chunk of the total profit. In other words, the size of the pie stays the same, but everyone gets a bigger piece because fewer people are eating the dessert. Buybacks are a good thing for shares you already have in your portfolio, but they tend to make the shares a little pricier if you're looking to buy.

Dividend stocks stage a comeback

The popping of the stock market's technology bubble in 2000 sent stock prices into a two-year freefall. Many technology companies went out of business. With nothing to show for their investments in growth companies, investors shifted to plan B. Suddenly the concept of earning profits in the form of dividends didn't seem so old-fashioned to investors. This time, the combination of factors showed how fleeting price appreciation can be:

- **Dividend-friendly tax laws:** The Jobs and Growth Tax Relief Reconciliation Act of 2003 has had the most influence on the increasing popularity of dividend investing. This tax law cut taxes on both dividends and long-term capital gains to 15 percent. This change made dividend income much more attractive. In the wake of the tax cut, dividend payouts on the S&P 500 jumped by an average of 8 percent. Dividend stocks helped spur the bull market of 2003 to 2007. With no taxation penalty, dividends gained equal footing with long-term capital gains and reemerged to their rightful place in the investment universe. For more about how taxes affect dividends, check out Chapter 20.

- **Buybacks backfire:** The buybacks that typically lift share prices (see the preceding section and nearby sidebar) had some unintended consequences. Many firms used this technique to boost the price of shares that had fallen significantly in value. In essence, a company would use the buybacks to prop up falling share prices, sending Wall Street a false signal that management was confident in the company's future. When investors failed to buy into the buyback, the company was sunk — if it was cash-poor before, it was flat broke after buying back all those shares.

- **Earnings scandals:** The stock market crash of 2000 also exposed the dirty underbelly of the bull market. Many companies weren't growing as fast as their management proclaimed. In fact, many were losing money. Realizing the only reason their investors stayed with them was for price appreciation, corporate managers broke the law to keep share prices, and hence their salaries, rising. Executives manipulated their companies' financial statements and perpetrated fraud to show bigger and faster profit growth than actually occurred. Some of the largest companies in the country — Enron, WorldCom, and Adelphia — were destroyed by earnings scandals. Investors learned the hard way that profits, but never dividends, can be faked.

- **Second stock market bubble pops:** Investors who didn't see the writing on the wall in 2000 received a repeat lesson on the value of dividends with the 2008 financial crisis. With stock market indexes plunging more than 50 percent off their highs, investors saw the unrealized profits in their portfolios disappear like smoke into the air twice in one decade. Thus, the steep declines in share prices and beneficial changes in the tax laws have made investing in dividend stocks much more attractive.

Part II

Selecting an Investment Approach and Picking Stocks

The 5th Wave   By Rich Tennant

Defining your investment risk with the
TOAST RETRIEVING RISK TOLERANCE TEST

LOW RISK | Waits for toast to pop up even though it's burning.

MODERATE RISK | Goes after toast with wooden toast prongs.

HIGH RISK | Goes after toast with all-metal butter knife.

ULTRA HIGH RISK | Goes after toast with metal butter knife wearing a wet swim suit and a stainless steel colander on head.

In this part . . .

*E*very investor has a unique stock-picking system. Many adopt a value approach, looking for what they believe to be undervalued stocks. Others prefer a crystal ball approach, attempting to predict a stock's performance based on market trends and investor sentiment. Some, usually the ones popping the most antacids, follow their guts.

This part presents a practical, low-stress approach to investing that accounts for your personality, risk tolerance, financial goals, and time frame. It reveals several standard approaches to investing that you may want to consider, shows you how to find potentially good dividend stocks to invest in, and guides you in carefully scrutinizing candidates to pick the best of the bunch.

Chapter 4

Risky Business: Assessing Risk and Your Risk Tolerance

*L*ife is a risk. In fact, most things people find worthwhile are risky — driving, flying, swimming, getting married, raising kids, starting a business, buying a house — but people often engage in these activities because the reward (or at least the promise of reward) is worth the risk.

Each individual has a different *risk tolerance* — a threshold beyond which she won't willingly venture. Some people draw the line at public speaking. For others, it's bungee jumping, whitewater rafting, or sealing themselves in a barrel to take a thrill ride down Niagara Falls. Investing is risky, too, but you get to choose the level of risk and can take steps to reduce your exposure to it.

In this chapter, you discover how to measure risk and reward, gain a deeper understanding of the tradeoffs, gauge your level of risk tolerance, recognize the factors that can increase risk, and pick up a few techniques for improving your odds.

 "When reward is at its pinnacle, risk is near at hand," says John Bogle, creator of the first index mutual fund and founder of the Vanguard Group. In life, the more dangerous the activity, the greater the risk of injury or death, but the greater the thrill. In investing, the riskier the investment, the greater the potential for big returns or big losses.

Weighing Risk and Reward

Barron's calls *risk* the measurable possibility of losing money. It's different from *uncertainty,* which isn't measurable. *Reward,* of course, is what you stand to gain if your risk pays off. Investors have a couple ways of measuring risk and reward. I use these methods in the following sections to demonstrate how risks and rewards generally interact in terms of investments.

Graphing risk versus reward

One way to gain a sense of how risk and reward generally play out in the world of investing is to look at a graph such as Figure 4-1 that shows how investments with different relative risk levels perform over time (this figure compares stocks, bonds, and cash with inflation from 1987 through 2007). Note the following types of investment vehicles:

- **Cash:** Parking your money in the bank or a money-market fund may seem pretty safe, but you can expect a return that's significantly lower than that for stocks and bonds and may not even keep pace with inflation.

- **Bonds:** By investing in bonds, you retain some security while enhancing the potential return on your investment.

- **Stocks:** Stock prices rise and fall, but when all is said and done, they generally provide you with an opportunity for a significantly higher rate of return. As I explain in Chapter 3, dividend stocks offer greater stability while still enabling you to score the higher returns stocks offer.

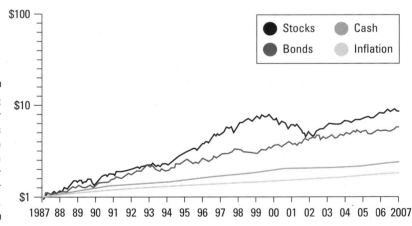

Figure 4-1: Riskier investments tend to produce higher returns over time.

Time can be your friend or foe. Young investors can take more risks than older investors because they can afford to spend some time waiting until the market recovers before withdrawing their money. Older investors are generally advised to play it safe and protect the gains they've earned over their many years, because soon they'll need to cash out their chips.

Assigning a number to investment risk

Assigning a number or a risk level to various endeavors can be quite a challenge. I suppose on a scale of one to ten, taking a nap would rank one and rock climbing may rank nine or ten. Investors have a much more precise measure of risk: *volatility* — the range in which an investment generally moves.

Calculating volatility is a task best suited for mathematicians. I mention it here only to make you aware that highly volatile investments are generally riskier than those that sail on a more even keel. (If you're really interested in more on volatility, head to the nearby sidebar.)

Fortunately, stocks that pay dividends are generally much less volatile than pure growth stocks. By following the guidelines for selecting dividend stocks in Chapter 8, you improve your chances of picking less-volatile stocks that deliver solid returns.

Volatility, relatively speaking

Volatility gauges the relative risks of different investment types and even individual investments. Volatility is expressed in terms of *standard deviation* — how far something tends to rise above or sink below the *mean* (average). *Spread* expresses the total swing (above and below), so if the standard deviation is 25 percent, the spread is 50 percent. Here's how stocks stack up against bonds in terms of volatility (on average):

✔ A growth stock may see gains of 100 percent or losses of nearly 100 percent — a *standard deviation* of about 100 percent or a spread of about 200 percentage points.

✔ The S&P 500 Index, which is probably the least volatile stock index, has a standard deviation of about 16 percent or a spread of about 32 percent.

✔ Long-term U.S. Treasury bonds (those with a maturity greater than 17 years) have a standard deviation around 8 percent, according to *Bond Investing For Dummies* by Russell Wild (Wiley). Short-term government bonds and investment grade corporate bonds experience volatility in the range of just 2 percent to 3 percent. Only the riskiest bonds have a standard deviation as large as that of the S&P 500.

Keep in mind that volatility measures the price swing — both up and down. Investments that have a bigger potential upswing generally have a bigger potential downswing.

Assigning a number to rewards

Assigning a number to investment rewards is easy — it's a dollar amount or a percentage. All you have to do is look at your statements.

- ✔ A positive number indicates reward — the bigger the number, the greater the reward.
- ✔ A negative number means you've just been spanked. Hey, it happens to the best of us.

Recognizing the risk of no risk

If you lie in bed all day doing nothing, your risk of not living a full life is 100 percent. The same is true when you're dealing with money. If you don't take some risk with it, it loses value. Unless you invest it in something that provides a decent return, inflation gnaws away at it with each passing day.

Stuffing your cash in a mattress, burying it in a coffee can, or stashing it in a savings account with an interest rate lower than the rate of inflation is risky. To protect your savings, put your money to work by investing it in something that offers a return at least equal to the inflation rate.

Remain aware of the risk of not taking a risk. It's one sure way to lose money.

Gauging and Raising Your Risk Tolerance

Investors are like parents of little children. Some parents send their kids out to play without a worry in the world. Others fret so much that their poor kids never get out of the house or have a chance to grow up. Before you send your money out in the world to earn profits for you, you need to determine how worried you're going to be about it — how much risk you can tolerate without getting sick over it.

How you perceive risks and respond to losses is very personal and not something you can assign a number to. It's purely subjective. However, you can gauge your risk tolerance to gain a clearer understanding of the types of investments you feel comfortable with. You can also stretch your comfort zone by adjusting your perspective. The following sections show you how.

Those who have never experienced financial hardship often become flippant about risk. After all, it's only money, right? Well, for some rare souls, money is really only money. For the rest, money represents more than that — having good credit, owning a car and a house, supporting a family, and even eating a couple of meals a day. Because of this gravity, realize what's really at stake before you make any investment.

Measuring risk tolerance in sleepless nights

You don't want to lose sleep over your investments, so try gauging your risk tolerance in relation to sleepless nights. Use the following guidelines to estimate your comfort level:

- **High tolerance:** You can handle extreme volatility in your investments and the possibility of massive losses, and you're able to sleep at night when the market is in turmoil.

- **Average tolerance:** You can handle average-sized drops in price for extended periods, but the extreme stuff makes you anxious, jumpy, and unable to sleep at night.

- **Low tolerance:** Losses of 5 percent keep you awake at night. It's mostly bonds and bank accounts for you. Don't lose faith, though — you may be able to expand your comfort zone, as I cover in the following section.

Boosting your risk tolerance with the promise of rewards

Whenever you're thinking about investing in anything, consider the potential rewards along with the risks to determine whether taking the chance is worth it to you. Risk tolerance isn't set in stone — the levels of risk and reward influence your decision. Nobody in their right mind, for example, would step into a cage with a hungry lion. But set $1 million in the cage and offer the person something to defend himself with, and you'll probably get a few takers because the reward is more proportionate to the risk.

The same is true for investing. If a complete stranger presents you with an opportunity to risk $10,000 to earn a buck, you're going to tell the guy to take a hike. On the other hand, if someone you trust completely in financial matters assures you that investing $10,000 will earn you $20,000 by the end of the year (and you have an extra ten grand sitting in the bank), you'd probably jump at the offer.

Table 4-1 provides some guidelines to help you decide whether a particular level of risk is right for you.

Table 4-1	Risk/Reward Guidelines
Risk Level	**Reward Level**
High	Potential for high returns or losses
Average	High potential for average returns or losses, but still a little potential for high returns or losses
Low	High probability of small returns or losses, average potential for average returns or losses, and very little potential for high returns or losses

Don't risk what you can't afford to lose. If you've saved $20,000 to send your daughter to college next year, investing in stocks, even "safe" stocks recommended by a trusted source, is probably a bad idea. If your share prices drop, you have little or no time to recover from the losses before you need to cash out.

Recognizing Factors That Can Increase Risk

Risk is ever present, but it's always variable and unpredictable. A host of factors can increase risk, some of which are within your control and others of which aren't. Although you can't eliminate risk, you can often reduce your exposure to it by becoming more aware of the factors that influence it. In the following sections, I introduce these factors, describe them, and provide a few suggestions on how to deal with them.

Dealing with risk factors you can control

Even the riskiest activities offer ways for participants to reduce the risk. For example, skydivers can pack their own parachutes. Racecar drivers can strap themselves in and wear helmets. In much the same way, investors mitigate their risks by dealing with factors they can control, as described in the following sections.

Reducing human error

Human error is the biggest risk factor with investing, and it can come in many forms:

✔ Insufficient knowledge

✔ Lack of research and analysis

✔ Choosing the wrong investment strategy for your stated goals

✔ Failure to monitor market conditions

✔ Choosing stocks emotionally rather than rationally (see the following section)

✔ Letting fear and panic influence investment decisions

The best way to remove human error from the equation is to do your homework. If you've ever taken an exam you haven't studied for, you know the risk involved in not being prepared. In addition to having no idea what the answers are, panic sets in to make matters worse. This book can assist you in preparing properly, thus reducing the risk of human error.

Investing less emotionally

One of the prevailing theories about the mechanics of the stock market is called the *Efficient Market Hypothesis.* It describes investors as rational people processing all the available information in the market to make logical decisions for maximum profits. But the truth of the matter is that most people aren't rational or logical investors. They buy stocks on tips from friends or even strangers, because of something they heard on the news, or because a company makes a product they love and are sure it's going to be a big hit. They know nothing about the company, its management, or the stock's history.

Don't let emotions govern your investment decisions. Remain particularly cautious of the following emotions:

✔ **Greed:** Greed often seduces investors into making terrible decisions. During market rallies, investors often succumb to a herd mentality, throwing their money into the hottest sectors and companies, inflating a bubble that invariably bursts. Greedy investors often tend to make bets they can't afford to lose and then fall into the trap of making even bigger bets to recover their losses.

✔ **Fear:** Fear is the flip side of greed. People who previously lost money in the market, or just witnessed the pain felt by others, can experience such a massive fear of losing money that it paralyzes them from doing anything. Instead of taking on some risk with suitable investments, they put their money in low-risk investments with poor rates of return.

✔ **Love:** Don't fall in love with your investments. They don't return your love but have a good chance of hurting and betraying you. All too often, people refuse to sell when stocks begin to fall because they really believe in the company. Maybe they found it themselves or received a hot tip from a friend. Yet, when a stock falls sharply on very bad news, you need to bail out. Remember, you're not married to a stock. On a regular basis, look at your stocks and ask them, "What have you done for me lately?" If the answer doesn't satisfy you, you can unceremoniously dump them without hurting anyone's feelings. And because stocks are very liquid, you can get rid of shares immediately.

Spreading your nest eggs among several baskets

Regardless of how promising a company is, you should never invest all your money in it. Management may be incompetent or corrupt. Competitors may claim more market share. Or the company or its entire sector can lose investors' favor for whatever reason.

The good news is that you have total control over where you invest your money. You can significantly reduce your risk by spreading it out through *diversification*. See "Mitigating Your Risks" later in this chapter for details.

Knowing factors outside your control

You can't always control what happens around you. Inflation can soar, the Federal Reserve can decide to raise or lower interest rates, bubbles can burst, and entire economies can crumble. However, by becoming more aware of these risks, you can develop strategies for dealing with them effectively.

In the following sections, I describe risk factors that you're unlikely to have any control over and offer suggestions on how to adjust to them.

Greed gone wild

The technology bubble of the late 1990s presents a perfect example of greed gone wild. The idea that a company run by two 24-year-olds with no business experience, one that didn't sell a product or produce any profits, was worth more than companies making millions of dollars in profits sounds preposterous. But that's what happened with a company called theglobe.com.

The day of theglobe.com's IPO (initial public offering), the stock's target price was $9. By the end of its first day of trading, shares stood at $63.50, giving the company a market value of $840 million. When other investors saw this and other dot-com stocks double and triple in value over a very short time, they sold shares in mature companies with long histories of making money and piled the cash into risky Internet companies, creating a huge bubble in the sector that eventually burst. Stories like this are why you should avoid speculative investing and buying into obvious bubbles. Bubbles *always* burst, and when they do, they smash a lot of nest eggs.

Beating inflation

Inflation is a silent killer, eating away at your savings unless you put that money to work by investing it in something that earns a higher rate of return than the rate of inflation. And it's worse than most people realize.

An inflation rate of 4 percent means that something that cost a dollar last year costs $1.04 this year. If your yearly expenses total $40,000 this year, next year you'll have to spend $41,600 to buy the same amount of groceries, clothing, gas, and everything else. The year after that, those same goods and services will cost $43,264. If your salary doesn't keep up and your investments don't make enough to cover the distance, you will have to dig into your savings to make up the difference.

When you hear that inflation is at 4 percent, that doesn't sound like much, but when you look at what a 4-percent inflation rate can do to your money over the course of 10 or 30 or 40 years, as shown in Table 4-2, the fallout is shocking.

Table 4-2	Inflation's Corrosive Effect on Purchasing Power			
Inflation Rate	**10 Years**	**15 Years**	**25 Years**	**40 Years**
2%	−18%	−26%	−39%	−55%
4%	−32%	−44%	−62%	−81%
6%	−44%	−58%	−77%	−90%
8%	−54%	−68%	−85%	−95%
10%	−61%	−76%	−91%	−98%

Dividend stocks provide a great way to offset inflation risk. Buying dividend stocks that yield as much as the rate of inflation keeps you even in terms of what your money can buy. Any stock price appreciation is pure profit. Buy stocks with dividends greater than inflation, and you always see your money grow in real terms.

Adjusting to interest rate hikes

When the Federal Reserve hikes interest rates, it hurts companies in a variety of ways, which can have a significant effect on dividends:

✔ **Interest rate hikes increase costs and slash the bottom line.** With a higher interest rate, a company that carries a high debt load must pay more the next time it borrows funds. This jump increases its cost of doing business, which may hurt the company's profitability and trigger a drop in share price.

✔ **Rising rates hurt business-to-business sales.** When companies are spending more to service their debt, they have less money to purchase goods and services from suppliers. Everyone suffers.

✔ **Stocks become less attractive.** When interest rates rise, safer investments earn a higher rate of return. If the yield on a bond or money market account equals the yield on a stock but carries a lot less risk, many investors sell their shares and move into bonds to maximize returns while lowering risk. This switch can send stock prices even lower.

Investing in dividend stocks provides some protection against interest rate hikes. Even if the share price drops, companies often continue paying dividends, which offset the drop in price.

Steering clear of companies with fuzzy financials

In the stock market, you can lose all your money if the companies you invest in go belly up or post significant losses. This situation is exactly what happened after the technology bubble of the 1990s popped and many Internet and telecommunications companies vanished. Investors had ignored the classic signs of risk: few or no sales and no profits. They decided that the old rules and risks didn't apply in the new Internet economy and that they could value a company by its revenues or projected revenues rather than profits.

If investors had researched these companies and properly evaluated their business prospects, they never would have gone near them. All they saw were rising stock prices. They didn't care why. The just wanted in before it was too late.

You can often avoid making similar mistakes by carefully researching the companies you plan to buy. At the very least, you need to look at a company's financial statements to see whether earnings and revenues are growing or falling. For more about evaluating dividend stocks, see Chapter 8.

Monitoring market risk

Market crashes are a fact of life. Between 2000 and 2009, the U.S. stock market experienced two of the biggest crashes since the Great Depression. From 2000 to 2002, the Dow Jones Industrial Average sank 39 percent, beating the 36-percent drop the Dow experienced during the crash of 1987. During that period, the S&P 500, considered the benchmark for the broader market, tumbled more than 50 percent, and the technology-laden NASDAQ plummeted 76 percent.

From October 2007 to March 2009, the Dow plunged 53.8 percent — the worst decline since the crash of 1929. The S&P 500 skidded 56.8 percent, and the NASDAQ fell 55.6 percent.

Stocks less risky than Treasury bills and bonds?!

In *Stocks for the Long Run,* 4th edition (McGraw-Hill), Jeremy Siegel, a professor at the University of Pennsylvania's Wharton Business School, says risk and return are the building blocks of finance and portfolio management. Most people think that fixed-income instruments such as Treasury bonds and bills are always safer than stocks. Although this belief is true over a short period of time (just two years), over a five-year period, the risks are about the same.

Professor Siegel studied returns since 1802 and found that in every five-year period since then, the worst performance among stocks was just –11 percent. Surprisingly, it came in only slightly below the worst performance in bonds or bills. Over the 10-year periods, the worst return for stocks actually beat the worst for bonds and bills. For the 20-year holding periods, stock returns have never fallen below inflation, but bond and bills for a two-decade period fell as much as 3 percent per year below the inflation rate. And for every 30-year period since the Civil War, stocks have always outperformed bonds.

The moral of the story is this: If you buy good companies and hold onto them long enough, they will come back. This fact is particularly true of companies that have a solid track record for paying dividends and increasing their dividend payments over time.

In addition, the market has fallen 10, 20, or even 30 percent many more times over the years. The main way to mitigate this risk is the same as for financial risk: research. Invest in good, profitable, stable companies because they tend to weather the storm better than most. And if you continue to invest during these stormy times, you can often find real bargains on your favorite shares.

Riding out a slumping economy

Like the stock market, the economy has its ups and downs. In fact, the stock market typically reflects current economic conditions. And, generally speaking, what's bad for the economy is bad for the stock market.

As a dividend investor, you can't control the economy or prevent an economic meltdown, but you can mitigate your losses and often gain ground in a slumping economy. Remember that a drop in share prices just may signal a perfect buying opportunity.

Reacting to changes in the tax code

The federal government often tries to influence consumer behavior and business practices through tax code. For example, when the government wants people to buy homes, it offers tax credits and other incentives to make homeownership more affordable. To stimulate economic growth, the government slashed the capital gains tax in 1981, which some analysts credit for triggering the bull markets of the 1980s.

Profits up in smoke

Sometimes law-abiding companies become the targets of both citizens and legislators. For years, the tobacco industry sold cigarettes, proven to be a deadly and addictive drug, without repercussions. Many people considered smoking to be a right.

In the 1990s, the political winds changed. The country experienced a cultural shift in which the people who sold cigarettes were vilified as common drug dealers. People blamed smoking for causing many health problems in the United States and said that the tobacco companies were responsible.

Facing rising health care costs, 46 states joined together in the mid-1990s to sue the four biggest tobacco companies for Medicaid costs. The result was an agreement by the tobacco companies to pay $206 billion over 25 years to the states. Needless to say, that wasn't good for their dividends.

As a voter, you have some control over the tax code, but not much. You have more control over developing an investment strategy that takes advantage of favorable changes and protects your investments against unfavorable changes. For more about monitoring and adjusting to changes in the tax code, check out Chapter 20.

Adjusting to shifts in government policy and actions

Although the stock market is filled with uncertainty, it does have a certain amount of predictability. When the government intervenes, however, predictability is tossed out the window. Yes, the United States does have a free market economy, but the government often steps in to influence it. And when the government steps in, the effects tend to ripple through the markets.

You may not be able to control or even predict changes in government policy, but it's a good idea to keep up on the news and try to understand how specific policies or even talk of policy changes may affect your share prices and investment strategy. In addition, a slow, steady approach to investing can help reduce the effects of policy changes on your portfolio, as I explain in the following "Mitigating Your Risks" section.

Remaining aware of credit risk

Keep in mind that banks aren't risk-free either. They may seem safe, at least until *credit risk* (the risk of a loss caused by failure to pay) rears its head. A bank can fail to have enough cash to meet capital requirements, essentially owing more than it owns. This situation can cause a bank to collapse, and as the crash of 2008 demonstrated, collapsing banks aren't just a historical phenomenon.

Mitigating Your Risks

You can never completely eliminate risk. Whether you choose to invest your money or not, you always risk losing at least some of it. You can, however, reduce your exposure to risk by following a sensible plan and doing your homework. The following sections suggest four risk-reduction techniques employed by the pros.

Matching your strategy to your time frame

One of the easiest ways to lose a significant chunk of change in the stock market is to make risky investments. An even easier way is to make risky investments when you have insufficient time to recover from any drop in share price. In other words, if you buy some shares, they drop in price, and you *have to* sell because you need the cash right now, you're going to lose money.

Choose investments according to your time frame. If you're young and can afford to leave your money in the market, you can also afford to take on more risk for the promise of bigger returns. If, on the other hand, you're going to need that money sometime in the near future, play it safe. Swing for the base hit or a double instead of striking out trying to hit a homer.

Performing your due diligence

Novice investors, and some greedy pros, attempt to ride the waves of investor enthusiasm by purchasing popular stocks. This practice is certainly okay if the company's fundamentals justify the share price. It's never okay if shares are way overvalued compared to the company's earnings and its realistic growth projections. You can significantly reduce your risks by carefully researching companies before investing in them.

Successful investing is hard work. It requires gathering company reports, crunching the numbers, and comparing results to other sectors and other companies in a sector. It may even require some additional research to determine whether market conditions are right. In Chapter 8, I show you how to perform your due diligence and pick companies that meet or exceed your minimum requirements.

Diversifying your investments

Diversification is just a fancy way of saying "Don't put all your eggs in one basket." It's one of the best ways to protect your portfolio from the many forms of risk. Diversification demands that you hold many different asset classes in your portfolio to spread the risk. (*Assets* are any items of value. An *asset class* is a group of similar assets.) With this strategy, a significant loss in any one investment or class doesn't destroy your entire portfolio. More importantly, it ensures that in the event of a loss, you retain at least some capital to make future investments — and hopefully recover what you lost.

Analysts often use the concept of correlation to guide their diversification decisions. *Correlation* determines how closely two assets follow each other as they bounce up and down on the charts. Analysts measure correlation on a scale from 1 to –1. The number 1 represents *perfect correlation,* and –1 represents *perfect inverse correlation.* For instance, when oil prices rise, nearly all the oil companies rise together, achieving perfect or near perfect correlation. When oil rises 10 percent, but automobile companies lose 10 percent, their relationship represents perfect inverse correlation. A correlation of 0 (zero) means the rise and fall of any two sectors or stocks are unrelated.

To diversify, follow a process of asset allocation. Populate your portfolio with a variety of asset classes with different degrees of correlation, as described in the following list:

- ✔ **Stocks:** Although stocks are considered an asset class of their own, the market offers several classes, including large cap, small cap, and foreign stocks, which allow you to diversify within the stock market. You can also diversify by industry — for example, consumer staples and telecoms.

- ✔ **Bonds:** Fixed income instruments such as bonds have an inverse correlation to stocks. When stocks fall in price, investors often make a flight to safety by purchasing government-backed Treasury bonds. Greater demand for bonds moves their price higher. However, rising interest rates can hurt stocks and bonds simultaneously. Returns on bonds often increase as stock prices sink.

- ✔ **Commodities:** *Commodities* are raw materials typically sold in bulk, including oil, gold, wheat, and livestock. In general, commodities have a zero correlation to stocks, meaning the risks that affect stocks have no bearing on what happens in the commodities markets.

- ✔ **Mutual Funds and ETFs (Exchange-Traded Funds):** An easy way to diversify investments is to buy shares of a mutual fund or exchange-traded fund that holds a large basket of many different stocks or bonds. Instead of purchasing 100 shares of just one stock, you can get one ETF share comprised of 500 stocks without having to pay costly brokerage commissions. Chapters 15 and 16 explain what to look for in mutual funds and ETFs.

Employing dollar cost averaging

Dollar cost averaging is a disciplined investment strategy that, over time, can prevent you from paying too much for shares. Here's how it works: You buy a certain fixed dollar amount of shares regularly — say every month, quarter, or year. As a result, you end up buying more shares when the price is low and fewer shares when the price is high, but you don't get stuck buying all of your shares at the higher price. Therefore, the price you pay is a reasonable average. For more about implementing dollar cost averaging in your overall investment strategy, check out Chapter 18.

Chapter 5

Setting Goals and Making Plans

. . . .

In This Chapter

▶ Discovering your preferred investing style

▶ Defining your goals

. . . .

Before you start plunking money into the stock market, realize that people don't invest in the stock market for the pure joy of owning stocks. Stocks are a means to an end, a way to parlay your savings into more money to finance what you want — a vacation home, a fancy car, your kids' or grandkids' education, a comfortable retirement, or whatever. To be a successful investor, you need to write down your financial goals and honestly analyze yourself. Does money burn a hole in your pocket? Are you a reckless spender? Are you afraid of taking risks or more of a high roller?

Perhaps even more important is having a goal and a realistic time frame in mind — what do you want and how long do you have to acquire the money for it? Whether you need the money two years from now or 30 years down the road can have a strong influence over how you choose to invest your money.

A sincere and honest evaluation now can save you much time and agony later. This chapter helps you figure out what kind of investor you are, how aggressive you are (or aren't), what your goals are, and how much time you have to achieve your goals, so you can begin to formulate and implement a practical investment plan for achieving your goals.

Examining Your Personality Profile

Whenever you're about to engage in anything worth pursuing — career, marriage, child-rearing, community service — consider how your personality factors in. A fair portion of unhappy people are unhappy because they live life against the grain. They pursue a career they're not passionate about, marry someone who doesn't share their goals and values, or buy things they really don't find fulfilling.

The same is true of investing. If you tend to be a high roller, socking away your savings in a CD or money market account will probably bore you to tears. If you're more conservative, gambling big in the hopes for big returns will turn you into a nervous wreck. To choose an investment style that's right for you, take a moment to analyze your personality.

What's your style?

Wall Street considers an investor any person or business that buys an asset with the expectation of reaping a financial reward. However, I think this all-encompassing use of the term *investor* blurs important distinctions between the various market participants: savers, speculators, and investors.

The first step on the road to becoming a successful dividend investor consists of becoming a money saver. Whether you've been saving money for years or are just starting today, the fact is that you need to save more. After you become a saver, the question becomes whether you want to progress to speculating or investing to make your seed money grow. The following sections examine savers, speculators, and investors to help you figure out which approach matches your personality.

When I talk about short-term and long-term investments, I use the following time frames:

- ✔ **Short-term is two years or less.** Why two years? Because it rarely provides enough time to recoup losses. Look at the 2008 market crash. The S&P 500 hit its high in October 2007. A year and a half later the index lost half its value. Two years later, even though the market struck a bottom and began to bounce back, it remained significantly lower.

- ✔ **Intermediate is two to five years.** This period usually gives stocks enough time to recover — still no guarantee of a recovery, but chances are much better.

- ✔ **Long-term is five years or more.** When you can leave your money in the market for five years or more, you have a significant buffer for the ups and downs of the market.

Also, I consider a savings account to be long-term/short-term vehicle: Long-term, because you plan to hold it for many years; short-term because it provides liquid funds for immediate needs.

Saver

Every investor starts out as a saver. After all, you have to have some money before you can invest it. Some people move past this stage to become speculators or investors, but others remain savers throughout their lives.

Saving for nest eggs and rainy days

Everybody should have a little bit of saver in them so that they have some cash on hand to deal with necessities and emergencies. I recommend the following saving investment strategy:

✔ **Establish a six-month savings buffer — enough money to cover monthly expenses for six months in the event you lose your job.** This buffer can help cover emergency bills, too; for example, if your house is damaged in a storm, you can pay for repairs immediately while waiting for the insurance company to process your claim.

✔ **Don't invest money needed for short-term goals in long-term investments.** Stocks and bonds are *liquid* — you can sell them on any business day and receive your money in three days. However, when you need the money may not coincide with the most opportune time to sell. You need to think of stocks as long-term investments; if you need to send a child to college or pay for a wedding in the next two years, don't put that money in the stock market. If your stocks lose 40 to 50 percent of their value and you have to sell to pay for previously scheduled expenses, you not only won't be able to recoup your losses but also may not have enough to cover the expenses. Remember, that six-month savings buffer could turn into a short-term need as well. The time many people lose their jobs and need cash occurs during or just after the stock market has posted serious declines. If your buffer is in the stock market, you may need to sell a lot more than you expect to cover the six months.

✔ **Invest the majority of your excess savings (anything above and beyond your six-month buffer) to maximize capital appreciation.** Interest earned in safe investment vehicles, such as savings accounts, rarely keeps pace with inflation. To grow your money, you must invest it in something that holds a promise of higher returns. See Chapter 4 for more about the inherent risk of inflation.

✔ **Gradually move toward safer investments over time.** As you age, your time frame shrinks, so capital appreciation begins to take a higher priority in your overall investment strategy.

What separates the saver from the speculator or investor is risk. The saver's main objective is capital preservation. After he's squirreled away some money from his paycheck, he wants to guarantee the cash will be there when he needs it. To achieve his goals, he tends to invest in safe vehicles — bank accounts, CDs, and money market accounts — because of their low risk, safety, and liquidity. The big down sides? Very little chance of capital appreciation and near certainty of inflation chipping away at that nest egg.

Speculator

Speculators attempt to capitalize on the market's short-term price movements — *volatility.* Capital preservation is a low- or no-priority item. The speculator jumps into the market and puts his principle at significant risk in the hopes of scoring a big return quickly. Unlike investors, speculators really have no interest in how long a company will be in business — their sole focus is share price.

Volatility can best be described as the size and frequency of extreme price moves over short periods of time. *High volatility* means an asset's price can experience dramatic moves up or down, and *low volatility* describes moves of less than 5 percent.

Speculation can be day-trading a variety of stocks many times every single day or buying and holding a blue-chip stock for 12 months. If it sounds a lot like gambling, that's because it pretty much is. Speculating demands a high risk tolerance because you can easily lose money. Over the long-term, the stock market climbs higher. But over the short-term, asset markets can be extremely volatile. It's very similar to what happened with real estate investors who were flipping houses in 2006 and 2007, banking on rising real estate values and hoping for big returns. When the housing bubble burst, many were stuck with homes worth significantly less than what they had paid for them. Even worse, most of them didn't have the cash necessary to continue making payments. Speculating in the stock market can lead to similar results — if you have to sell in a down market, you almost certainly stand to lose money.

Investor

Investors are in the stock market for the long-haul, seeking both capital preservation and appreciation. As such, they're willing to take more risk than savers but approach their investments more carefully than speculators. Following are the three actions that define investors:

- They have long-term financial goals — several years rather than several months, days, or hours.

- They plan to hold long-term investments, holding an investment vehicle for at least five years.

- They do extensive research because they plan on holding their shares for five years or more and want to invest in fundamentally sound companies.

Because of the volatile nature of most financial vehicles, you can never be sure of selling them at a profit when you need the cash. If the stock market suffers a major downturn, even conservative investments can experience significant price drops. However, if you give your investments many years to grow, even if the market suffers a downturn, a portfolio with stable, dividend-paying stocks will be worth more than when you started.

How aggressive are you?

In Chapter 4, I explain how you can determine your risk tolerance. Some investors tend to be more aggressive than others — they want more, expect more, and are willing risk more to get it. Conservative investors, on the other hand, are either fairly satisfied with what they have (assuming their investments are growing at a steady rate and earning a reasonable return) or are fearful of losing what they've already acquired. In the following sections, I describe these two types of investors in greater detail and show how differences in aggressiveness can influence investment styles.

Conservative

The word *conservative* has nothing to do with politics when used in an investment context. Political conservatives can be very aggressive investors, and liberals can be very conservative in managing their money. In the world of investing, *conservative* means careful. Conservative investors tend to play it safe to protect their lead — they don't like risk. They prefer to put their money in safe places, even if they have to accept a lower rate of return.

You can usually identify a conservative investor by the investments comprising her portfolio:

- ✔ 50 percent or less in equities (of this percentage, no more than 20 percent, and preferably 10 percent or less, in commodities or high-risk equities). The more conservative the person, the lower the portfolio's equity allocation.

- ✔ 50 percent or more in lower-risk investments, including treasury bonds, municipal bonds, bank accounts, certificates of deposit, and money market funds.

In general, the older you are, the more conservative you should be because protecting principal takes precedence over earning huge profits. This guideline is especially true the closer you are to retirement because you have less time to recover from a severe market crash.

Aggressive

Aggressive investors go for the gold, pursuing investments with higher rates of return. Because of this, a higher percentage of the investments in their portfolios is allocated to riskier investments:

- ✔ 70 percent or more in equities or other riskier assets
- ✔ 30 percent or less in lower-risk investments, including treasury bonds, municipal bonds, bank accounts, certificates of deposit, and money market funds

The classic definition of an aggressive investor is someone comfortable in taking on large amounts of risk. The longer you have to recover from a market correction, the more aggressive you can afford to be. Young people in their 20s and 30s can afford to be the most aggressive because they have the time to recover from significant losses.

Many aggressive investors hold commodities, such as gold or silver, stocks from emerging markets in Asia or Africa, or junk bonds from companies with poor credit.

Formulating an Investment Plan

You don't set out on vacation and then plan for it — that would be absurd. Yet this mindset is the equivalent of what many misdirected investors do: They start investing before they even have a destination or goal in mind, let alone a plan or a budget. Not knowing where they're going or how they plan to get there, they waste a lot of time and money trying to find their way.

To avoid this headache, you first need to ask yourself whether you really want to be an investor. If you plan on living fast and dying young, you should probably just spend all your money. Not to be too morbid, but if that's your plan, you have no reason to save your pennies for a rainy day. Carpe diem!

However, if you have any thoughts of longevity, building a family, and retiring, you should start saving money now. In the following sections, I assist you in defining your investment goals, developing a viable plan, and making sure all the pieces are in place before you set out on your journey.

Defining your goals

Most people have a goal in mind before they start investing. They want to save money to buy a home, finance their children's education, retire in comfort, or start their own business. When defining your investment goal, consider two things: the amount of money you need and when you need it. Then choose a time frame that best fits your goal:

- **Short-term:** *Short-term goals* include buying a new vehicle, taking a nice vacation, renovating a home, or paying off a debt.

- **Intermediate-term:** *Intermediate-term goals* may include saving for a down payment on a house, traveling the world for a year, or financing a new business venture.

- **Long-term:** *Long-term goals* are beyond the foreseeable future (about five years out) and include things such as paying for a child's college education or retiring in the manner to which you've become accustomed.

A comfortable retirement should be everyone's number one long-term goal. Stocks provide a great place for investing toward long-term goals because they need a long time horizon to maximize returns while minimizing risk.

Putting a plan in place

After you have a goal in mind, you have two points: where you are now and where you want to be when you reach your destination. Your next job is to develop a plan that moves you from point A to point B within your pre-established time frame without derailing the train.

One of the best ways to determine how much money you need to invest toward reaching your goal is to play what-if with a financial calculator. You can find financial calculators all over the Web. Using a simple investment goal calculator, like the one from AARP (`www.aarp.org/money/toolkit/articles/investment_goal_calculator.html`), you can play with the following numbers to determine how much you need to invest per month to achieve your goal:

- ✔ **Investment goal:** The total amount of money you need

- ✔ **Number of years to accumulate:** Your time frame

- ✔ **Amount of initial investment:** The initial amount you plan on investing, if any

- ✔ **Periodic contribution:** The amount you plan on contributing on a regular basis

- ✔ **Investment frequency:** How often you plan on making a periodic contribution; for example, monthly or quarterly

- ✔ **Rate of return on investment:** The percentage return you realistically expect from your investments per year

- ✔ **Expected inflation rate:** The average inflation rate over the time frame in which you plan on investing

- ✔ **Interest is compounded:** Whether the returns on your investment are compounded, and if so, how frequently (monthly, quarterly, or annually)

- ✔ **Tax rates:** Federal and state tax rates on your dividends and any capital gains

Even more common on the Web are short-term investment calculators, such as the one at SmartMoney.com (`www.smartmoney.com/Investing/Bonds/Set-Your-Goals-7975/`). You simply plug in the current cost of whatever you want to purchase, the inflation rate for that item, your time frame (in years), your state and federal tax rate on your dividends or capital gains, and the percentage yield you expect from your investment, and the calculator determines how much money you need to invest today to reach your goal. `Bankrate.com` is another good source of financial calculators.

"Pay yourself first" is cliché for financial advisors, but it's the best strategy for achieving financial goals on time. After setting your goals, make sure you're setting aside enough money each month (or each payday) to achieve those goals according to the time frame you set. For more about financial goal setting, see *Personal Finance For Dummies,* 6th Edition (Wiley), by Eric Tyson.

Budgeting to stay on course

After you've established how much money you need to invest to reach your financial goal, develop a budget to cover the rest of your expenses. Otherwise, you're likely to overspend on living expenses, which can put your entire investment plan in jeopardy.

Careful budgeting can help you achieve your investment goals sooner. By trimming the fat from your household budget, you may find that you have more money to invest.

A detailed budget lists all income and expense categories. For example, you may have income from one or more jobs along with investment and interest income. Your expenses may include groceries, rent or a mortgage payment, taxes, auto fuel and maintenance, insurance, utilities, gifts, entertainment, dining, and even personal items. Be sure to include, as an expense, the money you're setting aside for investments. If your budget is in the black, good for you. If it's in the red, you need to start trimming your expenses or looking for an additional (or better-paying) job.

Start using a personal finance program, such as Quicken or Microsoft Money to track your income and expenses. When recording transactions, you can assign them to specific categories, including Groceries, Utilities, Automobile, Gifts, Dining, and so on. These programs can help you develop a budget and generate reports that clearly show whether you've been overspending in a particular category.

Planning Specifically for Retirement

Planning for retirement is often more complex than simply setting a goal and using a single, solitary investment vehicle to reach it. You may need to account for money from several sources, including Social Security, a pension, a company's 401(k) plan, and your own individual retirement account (IRA). Through some of these accounts, the federal government encourages citizens to invest for retirement and provides some tax incentives for doing so.

In the following sections, I point out the various types of accounts you may be able to rely on for retirement income so that you can take into consideration all likely sources of income and discount some sources you'd be better off *not* relying on.

Consult a tax expert when planning for retirement so that you can take full advantage of the federal government's tax incentives. By paying less income tax on your earnings, you may be able to afford investing more to reach your retirement goals much sooner.

Because Social Security and pensions aren't guaranteed in the end, the only money you can count on for retirement is the money you bring into your household. Whatever you don't spend today may be all you have to live on later. Be wise about how much you spend and how you invest the money you earn.

Social Security

Social Security is a federal social-insurance program with a variety of benefits, including providing retirement income. Developed in 1935, it became a cornerstone of President Franklin D. Roosevelt's New Deal created to pull the United States out of the Great Depression. The program bases your retirement income on the average wage you earned over your working life. You can begin collecting retirement benefits as young as 62 years or wait until the age of 67 to qualify for significantly higher payments.

If the Social Security Administration (SSA) isn't already keeping you posted about your estimated retirement benefits, contact it and request a copy of your Social Security statement, which shows how much Social Security income you can expect per month upon retirement. You can visit your local SSA office; call 800-772-1213 (TTY 800-325-0778); or request a copy of your statement online at www.ssa.gov.

Pensions

For a good part of the 20th century, companies in the United States funded pension plans for their workers. The workers didn't need to worry about 401(k)s, IRAs, and all that other complicated stuff because their companies took care of depositing money into the pension fund and hiring a manager to invest the money and make sure enough would be available for retirees.

Unfortunately, those days are long gone. Although a few companies still pay pensions, most of the companies that offered pensions have either eliminated them or been eliminated themselves. Some companies simply mismanaged their pension funds and ran out of money to cover their obligations. Many companies have elected to scale back benefits to avoid running out of money, and some have simply gone out of business or been acquired by other companies that suspended the pension programs.

When planning for retirement, assume you're not going to receive a pension, even if you're scheduled to. If you have a pension, good for you, but you can't count on it paying benefits throughout your retirement. Even historically reliable pension funds have been known to disappear during troubled economic times. By planning for the worst-case scenario, you get an added bonus if you do end up receiving a pension.

How secure is Social Security?

You've probably heard that unless the U.S. Congress takes some drastic measures, the Social Security program is in danger of running out of money by about 2040. Why? The reasons basically boil down to the following three:

✔ Social Security is a pay-as-you-go program, so the working stiffs finance Social Security payments for retirees and others claiming benefits.

✔ People are living longer, so more people are collecting payments and drawing money out of the till for more years than originally intended.

✔ 80 million baby boomers recently started retiring. In about 30 years, the United States will have twice as many retirees as it does now. By 2035, the number of workers paying into Social Security per person drawing benefits will drop from 3.1 to 2.1.

In short, Social Security is on the fast track to bankruptcy, so don't count on collecting any benefits after 2037. You may get lucky and be able to collect benefits after 2037 — I'm just cautioning you not to count on it. And if I were a betting man, I'd wager that retirement benefits will be slashed long before the money runs out.

Even if you could count on Social Security for supplemental income during your retirement years, keep in mind that it replaces only about 40 percent of the average worker's preretirement earnings. Unless you drastically scale back your lifestyle, you'll need about 70 percent or more of your preretirement earnings to live comfortably.

Defined contribution plans

The federal government realizes that Social Security may run out of funds to cover retirement benefits. In order to prevent a financial calamity with millions of retirees having no money, the feds have put programs in place to encourage citizens to start saving for retirement. At the center of the government's efforts are tax-deferred retirement savings plans named after numbers, including 401(k), 403(b), and 457.

✔ **401(k) plan:** A defined contribution retirement plan provided by a commercial entity

✔ **403(b) plan:** The equivalent of a 401(k) plan for nonprofit enterprises such as colleges, school districts, hospitals, and other organizations

✔ **457 plan:** A defined contribution plan for employees of state and local governments

Calling a tax-deferred retirement savings plan a 401(k) plan may seem a little weird. It sort of begs the question of what happened to the 400 plan, or the 300 or 200 plan, for that matter. The name comes from paragraph (k) in Section 401 of the Internal Revenue Code. Added in 1978, this arcane passage explains in detail how the plans work. Collectively, the 401(k), 403(b), and 457 plans are referred to as *defined contribution plans*. In the battle of nomenclature, pensions are now called *defined benefit plans*. Unlike a defined benefit plan, which a company provides for you, you contribute the money in defined contribution plans.

The key benefit of the defined contribution plan, other than a nice retirement nest egg, is that you can invest pretax dollars, so presumably you have more money to invest; for example, if you earn $100, you can invest all of it instead of having to pay $25 in federal income tax (leaving you with only $75 to invest). The major disadvantages to defined contribution plans are the limitations on how much you can invest each year and the narrow selection of investment opportunities offered. Some 401(k) plans offer the opportunity to buy stocks, but most plans offer you a limited selection of mutual funds you probably would never buy on your own.

Some employers offer matching contributions; for example, they may contribute 50 cents or even a dollar for every dollar you invest up to a certain annual dollar amount. This setup allows you two ways to build your nest egg much more quickly — by investing pretax dollars and collecting matching contributions. If your employer offers matching contributions, try to take full advantage.

If the option is available, I recommend that you manage your own fund. Of course you don't have complete control. You're restricted to investing in only the options available inside the plan and probably don't have the option of buying individual stocks. However, the more control you have over the fund, the more control you have over the outcome.

Accounts you create yourself

All the accounts I mention in the preceding sections can help you achieve your financial goals. But with the exception of the rare 401(k) plan, none of those plans gives you the freedom to invest as much as you want in anything you want. The only place you can execute a dividend-stock strategy exactly to your specifications is in an account you set up. Your choices include an Individual Retirement Account (IRA), Roth IRA, Keogh, and a taxable account set up at a brokerage firm.

- ✔ **Individual Retirement Account (IRA):** An IRA is a tax-deferred retirement savings account; that is, you pay taxes only when you withdraw money, so you contribute tax-deferred dollars and your investment grows tax-free. Assuming you earn less than a specified amount and don't belong to an employer-sponsored retirement plan, such as a 401(k), the government allows you to deduct from your income taxes the annual contribution to the account. You can set up an IRA at a bank or brokerage.

To use your IRA to invest in dividend stocks, set up the IRA with a discount broker, as I explain in Chapter 19.

IRAs do have limitations. Currently, the maximum annual tax-deductible contribution is $5,000 for people younger than 50 years of age and $6,000 for people older than 50. The restrictions on how much you can earn to qualify for an IRA and the contribution amounts change often, so contact the people where you set up the account to get the current details.

✔ **Roth IRA:** Like an IRA, the Roth IRA offers some tax benefits. Unlike an IRA, you pay your taxes on the money going in and withdraw it tax-free on the way out. Assuming you take more money out than you put in, the Roth IRA actually offers a better tax break.

✔ **Keogh account:** Similar to an IRA but exclusively for the self-employed, this tax-deferred account allows you to deduct much higher contributions from your taxable income. Like the IRA, the withdrawals are taxed as ordinary income, but you're allowed to invest much more in pretax dollars.

✔ **Brokerage account:** The brokerage account offers the most freedom, but no tax benefits. You can invest as much as you want into anything you want — no restrictions. However, every year your earnings are subject to capital gains and/or dividend taxes, so your investment can't benefit from tax-deferred growth. See Chapter 19 for more about setting up a brokerage account.

Chapter 6

Choosing the Right Approach for You

. . . .

In This Chapter

▶ Banking on the prospects of future growth

▶ Securing steady cash flow with the income approach

▶ Shopping for value in dividend stocks

. . . .

The goal of every investor is to make money. As with most things in life, several paths lead to the same destination. When you're an investor, you can make money through any of the approaches I discuss in this chapter — growth investing, income investing, or value investing — or a combination of all three. In this chapter, I delve into each of these investing strategies so you can figure out which suits your needs.

The dividend investing approach I recommend combines the best of all three of these methods, starting with income. After identifying some stocks with acceptable yields, you can begin to search for bargains that offer a good potential for both price appreciation and dividends. In Chapter 7, I start you on your search. In Chapter 8, I show you how to perform your own company analysis and spot potential bargains.

Go for Broke with the Growth Approach

With *growth investing,* you buy stocks in companies with earnings and revenue growth rates that exceed the market average in anticipation of big jumps in the share price; these stocks are typically young or small companies that reinvest their earnings to maximize growth and typically don't pay dividends. Growth investors are like scouts for professional sports — their job is to evaluate the up and coming talent and identify the most promising athletes.

Growth investors want to see companies with potential — companies that are growing faster than the competition and other companies in their industry. They're interested in companies that plow every penny of profit back into the company to fuel future growth. Because of this focus, growth investors care little or nothing about dividends.

In the following sections, I reveal the criteria growth investors consider in picking good growth stock candidates.

Don't confuse growth with share price appreciation. Growth is a measure of a company's earnings and revenue increases relative to similar companies. Share price merely reflects what investors are willing to pay for the stock, which may have nothing to do with the company's actual performance.

Seeking potential in the young and small

Small things tend to grow at a faster rate than big things. Plant a pea, and after it germinates, it can double or triple its size in a single day. After that pea plant is mature and begins producing fruit, however, it barely grows at all. A typical baby boy doubles his size (by weight) in about five months. The same isn't true of the average adult or even the average teenager — at least I hope not!

Likewise, companies with the most growth potential are generally the smallest and youngest — companies that have been around less than 15 years and post profits in the millions as opposed to the billions. If Company A earned $1 million last year, it may quite easily double its business and post a profit of $2 million this year. However, if Company B earned $1 billion last year, it has to come up with 1,000 times more money than Company A does to post the same growth rate.

Profiting from share price appreciation

Small companies are sort of like mom and pop operations — if they want to grow, they don't borrow a bunch of money. Instead, they use a portion of their profits to finance their growth. After all, borrowing money is an added expense. Because small businesses often reinvest their profits, they have little or nothing left to return to shareholders in the form of dividends. The only way for shareholders to see a return on their investment is through *share price appreciation*, also known as *capital appreciation*.

Growth stocks are typically in newer industries that provide products few people have but everybody wants. If you sell something that more people want to buy this year than did last year, you should see your sales rise significantly. And if you run your company well, this sales increase should lead to a sharp rise in earnings. When a company starts to make more money, investors see the potential to make more money for themselves, so they start increasing the demand for the company's shares. Greater demand for the stock sends the price rising, which is how growth stocks see big jumps in share price.

Focusing on growth

Growth stocks get their moniker if their earnings and revenues grow at a faster pace than their particular end of the market. For instance, a large-cap stock growing at a faster rate than the S&P 500 is considered a growth stock. Small-cap stocks have to show a greater growth rate than the index for the small-cap market, the Russell 2000, to be considered growth stocks.

Large-cap is short for large market capitalization. Small-cap is the abbreviation for small market capitalization. Market capitalization is a fancy phrase for a company's market value, determined by dividing its share price by its number of outstanding common shares. The definitions aren't set in stone, but currently, a large market cap is greater than $10 billion. A small market cap is between $300 million and $2 billion.

Because the focus is on growth, certain measures, including a company's price-to-earnings ratio or price-to-sales ratio (see Chapter 8) carry less weight. Growth investors are more concerned with how the company did this quarter compared with how it performed in the quarter 12 months earlier. Here's the formula:

Growth Rate = (This Year's Profit – Last Year's Profit) ÷ Last Year's Profit

For example, say Dubois Foods earned $1 million last year and $1.25 million this year:

($1.25 million – $1 million) ÷ $1 million = 25 percent

Growth investors generally evaluate growth stocks based on the following criteria:

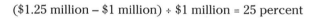

- ✔ **Earnings and revenue growth rates higher than the broader market and other companies in the same industry:** Growth rates should be at least 10 percent. If the earnings growth rate is faster than the revenue growth rate, the company is also keeping costs down.

- ✔ **Consistent growth rate for several consecutive years:** A one-year jump is a fluke. Five years of consistent growth is a trend.

Growth investors aren't scared by P/E (price-to-earnings) ratios in the 20s, 30s, and 40s — meaning the price of each share is 20, 30, or even 40 times higher than each share is earning. If the earnings are growing fast enough, the price is warranted.

Comparing this year's results to last year's results provides the annual growth rate, but what if you're in the end of the third quarter? Over nine months, a lot can change. Are those numbers still relevant? The most recent growth rate compares the most recent fiscal quarter to the same fiscal quarter last year. The reason you compare the current quarter to the *year-ago* quarter is that business can be cyclical. Ice cream shops sell a lot more in the summer than the winter. So, comparing this summer quarter to the year-ago summer quarter gives you a better comparison of a company's growth because business conditions should be similar.

Securing a Steady Cash Flow with the Income Approach

The *income investing* approach encourages you to buy investments, such as stocks or bonds, that promise a steady stream of income; among stock investors, income and dividend investing are one and the same. For most of history, investing was income investing. Whether investing in stocks or bonds, in small or large businesses, investors needed income from their investments to cover their daily expenses. They simply didn't have the surplus cash on hand to let it sit in the market for several years until they could sell and reap their profit.

Many investors still rely on income investing to some degree to profit in the stock market. Income investing tends to attract the following types of investors:

- ✔ Conservative investors
- ✔ Novice investors
- ✔ Retirees

Don't look at this list and say "I'm a sophisticated investor with many years until retirement looking for significant returns, so why do I need dividends?" Dividend investing is a sophisticated strategy, but more than that, it's a smart strategy. As my grandmother used to say, "The money is better in your pocket than in theirs." Dividend investing puts the money into *your* pocket now rather than later.

In the following sections, you explore the various income-investing options and then, assuming you want to take this approach, discover how to target specific dividend stock categories.

Comparing income-investing options

When you're investing for income and looking for a relatively safe and steady cash flow, you have several options, ranging from socking away your money in a savings account to investing in dividend stocks. The following list identifies the most common income-investing options and shows you how dividend stocks fare in comparison:

- ✔ **Savings account:** Sticking money in a savings account is one step up from stuffing it in a mattress, in terms of liquidity, security, and potential return on your investment. You can withdraw your money at any time without penalty, and your savings are guaranteed by the Federal Deposit Insurance Corporation (FDIC) up to a certain amount. However, the rate of return is the least of any investment alternative.

- ✔ **Money market accounts:** Money market accounts have many of the advantages of savings accounts but not to the same degree. Liquidity is about the same, because you can withdraw money at any time, typically by writing a check. Your money is slightly less secure because it's not federally insured, but you can expect a slightly higher return on your money. Interest rates pretty much stay in line with the Federal Reserve Bank's discount rate, which is the minimum commercial interest payment around.

- ✔ **Certificates of deposit (CDs):** Less risky and less liquid than money market accounts and more profitable than savings accounts, CDs give you a way to stash your money in the bank and earn a slightly higher interest rate in exchange for your promise not to touch the money for a specific period of time — 30 days to five years. Sell before the agreed-upon time limit expires, and the bank slaps you with a penalty.

- ✔ **Bonds:** These fixed-income IOUs provide a fairly secure income stream and generally pay higher interest than you can expect from a savings account or CD. They do have some drawbacks, however. Bond prices can fall, typically when interest rates rise, while the interest rate you receive remains constant.

- ✔ **Dividend stocks:** The riskiest of the commonly used income-investing options, dividend stocks also feature plenty of potential benefits. Investors can see returns rise both in terms of share price appreciation and dividend increases. On top of that, dividends are taxed at the low rate of 15 percent regardless of income tax bracket.

The main attraction of most conservative, income-investing options is that they help protect your principal — when the game is over, you can expect to walk away with at least as much money as you started. However, principal protection and risk management come at a price:

- ✔ **A low yield** can prevent the investment from keeping pace with inflation, which means you may walk away with the same amount of money but less purchase power because that money is now worth less.

✔ **Taxes** can chip away at any gains. Don't forget that anything not in a tax-deferred account is subject to tax. Interest from savings accounts, CDs, bonds, and money market accounts is usually treated as standard income and taxed accordingly. For more about taxes, see Chapter 20.

Focusing on yield, payout ratio, and dividend growth

When you're focused on income investing, particularly through dividend stocks, three criteria step into the spotlight:

✔ **Yield** is the percentage return on your investment you see exclusively from dividends. If you buy shares for $20 each and the company pays $2 per share for the year, the yield is 10 percent: $2 ÷ $20 = 10 percent. When you're investing solely for income, make sure the yield is greater than the inflation rate; for example, if inflation is at 3 percent, eliminate most stocks yielding less than 4 percent. (I explain some exceptions in the following section, "Targeting a dividend category.") See Chapter 8 for more about yield.

✔ **Payout ratio** is the percentage of its profits a company pays out as a dividend to shareholders. I show you how to calculate a company's payout ratio in Chapter 8. For now, just keep in mind that anything over 50 percent is good. Most companies pay between 50 and 75 percent. Higher is usually better, but anything more than 100 percent is a red flag, because it means the money is coming from someplace other than profits.

✔ **Dividend growth** demonstrates a company's ability to earn ever-increasing profits and share ever-increasing dividends with shareholders. Dividend growth is just as important as, if not more important than, yield. A low-yielding stock with a steady stream of increases may be a better investment than a high-yielding stock that hasn't increased the dividend in years.

For all the extra risk you accept with the purchase of dividend stocks, you receive a huge benefit — the potential for income growth from a steadily increasing dividend. This advantage can be more important than a high yield because every time the dividend increases, the yield on your initial investment increases. If you buy a $10 stock with an annual dividend of 20 cents, you receive a 2 percent yield. If the company increases the dividend by a nickel every year, after four years the yield on your initial investment will have doubled to 4 percent.

Targeting a dividend category

When you start shopping for dividend stocks (covered in Chapter 7) and evaluating candidates (Chapter 8), consider targeting a specific dividend category to narrow the field. After identifying a few prospects that meet your minimum dividend requirements, you can then dig deeper into each company by using valuation, growth, liquidity, and solvency ratios, as I explain in Chapter 8.

Low-yielding stocks

In general, low-yielding stocks are those with a yield less than the average yield of the S&P 500 Index — 2 percent or lower during the writing of this book. These yields are unlikely to keep pace with inflation.

You can find the yield on the S&P 500 on the Standard & Poor's Web site (www.standardandpoors.com/indices/market-attributes/en/us). Under the heading Latest Standard & Poor's 500 Market Attributes, click S&P 500 Earnings and Estimates. An Excel spreadsheet will appear; the yield is in the middle of the spreadsheet.

Don't ignore low-yielding stocks and low payout ratios as a starting point for your research. A low payout ratio from a company just starting to pay dividends may show that the company is still reinvesting a considerable portion of its profits. Taking share price appreciation into account, a low-yielding stock may eventually outperform a high-yielding stock.

Steer clear of low-yielding stocks accompanied by high payout ratios. If the company is distributing 50 to 75 percent of its profits to investors and the yield is still below two percent, that's not a good sign.

Medium-yielding stocks

Stocks posting yields between the average yield of the S&P 500 and up to 3 percentage points greater than the index's yield are medium-yielding stocks, typically keeping pace with inflation and paying out between 30 and 50 percent of their earnings in dividends.

Investors usually buy medium-yielding stocks only if they expect to see share price appreciation as well as income.

The key issue when buying a dividend stock with a low (see the preceding section) or medium yield is income growth. You want to see a steady stream of dividend increases.

High-yielding stocks

High-yielding stocks are those with yields at least 3 percentage points higher than the average yield of the S&P 500 Index, which typically means higher than the inflation rate and returns from safer investment vehicles, including CDs and Treasury bonds. Companies that fall into the high-yield category are usually mature and have a limited growth potential. You can find them in a variety of industries, including utilities, energy, and real estate investment trusts. If you're primarily an income investor, high-yielding stocks are the stocks for you.

Look for the sweet spots: high-yielding, undervalued companies where growth, income, and value all meet. Yield can increase as a result of an increase in dividend payment or a decrease in share price or both. A high-yielding stock can mean the shares are selling for less than they're worth, signaling a potential buying opportunity. When management increases the dividend as the share price drops, they're sending a message that they believe the share price will rise to a point at which the dividend is at an appropriate level. Buying the stock at this point may help you reap the benefits of both share price appreciation and high yield.

Just as a low yield alone isn't reason enough to avoid a particular stock, a high yield isn't reason enough to buy it. A high yield may indicate that the company is having problems and the share price is in a nosedive. Chapter 8 and the nearby sidebar help you ask yourself why that yield is so high and consider other factors when evaluating the stock.

High yield? High alert!

When companies declare dividends, they aim for the middle. They want to set the yield at a level that the share price justifies and that the company can maintain long term. If they shoot too high, they risk creating a situation in which they may need to decrease the dividend somewhere down the line, which may spook investors.

As with bonds, a high yield is often evidence that the stock's price has been depressed. The question then becomes "Why?" Does the company's balance sheet show a dramatic change? Are earnings down? You can often gain some insight by inspecting the company's quarterly reports, which I show you how to do in Chapter 8.

When you see a yield well above average, be prepared for the dividend to be cut or eliminated in the near future. It usually means bad news. Examples abound from recent market crashes.

In 2008 and 2009, most financial companies saw their balance sheets severely affected by the subprime mortgage meltdown. Companies that had declared huge profits just one year before the lightning struck suddenly posted huge losses. Share prices plunged. The government eventually came in and bailed out most of the financial sector. As the stock prices plunged, most of the dividend stocks in the financial and real estate industries cut their dividends by 90 percent!

If the company has none of these problems, other issues to be aware of include dividend cuts — because the company may think itself too generous and feel comfortable cutting the yield to a number closer to the industry average — and regulatory rate cuts to companies such as utilities if regulators think the company is paying out too much.

Establishing a Balance with the Value Approach

Ever feel underappreciated? You're intelligent and talented but can't find a job? You're personable and good looking but can't get a date? You're a good neighbor but can't seem to drum up enough friends for a game of Parcheesi? Well, that happens to companies, too. A perfectly good company can fall out of favor with investors or simply go unnoticed. For a value investor, such a company can become a real catch.

In a *value investing* approach, you buy stocks with steady profit streams selling at prices below their true market value. Value investors search for *underappreciated* stocks — companies with a total stock value lower than the value of the shareholder equity, also known as working capital. (I explain shareholder equity in Chapter 8). These stocks are typically well-established companies that pay dividends, especially companies way down in price compared to their historical average share price. The more beaten-down the stock's price, the better the value.

The value approach seeks to identify these underappreciated stocks and purchase them at bargain-basement prices. In the following sections, I reveal the basics.

Valuing stocks: Two approaches

On the stock market, supply and demand generally rule the roost. As a result, a stock's worth at any given point in time is determined by whatever investors are willing to pay for it. The key to value investing is to follow a less biased and less emotional approach in estimating the true value of a stock. The following sections describe two schools of thought that attempt to do just that: Efficient Market Theory and Fundamental Analysis.

Efficient Market Theory

According to *Efficient Market Theory,* the stock market is an efficient marketplace where a stock's price reflects its true value at all times. The theory states that the market is efficient for two reasons:

🖝 **Investors are rational.** Every investor is a rational human being using her skills and knowledge to the best of her ability to maximize her own profits. Don't laugh. Some people actually believe this statement.

✔ **All public information has been factored into the price.** All the information the company made public already has been factored into the price of the stock. A stock's price may move in the future as new information becomes available, but because you can't know what that information will be, you have no way of knowing whether that move will be up or down.

According to Efficient Market Theory, you can't possibly gain an advantage over other investors because investors are rational and all of them have access to the same information. In other words, you may as well just buy an index fund.

Personally, I like index funds. Even if you don't believe the Efficient Market Theory, index funds carry several potential benefits. You're guaranteed the same rate of return as the market you invest in, the better ones don't charge a commission to invest in them, and the management fees are tiny. The best part is that someone else does all the research. For more on dividend investing with index funds see Chapters 15 and 16.

Fundamental Analysis

Fundamental analysts believe the Efficient Market Theory is a bunch of hooey. Although the market may be efficient on a yearly basis, it sure isn't on a daily, weekly, monthly, or quarterly basis. Value investors are fundamental analysts. They analyze a company's past results to evaluate its current financial health and then to predict the company's future growth in earnings, revenues, and stock price.

Although past results are certainly no guarantee of future performance, past performance can be a good *predictor* of future performance. A company with a proven history of good management, innovation, and revenue and earnings growth can be expected to continue along that path until experiencing a drastic change.

Value investors use the equations of Fundamental Analysis (see Chapter 8) to predict where a stock's future price should be, based on expected earnings and revenues. According to Fundamental Analysis, the stock market is inefficient because both of the core assumptions of Efficient Market Theory are wrong. Fundamental Analysis relies on the following theories:

✔ **Investors are irrational.** Many individual investors don't use their skills and knowledge to the best of their ability to maximize their own profits. They follow hot tips and rarely research their investment choices. Typically, most people spend more time planning their next vacation than they do researching their next investment. In addition, many investors run between the two extremes of fear and greed — buying when they should sell and selling when they should buy. Examine any bubble burst, and you quickly realize how irrational investors can actually be. Value investors use this knowledge to their advantage.

✔ **All available information has *not* been factored into the price.**
Although all the information is out there, the majority of investors, including the big Wall Street firms, ignore most stocks. Retail investors typically buy what is hot at the moment. Institutional investors, such as mutual funds, pension funds, endowments, and charitable trusts, often have tight restrictions on what they can own. So, the market contains a lot of hidden gems waiting to be discovered. Finding a bargain is often a matter of simply doing the research. If you find one before everyone else, you can see some nice capital gains.

Fundamental Analysis isn't foolproof. Trying to predict the future is always risky, but thorough research and careful analysis significantly improve your odds.

Spotting a bargain

Some people are better at bargain hunting than others. What usually separates the clueless from the pros is that the pros know what something is worth. The same is true for finding bargains on Wall Street. You need to know what a stock is worth, and low price isn't always a bargain.

Banking on irrational behavior

Irrational investors make two mistakes. First, they invest emotionally, letting greed or fear taint their decisions. Second (often because of the first reason), they fail to perform their due diligence, so even if the information is readily available, they don't look at it.

These two mistakes clearly contributed significantly to the formation and bursting of the dot-com bubble in the 1990s. Both professional and individual investors bought shares of companies that had no earnings at all and few if any revenues, run by inexperienced managers with no real, clear business plans. Incredibly, investors would pay upwards of $100 per share for these companies, scoffing at the readily available data screaming "Not worth it!" People just felt it didn't matter. The often-heard refrain during this bubble was, "It's different this time. Earnings don't matter in the new economy."

When these stocks eventually fell to pennies a share, people realized the market hadn't efficiently priced these shares. Greed and investing mania had pushed the prices higher. When the bubble burst, these same investors didn't know a good stock from a bad one. Indiscriminately, they dumped stock in good companies and bad, pushing share prices lower across the board. Savvy, less-emotional value investors were then able to scoop up shares in good companies for pennies on a dollar.

Do your homework and keep a cool head when everyone else is losing theirs. When you see the share price fall on companies you know are good investments, load up on the shares, don't sell them.

For example, Warren Buffett, the second richest person in the world, is considered the world's best value investor. He runs Berkshire Hathaway — an insurance company that serves as his investment vehicle. In the summer of 2009, Berkshire Hathaway (BRK.A) shares sold for around $100,000 each. Meanwhile, eDiets (DIET), a provider of Internet-based diet and fitness programs, sold for about $2 a share. Although shares of eDiets cost a lot less than those of Berkshire Hathaway, that $2 a share wasn't a bargain.

Investors were buying Berkshire Hathaway because they thought it was cheap. They determined its *intrinsic value* (actual value) was $125,000. It had a great management team, consistently produced profits, and had a long history of capital appreciation. Plus, it held stock in growing businesses. Meanwhile, investors thought eDiets was overpriced at $2 and expected it to lose half its value over the year. Revenues were falling. It was on its way to its fourth consecutive annual loss. Its current liabilities were double its current assets, and it had negative shareholder equity.

At first glance, paying $2 per share for a company looks a lot better than paying $100,000 per share, but some fundamental analysis shows that in this case, that $100,000 per share is the better bargain.

Value investors hunt for bargains, but they buy only after performing some careful research and crunching the numbers, as Chapter 8 explains. When you spot a stock that seems to be underpriced, ask the following questions to determine whether it's a real buy:

- **Is this stock down due to market conditions?** If the broader stock market is down, possibly due to an economic slowdown or recession, chances are good that most other stocks are down too. If the share price falls but the company's fundamentals remain strong, this stock may be the bargain you've been looking for. (If the market is up but the stock is down, the stock isn't necessarily a loser. The drop in share price may be an anomaly representing a good buying opportunity. Ask more questions.)

  When market conditions turn sour, a rational reason for indiscriminate selling is when investors experience a liquidity crisis. Desperate for cash but unable to sell their worst money-losing investments, investors in this situation sell what they can, typically their most liquid stocks and bonds. Often these may be their best investments, but the need for cash forces them to sell. This scenario provides a bargain for the value investor.

- **Is this stock down because of sector news?** If bad news comes out of one stock in the sector, traders may flee from stocks in the same sector. If a good company's stock takes a hit because of another company's misfortune, that's a bargain waiting to happen.

✔ **Is the stock down because it's not in a sexy industry?** At the peak of the tech bubble, anything that wasn't a technology stock (pretty much anything that functioned as a part of the economy prior to 1980) was considered out of fashion, and their stock prices fell as a result. However, they continued to post earnings and revenue growth. The industrials, manufacturers, food processors, and other standard bearers became value stocks in the late 1990s. Value investors were rewarded for their patience and conviction when the tech bubble burst and investors returned to more traditional companies.

✔ **Is this stock down because of problems specific to this company?** If investors have fled for good reason, sell shares in the company if you own them or avoid buying if you don't. However, keep in mind that the market tends to overreact and that some negative news can be very short-lived, especially if it's not true. A passing bit of bad news can trigger a good buying opportunity, but if the news points out fundamental problems in the company's success or operations, watch out. Be wary of the following:

- Declining sales or earnings

- Excessive debt

- Little or no cash flow

- Scandal

- Illegality, such as falsifying documents or insider trading

If this stock has a lot of issues, the beautiful thing about the stock market is you don't have to hang around. Money can stagnate or even rot in a dead stock, but if you sell and put the money into a true value stock, you may be able to recoup some of your losses.

Finding the Sweet Spot: Dividend-Paying Growth Stocks at Bargain Prices

Value, income, and growth aren't mutually exclusive. Even growth investors are looking for bargains, and all investors are ultimately trying to score some income. No investor is going to pass up a true bargain.

The sweet spot of stock investing occurs when you find a company exhibiting characteristics of all three approaches — a hot stock at a cheap price.

When shopping for stocks (see Chapter 7), use all three criteria to narrow the field. You can start by looking for dividend stocks with a minimum acceptable yield (for example, 1 or 2 percent higher than the current inflation rate) and then screen for growth and value. Or, start by searching for undervalued stocks and then screening your list for candidates that meet or exceed your minimum acceptable yield. When you find a stock that meets all of your criteria, you have a true gem that embodies all the positive characteristics of a dividend stock:

- ✔ Steady income stream
- ✔ Good management
- ✔ Fiscal discipline
- ✔ Earnings transparency
- ✔ Dividends increases

Plus the benefits of growth:

- ✔ Strong earnings growth
- ✔ Strong revenue growth

With a steady income stream from dividends and good potential for capital appreciation from growth, you've found a real bargain that promises to limit your exposure to risk while maximizing your profit potential.

Don't automatically eliminate small-yield stocks. If a company is managed well and demonstrates consistent growth, chances are pretty good it will eventually start increasing its dividend payments. Once it makes that commitment, it's very likely to increase dividend payments on a regular basis.

Chapter 7

Searching for Promising Candidates

*T*he stock market is really big. How big depends on when you measure, what you use to measure it, and who's doing the measuring. On October 31, 2007, the Dow Jones U.S. Total Stock Market Index, which contains all U.S. equities that have readily available prices, held 4,875 stocks valued at $18.9 trillion. By December 2009, it held 4,209 stocks and its value had plunged 30 percent to $13.2 trillion. Thousands more trade over the counter (OTC), where stocks for newer and smaller companies are more likely to be traded.

Any way you count 'em, that's a lot of stocks to sift through to find a few nuggets of gold, even if you scratch non-dividend stocks off your list. Fortunately, several resources are available to help investors screen out the poorest prospects and focus on only the most promising candidates. In this chapter, I reveal useful sources for tools and information so that you know where to find them and how to use them to track down potentially good dividend stocks.

Focusing on What You Know

The best investors focus on businesses they know and understand, or they carefully research an industry prior to evaluating specific companies in that industry. They get to know the company's business model and how it stacks up to other companies in the same business. They develop an understanding of the company's opportunities, challenges, and the resources it has in place to overcome any challenges and maximize its opportunities.

Inspecting the company's fundamentals (financials), as I explain in Chapter 8, is critical, but it takes you only so far. By knowing the industry and how well a company is positioned in that industry, you have a significant edge over other investors. For example, prior to the mortgage meltdown that began in 2007, plenty of investors believed that the financial sector was rock solid. Examining quarterly reports gave them little reason to believe otherwise.

Savvy professionals in the real estate and mortgage industries and well informed investors knew better. They looked beyond the financials to the broader economy and noticed housing values soaring beyond belief, lenders approving loans to borrowers who obviously wouldn't be able to afford the payments, and homeowners lining up to cash out the equity in their homes just to cover their bills. They knew something had to give. They sure weren't buying financials — most were selling them.

When you're looking for dividend stocks to invest in, start with what you know. If you're in the medical field, you're probably more aware than most people which pharmaceutical companies are the leaders and how effective they are in terms of sales and customer service. If you work for a power company, you may have better insight into what's required to run a profitable business in that industry. You may hear things about new regulations that may affect profits and a company's ability to pay dividends. Be careful, because any nonpublic information you receive in an official capacity may be considered insider information. However, any information that is public but not widely disseminated can give you an advantage.

The more you know about a particular sector or company, the more your head is in the game. You can make better investment decisions even before the data shows up on a quarterly report. Write a list of all the industries you come in contact with through your profession. Your list can include the company where you work, its vendors, and any companies your company serves. Then add hobbies and interests and companies you've heard about through your pursuit of these extracurricular activities. If you're a video game aficionado, for example, you may have valuable insights about the video game industry you didn't even know about! Your list can serve as a valuable tool in identifying leads.

Be an information sponge. Everything you see, hear, read, consume, and experience can help you identify potentially good dividend stocks and make better investment decisions. Seek out credible information, remain skeptical, and verify all the information against other credible sources. Just because a top analyst rates a stock as a strong buy doesn't make it so — conditions on the ground may prove the stock was more like a strong sell.

Just because you're well informed on a few industries doesn't mean you should concentrate too much of your investments there. Putting too much of a portfolio in one company or industry that turns sour can destroy the portfolio, so you still need to diversify. And be especially careful of buying too much stock in the company where you work. Take a look at the employees of Enron, who invested most of their 401(k) plans in Enron because they thought they knew it best. You already have your livelihood based on one company; you don't want all your investments tracking the same thing. When Enron went under, employees lost not just their jobs but their nest eggs, too.

Digging Up Dividend Stocks on the Internet

Stock trading has come a long way since the days of stock certificates and tickertape machines. Tools, data, and analysis previously accessible only to investment professionals are now readily available on the Web 24/7 and are better and faster than ever. Many Web sites even provide free stock screeners that enable you to search for stocks by price, dividend yield, price-to-earnings ratio (P/E), earnings per share (EPS), and more. You can quickly whittle a list of 4,000 stocks down to about 25 in less than a minute. In the following sections, I provide a sample of some of the best tools available for tracking down dividend stocks on the Internet.

Hunting on Yahoo! Finance

The first finance *aggregator* (easily accessible collection of headlines, articles, and other newsworthy materials from a wide variety of sources), Yahoo! Finance remains the king. It's chock-full of information on every company, with news and commentary from 45 well-known financial Web sites. It also provides personal finance stories and exclusive videos.

To narrow your list of candidates, you start by entering selection criteria in Yahoo's Stock Screener. Go to `finance.yahoo.com`, mouse over the Investing tab, click Stocks, click Stock Screener, and then click Launch HTML Screener. The Stock Screener appears, prompting you to enter selection criteria.

You can pick any or all of the following criteria:

- **Category:** You can focus on one specific industry or market index.
- **Share Data:** Pick a minimum and maximum level for share price, market cap, dividend yield, or volatility (beta).

✔ **Sales and Profitability:** Choose the sales and profit range you want.

✔ **Valuation Ratios:** Enter a maximum and minimum value for a P/E ratio, price-to-book ratio, price-to-sales ratio, and/or PEG ratio. Most of these are explained in Chapter 8.

✔ **Analysts Estimates:** You can also make your picks according to the earnings per share growth rate expected by Wall Street analysts.

The Stock Screener displays a list of companies that match the search criteria you entered. Click the ticker symbol for one of the companies in the list, and a new browser window opens with charts and information about the stock and the company.

Googling on Google Finance

Fans of Google can celebrate the fact that in addition to serving as a killer search engine, Google offers an outstanding and very easy-to-use stock screener. To access it, fire up your Web browser, go to `www.google.com/finance` and click Stock Screener so that the Google Stock Screener appears. You can start narrowing your list of candidates by entering selection criteria near the top of the page:

✔ **Exchange:** All, AMEX, NASDAQ, or NYSE

✔ **Sector:** All, Basic Materials, Capital Goods, Conglomerates, Consumer cyclical, Consumer Non-cyclical, Energy, Financial, Healthcare, Services, Technology, Transportation, or Utilities

✔ **Market cap:** Minimum and maximum size of the company in terms of dollars, calculated by multiplying the price per share by the total number of shares outstanding

✔ **P/E ratio:** Minimum and maximum price-to-earnings ratio (see Chapter 8 for details)

✔ **Dividend yield:** Minimum and maximum desired percentage return on the investment based on dividends alone, not accounting for any share price appreciation (flip to Chapter 8 for details)

✔ **52w price change:** Minimum and maximum percentage of share price increase or decrease over the last 52 weeks

✔ **Add criteria:** Click Add criteria for specific dividend factors such as dividend for recent quarter, dividend per share (DPS), and dividend from cash flow. You can also specify a host of other criteria such as return on equity (ROE), net profit margin, or earnings per share (EPS).

As you adjust your criteria, Google's Stock Screener updates a list of all and only those stocks that match your search criteria. (If the list doesn't automatically update, press Enter after you change your criteria.)

Click one of the company names in the list, and Google displays a page packed with charts and information about the stock, the company, and its likely competitors. You can even click links to access additional news and information about the company.

For a quick stock price, go to the Google Finance homepage (`www.google.com/finance`), type the ticker symbol into the search box, and click Search.

Shining a light with Morningstar

Well known as the one of the best firms for the analysis of mutual funds and exchange-traded funds, Morningstar also analyzes individual stocks. On top of a stock screener and much of the same information provided by Yahoo! Finance and Google Finance, Morningstar also provides a staff of unbiased analysts offering commentary on the markets and 1,700 individual stocks. The best part is, these analysts don't have the potential conflicts of interest that can affect stock analysts at Wall Street investment banks (flip to "Picking the Brains of Professionals" later in the chapter for more). Check it out at `www.morningstar.com/Cover/Stocks.html`.

Finding the real data at the SEC

No matter where you get your stock ideas from, the real hardcore data comes from the companies themselves. According to U.S. law, all publicly traded companies must file financial statements with the Securities and Exchange Commission (SEC) every quarter. These quarterly reports contain the company's income statement, which tells you if the company posted a profit, and its balance sheet, which lists the company's assets and liabilities. I explain these documents in detail in Chapter 8. You can also find filings listing all legal stock sales and purchases by company insiders.

To find a company's filings, go to the SEC's Web site (`www.sec.gov/`) and follow these steps:

1. **Scroll down to Filings & Forms and click Search for Company Filings.**

2. **Click the first search option.**

   This step takes you to a page where you can enter the company's name or ticker symbol.

3. Enter the company's information and press Enter.

You now have a listing of all the company's SEC filings, starting with the most recent.

Picking the Brains of Professionals

Obviously, one of the best places to get information on stocks is from Wall Street itself — in particular, your broker. Part of your investment advisor's job is to come up with good ideas for your portfolio. Whether you use a full-service broker or a discount broker, both should be able to provide you with access to proprietary research from Wall Street's professional stock analysts.

- ✔ **Full-service broker:** Because your stockbroker or investment advisor is most intimately involved with your risk tolerance, portfolio needs, and financial goals, she should be one of the first people you talk to about stock ideas. After you make some choices, a broker at a large brokerage can provide you with research available exclusively to that firm's customers, such as analysis of an industry, the economy, or a specific company. Company research from investment banks is great, because the analysts do a lot of the fundamental analysis you'd otherwise have to do on your own and they offer some educated predictions. Also, they visit and talk to each company's management to get an in-depth view of what's really going on. If your investment advisor doesn't work for a brokerage, she should be able to get reports from the brokerage she deals with.

- ✔ **Discount broker:** With a discount broker, you don't have a person assigned to your account, but most discount brokers have stock screeners for coming up with ideas. Even though most don't have their own research departments, discount brokers do have access to some proprietary stock analysis from investment banks.

Check out Chapter 19 for more on which kind of broker is right for you.

Make sure your broker is a *fiduciary*; that is, the broker is required by law to act in accordance with his client's best interests rather than his own or the brokerage's best interest. Many brokers pass themselves off as financial advisors, but they're encouraged to sell stocks and other investment products that earn higher commissions for the brokerage and not necessarily higher returns for their clients.

Don't blindly follow your broker's recommendations or Wall Street reports. Your broker's advice isn't the last stop on the road — it's just the start of the journey. Do some research on your own. The SEC legally requires companies to provide you with the most accurate data and information. Meanwhile, in addition to data, Wall Street analyst reports contain a lot of commentary and opinion. Although stock analysts at investment banks do very deep research on a company, these reports are written for the specific purpose of selling stocks. Because many reports are written about clients of the analyst's firm, you rarely see an analyst recommend that you sell a stock. Thus, conflicts of interest aren't unusual. So don't accept everything a Wall Street stock analysis says as the end-all and be-all.

Scrolling Through Investment Publications

Increasingly, information is migrating to digital venues, including the Web, but don't overlook traditional media, including newspapers and magazines. Most of the up-to-the-minute and big business news still comes out of the two main daily business papers — the *Wall Street Journal* and the *Financial Times,* and their Web sites. Other options include *Investor's Business Daily,* a financial newspaper aimed specifically at investors, and the *New York Times,* a general-interest newspaper with a well-respected business section.

Consider subscribing to a few financial publications and reading them regularly. With most publications, you can choose to access your subscription online or off. You can even have issues delivered to your e-reader, such as Amazon's Kindle, instead of receiving a paper copy.

In the following sections, I take you on a tour of some of the more traditional media where you can find valuable investment advice and recommendations for specific companies to invest in.

The Wall Street Journal

The *Wall Street Journal* (WSJ) isn't only one of the best newspapers for financial and business news but also one of the best newspapers in the United States. As such, it provides readers with the information they need to interpret the business news in the context of everything else that's going on in the world. In addition to covering national and international business and financial news, it covers politics, science, government, health, arts, law, social issues, entertainment, and (on Fridays) even sports.

The Money & Investing section contains analysis and reports on the financial markets, along with stock-market tables that list the most widely held companies. However, the newspaper's tables are not nearly as informative as they used to be. With a subscription to the paper, you also receive a subscription to the paper's Web site, WSJ.com (`online.wsj.com/home-page`). There you can find a lot of data for each company, including industry comparisons, news stories, key facts, insider transactions, institutional holdings, and financial statements. You can subscribe to the *Wall Street Journal* print and/or online version at the Web site listed earlier or by calling 800-568-7625 or 609-514-0870.

Financial Times

In the midst of a global economy, having a global perspective often helps. Short of sailing across the Atlantic, you can often gain this valuable perspective by reading the *Financial Times* of London. Although you may read many of the same stories in the *Wall Street Journal,* the *Financial Times* sees it from a different angle that's often enlightening for investors. To check out what the *Financial Times* has to offer or to subscribe to the U.S. edition of the newspaper, visit its Web site at `www.ft.com`.

Investor's Business Daily

Nicknamed IBD, this daily financial paper aims to help investors make money. Its second section is chock full of charts and data. For each stock, the tables include five IBD ratings on different parts of the business. The paper also provides a section on the IBD 100, an in-depth ranking of the nation's leading companies based on profit growth, return on equity, sales growth, profit margins, and relative price strength. Its Web site is `www.investors.com/default.aspx?fromad=1`.

The magazine rack

Check out the magazine racks in your neighborhood, and you're likely to find a wide selection of personal finance and investing publications. In the following sections, I introduce the best of the bunch.

Barron's

Barron's is a weekly publication with market analysis and articles about the economy, Wall Street trends, and innovative technologies. Most people buy Barron's for investing ideas from its investor-oriented company profiles and interviews with successful portfolio managers. The magazine also prints extensive financial tables that list the following data for most public companies, widely held mutual funds, ETFs, and bonds:

✔ Stock name and ticker symbol

✔ 52-week high and low share prices

✔ Annual dividend, if any, based on the rate of the most recent quarterly payment

✔ Yield based on the previous closing price

✔ P/E ratio

✔ Volume, indicating previous day's trading activity

✔ Latest week's price data — close and change

✔ Earnings for last year, this year, and next year

Visit its Web site at `online.barrons.com`.

Fortune

Aimed at business professionals, this monthly magazine typically offers long in-depth profiles on companies and individuals. You can access it at `money. cnn.com/magazines/fortune`.

Forbes

Forbes monthly magazine tends to be politically conservative and pro-business, containing more political commentary than most other financial publications covered in this chapter. It also seems to be written for a more affluent audience, although the articles and insights are useful for the aver-age investor, too. The Forbes.com Web site (`www.forbes.com`) is currently one of the most comprehensive financial news sites for a magazine-based publication.

Kiplinger's and Money Magazine

Kiplinger's and *Money* are exclusively for individual investors. Although they offer stock picks, they're more general personal finance magazines address-ing budgeting, taxes, retirement planning, and even career advice. *Kiplinger's* is at `www.kiplinger.com`; even if you subscribe to the magazine, I encour-age you to visit the Web site, where you can find additional information and online tools. *Money* resides at `money.cnn.com`.

SmartMoney

Of the monthly personal finance magazines, *SmartMoney* spends the most space investigating stock ideas. The Web site (`www.smartmoney.com`) offers original content daily with investing ideas and stock screens. In addi-tion, SmartMoney.com offers some of the best stock evaluation tools for investors. It provides stock charts you can program from and to any date in the last five years. In addition, it's the only site that allows you to rank a company against five competitors in 25 fundamental metrics on a daily basis:

1. **Type a ticker symbol into the Search or Quote box.**

2. **When the stock's page comes up, click the Compare tab.**

Checking out some other investing sites

On the Web, sites for investors abound, offering news, information, analysis, discussion forums, advice, and just about everything else you need to get started and rise to the next level. In the following sections, I highlight some of the better Web sites and blogs specifically for dividend investing.

Web sites

Following is a selection of professionally produced Web sites that offer commentary focused on dividend investing:

- **Dividend.com** (www.dividend.com) provides daily articles on dividend-investing ideas. The site rates 1,700 dividend stocks and provides data that includes a list of the highest-yielding stocks. It also provides a handy reminder on its home page to let you know which companies are going into *ex-dividend* the following day, so you know the specific date you must purchase stock by in order to get the most recent dividend. See Chapter 2 for details about the ex-dividend date and other important dates in the life of a dividend stock.

- **The Motley Fool** is a broad investing site. However, it has a category on its stock tab focused on dividend and income investing. Go to www.fool.com, mouse over Investing, and click Dividends & Income.

- **Seeking Alpha** is an aggregator of stories from writers who aren't staff members of a financial publication — many are bloggers. Although it doesn't focus on dividends, the site offers a variety of opinions from a wide swath of the investing world outside of Wall Street. To reach its page for dividend stocks, go to seekingalpha.com/tag/dividends.

- **Wall Street News Network** provides a lot of stock databases, including lists of which stocks go ex-dividend in each month and the highest-yield stocks in a variety of industries, all compiled in Microsoft Excel spreadsheets. Take a look at wallstreetnewsnetwork.com/.

- **Dividend Investor** also provides a lot of data at dividendinvestor.com.

Blogs

Blogs differ from Web sites in that they're typically the work of a single individual with a specific viewpoint. These personal commentaries sometimes don't uphold the journalistic convention of accuracy as their highest ideal, so always back-check their facts. The following blogs come from investors — some of whom are professional investment advisors and some whom are just very knowledgeable individuals — who follow an income-based strategy of buying dividend-paying stocks and reinvesting the payments. They're listed in alphabetical order:

- ✔ **Dividend Growth Investor:** www.dividendgrowthinvestor.com
- ✔ **The Dividend Guy:** www.thedividendguyblog.com
- ✔ **Dividend Tree:** dividendtree.net
- ✔ **Dividends Value:** dividendsvalue.com

Steer clear of online investment scams. The Internet is a great resource for investors, but it also has a dark side populated with spammers, hackers, crackers, phishers, and other low-life scumbags bent on generating chaos and stealing money. As you perform your research, be careful of any investment opportunities designed solely to part you from your money. The best way to protect yourself from investment scams is to keep the following in mind:

- ✔ **Nobody will protect you, so protect yourself.** Far too many consumers place blind trust in professionals, believing that if the professionals are licensed and certified, they're legitimate. Otherwise, regulators would have shut them down, right? Wrong. The SEC was useless in stopping Bernie Madoff from ripping off investors, even after receiving numerous tips.

- ✔ **If an opportunity sounds too good to be true, it probably is.** A low-risk, high-return investment is a contradiction. If someone guarantees you an annual return of more than 10 percent or that your portfolio NEVER loses money, somebody is definitely trying to rip you off.

- ✔ **If someone contacts you, be skeptical.** Work only with people you seek out and contact. If someone goes out of his way to contact you, unsolicited, with an unbelievably great investment opportunity, he probably didn't approach you out of the kindness of his heart.

Chapter 8

Sizing Up Potential Picks

· ·

· ·

*O*n Wall Street perhaps more than anywhere else, knowledge is power, which is why insider trading is illegal — insiders know way too much to play a fair game. As an outsider, however, you want to know as much about the industry, the company, and its stock as possible so you can make a wise purchase decision, maximize your return, and minimize your exposure to risk.

This chapter shows you how to perform your due diligence so you have the information you need to keep from getting burned by your neighbor's hot tip. Not all dividend stocks are created equal, and the more you know about a company, the better you can judge whether it will continue to pay dividends and how likely it will be to increase its dividend payments.

Digging Up Key Facts and Figures

Publicly traded companies are required by law to publish reports — sort of like report cards — that tell current and prospective investors how well (or not so well) the company is doing. The most important of these reports are the following:

✔ **Annual Report:** Public companies send this attractive, colorful publication to all of their shareholders once a year. It contains many of the company's year-end financial statements as well as a chronicle of the company's activities during the previous year.

✔ **10-K Form:** Similar to the annual report, the *10-K* contains the same financial statements plus a bit more, such as how much the executives get paid and how much stock they own. The Securities and Exchange Commission (SEC) requires companies to file this comprehensive financial statement within 60 days after the end of the company's fiscal year.

✔ **10-Q Form:** This document is a quarterly report (hence the *Q*) that contains a company's financial statements, a discussion from management, and a list of "material events" that have occurred during the previous quarter. The SEC requires companies to file a 10-Q within 35 days after the end of each of the first three fiscal quarters. The 10-K contains the fourth-quarter along with the annual results.

✔ **8-K Form:** The *8-K* reports any significant events and/or material changes not made in the ordinary course of business. These material events include a change in auditors, the resignation or election of a director, the completion of asset acquisition or disposition, a bankruptcy, and other material impairments and must be reported within four days of their occurrence.

Don't ignore the most recent 8-Ks. These have potential to be the most important of all the forms. Depending on the news reported, such as a need to restate earnings, an 8-K can make all the other forms useless.

You can obtain a company's most recent annual report by visiting its Web site or contacting the company and requesting a copy. The best place to find the 10-K, 10-Q, and 8-K forms are on the SEC's Web site at www.sec.gov. Companies also typically release their balance sheets and income statements in press releases when they announce their quarterly earnings. You can find press releases on the company's Web site or on financial Web sites such as Yahoo! Finance (finance.yahoo.com) or Google Finance (www.google.com/finance).

Examining Company Fundamentals

When you buy shares in a company, you're not just buying pieces of paper — you're buying ownership of that company. It's sort of like loaning money to a relative who's looking to start a business. If his idea for a business sounds wacky and unprofitable, his home is in foreclosure, and he can't manage his own life let alone a business, you'd probably be reluctant to loan him any money. Just like you consider the financial soundness of your relative, you want to make sure that a company you're thinking about investing in is financially sound and that management seems to have its act together. You make this determination by examining the following three documents:

✔ Balance sheet

✔ Income statement

✔ Cash flow statement

The numbers on these statements are the company's *fundamentals* — things like revenues and expenses. In the following sections, I describe each of these documents in greater detail and show you how to decipher them.

After you understand the fundamentals, you can compare these metrics against others to calculate ratios specific to dividend investing. These calculations help you determine the health of the company and make educated predictions about future appreciation and dividend growth. I give you the lowdown on some of these ratios later in the chapter.

Company reports measure past performance, but a stock's value depends entirely on what people expect it to do in the future. Because of this discrepancy, stock analysis pretty much consists of predicting future performance based on current conditions and past performance. Although past performance is all you have to go on, it's no guarantee of future results; last year's big winner may be this year's big loser, and vice versa. If it sounds like trying to predict the weather, it is, and even the best meteorologists and stock analysts get it wrong sometimes. At the end of the day, staying on top of stocks is like keeping tabs on the weather: You can see most storms from miles away if you take the time to look, and you'd rather be ready for a storm than surprised by one.

Getting a financial snapshot from the balance sheet

The balance sheet presents a financial snapshot of what the company owns and owes at a single point in time, typically at the end of each quarter. It's essentially a net worth statement for a company. The left or top side of the balance sheet lists everything the company owns: its *assets*, also known as *debits*. As you can see in Figure 8-1, the right or lower side lists the claims against the company, called *liabilities* or *credits*, and shareholder equity. The following sections delve into some of the balance sheet's info.

Liabilities may not seem like credits to you, but that's not a typo. In accounting lingo, a credit is a loan. A credit brings cash in that the firm can use to purchase an asset. However, this credit is a liability, a debt that must be paid back at a later date. We use *assets* and *liabilities* as our main terms, so don't worry too much about keeping the debits and credits straight.

It's called a balance sheet because each side must equal the other. Assets equal liabilities plus shareholder equity. In other words, whatever assets aren't being used to pay off the liabilities belong to the shareholders. See the later "Shareholder equity" section for more information.

A company's balance sheet is only one item to consider when deciding where to invest your money. You also need to look at the other facts and figures covered in this chapter, along with how the sector (industry) is doing as a whole and the company's outlook as compared to that of other companies you're investigating. For more about using data on the balance sheet and other reports to evaluate a company, check out "Calculating a Dividend's Relative Strength" later in this chapter.

Carrel Industries, Inc.	
Balance Sheet	
	March 31, 2010
Assets	
Current Assets	
Cash and Cash Equivalents	4,434,000
Accounts Receivables	5,744,000
Inventory	7,615,000
Other Assets	4,215,000
Total Current Assets	22,008,000
Property, Plant, and Equipment	18,531,000
Goodwill and Intangible Assets	87,445,000
Other Noncurrent Assets	4,411,000
Total Assets	**132,395,000**
Liabilities	
Current Liabilities	
Accounts Payable	5,138,000
Other Current Liabilities	7,996,000
Current Long-Term Debt	18,366,000
Taxes Payable	1,329,000
Total Current Liabilities	32,829,000
Long-Term Debt	20,452,000
Other Liabilities	18,339,000
Total Liabilities	**71,620,000**
Total Shareholders' Equity	**60,775,000**
Total Liabilities and Equity	**132,395,000**

Figure 8-1:
Sample balance sheet for a healthy company.

Assets

Assets are items of value that the company owns. The major components that make up the asset side of the balance sheet include current assets, fixed assets, investments, and intangibles. Here's a breakdown:

✔ **Current Assets:** All liquid assets — cash or anything that can easily be turned into cash:

- **Cash equivalents:** Highly liquid, short-term investment securities with a high credit quality. These assets are typically low-risk, low-return instruments, such as bank accounts, money market accounts, and marketable securities, including U.S. Treasury bills and *corporate commercial paper* (short-term debt instrument) that matures within 24 hours.

- **Accounts receivables:** Funds owed to the company. These assets represent unsettled bills customers have yet to pay on goods or services already delivered.

- **Inventory:** The value of everything the firm is ready to sell.

✔ **Investments:** Stocks, bonds or derivatives. Some are long-term investments, but any investment that can be sold for quick cash goes under current assets.

✔ **Fixed Assets:** Tangible, permanent items necessary for the business to operate. Fixed Assets include real estate, buildings, vehicles, and equipment. These assets typically have a long life.

✔ **Intangibles:** Anything that has value but isn't involved in the actual production of the good or service. Intangibles include copyrights, patents, trademarks, licenses, and *goodwill* (the company's standing in the community, based on the company's relationship to customers and suppliers and people's view of the company's brand name).

Together, these items add up to total assets. Ideally, assets create income, which pays for future dividends.

Liabilities

Liabilities are sort of like IOUs — together, they represent the total cash value of what the company owes to other entities. Liabilities aren't necessarily a bad thing. After all, companies have to spend money to make money. They only become a problem when a company is consistently spending more than it's earning and has no clear and viable strategy to reduce that trend. Here's how liabilities typically break down:

✔ **Current Liabilities:** All short-term debt that must be paid back within the next 12 months, such as

- **Accounts Payable:** Unpaid bills for goods already received from the company's suppliers. These debts typically require payment within 90 days.

- **Current Long-Term Debt:** Any long-term debt that will be retired in the next 12 months and its interest payments.

✔ **Long-Term Debt:** Any borrowed money that the company will pay back over a time period longer than 12 months. Long-term debt includes bonds, loans from banks, and mortgages.

✔ **Other Liabilities:** Everything else the company owes.

Add current liabilities to long-term debt and other liabilities to calculate total liabilities.

Shareholder equity

Subtract total liabilities from total assets, and you end up with the company's *net worth,* also known as *shareholder equity* — the shareholders' ownership stake after all the debts are paid. (That's why stocks are also called equities.)

Common stock, preferred stock, and retained earnings comprise the three major parts of shareholder equity. (See Chapter 2 for details about common and preferred stock.) These items may not be listed in the annual report or press releases, but they can be found in the 10-Q and 10-K SEC filings I discuss earlier in the chapter. They ultimately determine how much each share receives in dividends:

✔ **Common stocks:** The number of common shares outstanding.

✔ **Preferred stock:** The number of preferred shares outstanding.

✔ **Retained Earnings:** The profits left over after dividends have been paid. Also called *undistributed profits* or *earned surplus,* retained earnings provide the funds to make investments and purchase new assets.

To help you evaluate the company's financial health, you plug the balance sheet's asset and liability values into a variety of ratios I explain later in the chapter. All other things being equal, the balance sheet in Figure 8-1 indicates a healthy company — a potentially good pick.

Tallying profits and losses with an income statement

The *income statement* (also known as the *profit-and-loss* or *P&L statement*) details all of the company's revenues and expenses —how much the company receives in sales and how much the company spends to make those sales. After all the additions and subtractions, the final tally tells you whether the company earned a profit or suffered a loss and how much. The income statement contains the fundamental equation for every business:

Sales – Expenses = Net Income

A positive net income indicates the company is profitable. Zero means it broke even. A negative number shows the company lost money. That's all pretty straightforward, but the income statement usually contains more detail, covering the following items (among other things):

- ✓ **Revenues:** Total dollar amount brought in from sales. Called the *top line* because it's the top line of the income statement, revenues record the company's total (gross) sales of products and services.

- ✓ **Costs of products sold:** Also called *cost of revenue* and *cost of goods sold,* this figure represents the costs of buying raw materials and producing the finished products.

- ✓ **Gross profit:** Deduct the cost of products sold from the total revenues to arrive at gross profit.

  The first benchmark comes right here, the *gross margin* or *profit margin,* also known as the *return on sales.* Divide gross profit by revenues to get profit margin. When it comes to dividend stocks, a profit margin of 50 percent of total revenues keeps me interested. Less that 50 percent and I toss it.

- ✓ **Selling, general, and administrative expense:** This category includes all costs to maintain the business:

  - **Selling costs** include all expenditures to sell the product, such as marketing and travel.

  - **Administrative** includes salaries and other services such as accountants and lawyers.

  - **General costs** encompass the costs to maintain plants and equipment.

- ✓ **Operating income:** The difference between gross profit and selling, general, and administrative expenses. Operating income represents the total amount of profits that came from the actual performance of the company's business.

- ✓ **Earnings before interest, taxes, depreciation and amortization:** These earnings, often referred to as EBITDA, combine operating income with income from investments.

  EBITDA is useful in giving a view to profits before non-cash accounting calculations, such as depreciation and amortization, are deducted. However, EBITDA is not an official number under the Generally Accepted Accounting Principles (GAAP), so it can be manipulated to suit management's goals.

- ✓ **Interest expense:** The interest paid on debt.

- ✓ **Non operating income:** Any income that doesn't come from the company's operations, such as the sale of assets or investment income.

✔ **Earnings from continuing operations:** Profits from the company's current businesses.

✔ **Earnings from discontinued operations:** Profits from any businesses the company closed or sold this quarter.

✔ **Net Income:** The true profit after every other possible expense has been paid. The profit is the _bottom line_, because it's the last line on the income statement and what really matters at the end of each quarter. In the end, does this company make a profit or loss, and how big is it?

Another key number to check on an income statement is _earnings per share._ You want to see this number going up rather than down, as it does in the income statement shown in Figure 8-2. In this example, even though the net income fell in the first quarter of 2009 to $2.6 million, compared with $2.7 million in the first quarter in 2008, earnings per share actually grew to 88 cents from 87 cents. That happened because Carrel Industries bought back some shares, lowering the number of shares available for sale on the stock market to 3,104,600 from 3,301,200. Fewer shares can boost earnings per share even when net income falls. For more about using data on the income statement to evaluate a company, check out "Calculating a Dividend's Relative Strength" later in this chapter.

Earnings per share and net income are different ways to measure the same thing — profits. If they move in different directions, wonder why. Whenever you notice discrepancies like this one, you need to investigate. When a company buys back its own shares, it lowers the number of shares outstanding, which means the profits are spread out among fewer shares. Did management lower the number of shares outstanding to artificially boost earnings per share and give investors a false impression about the company's health? Quite possibly. But that's not the only possible reason for a buyback. Buybacks and insider purchases are often signs that management believes the company's share prices will soon rise. In this case, the company bought back the shares because it felt they were underpriced. Carrel Industries, a provider of consumer products, saw profits fall because of problems in the economy, not inside the company. The recession and stock market crash of 2008 and 2009 caused consumers to reduce their spending, and share prices of Carrel Industries fell too. Realizing the company was worth more than the stock market was pricing it, management decided the shares were selling at a bargain price and bought some back.

Any time you see a number in parentheses, it means that's a negative number, or outflow of money. If the net income figure is in parenthesis, the company recorded a net loss for the quarter.

Income statements compare the most recent quarter to the same quarter a year earlier. Some businesses are cyclical. For instance, retailers make a lot more money during the winter holidays than the first three months of the year. So, to compare the January-to-March quarter to the October-to-December quarter wouldn't be a fair comparison.

Carrel Industries, Inc.		
Income Statement		
Period Ending	**March 31, 2010**	**March 31, 2009**
Total Revenues	18,417,000	20,026,000
Cost of Products Sold	(9,161,000)	(9,679,000)
Gross Profit	9,256,000	10,347,000
Selling, General, and Administrative Expenses	(5,526,000)	(6,334,000)
Operating Income	3,730,000	4,013,000
Interest Expense	(336,000)	(364,000)
Non Operating Income	93,000	10,000
Earnings Before Taxes	3,487,000	3,659,000
Income Taxes	(902,000)	(1,009,000)
Earnings from Continuing Operations	2,585,000	2,650,000
Earnings from Discontinued Operations	28,000	60,000
Net Income	2,613,000	2,710,000
Basic Earnings per Share	88 cents	87 cents
Diluted Earnings per Share	84 cents	82 cents
Dividends per Share	40 cents	35 cents
Shares Outstanding	3,104,600	3,301,200

Figure 8-2: Sample income statement for a healthy company.

Watching the money stream with a cash flow statement

The *cash flow statement* is like the company's checkbook register. It records the actual movement of all the cash in the company, showing which activities generated the money coming in and what was actually paid for in that quarter. The balance sheet and income statement summarize *how much,* but the cash flow statement provides more details about *where* the cash came from, *what* it was spent on, and (perhaps most importantly) *whether* the company spent more money than it generated.

The cash flow statement measures the movement of money from three different activities — operations, investments, and financing (see Figure 8-3).

- ✔ **Operating activities:** The cash flow statement starts with the net income from the income statement, making it the top line. It then adds back in *depreciation* (an accounting device in which no actual cash moves), other operating expenses that don't involve cash, and gains from the sale of assets. These items add up to the net cash generated from operating activities.

- ✔ **Investing activities:** Any money spent on the purchase of new assets such as machinery, plants, or land gets classified as a *capital expenditure,* or *CapEx.* These new assets go to the future production of income. Companies invest in capital expenditures to maintain and grow the business. Cash flow from investing activities subtracts capital expenditures from all income generated by these assets.

- ✔ **Financing activities** records the financing of the company's operations, including the payment of dividends, the sale or purchase of stock, and the net amount the company has borrowed.

Although seeing the change in total cash flow over the time period listed is good, the more important take-away number is called *free cash flow.* Here's the formula:

Free Cash Flow = Net Cash from Operating Activities – Capital Expenditures

For Carrel Industries in Figure 8-3, the free cash flow ends up being $4.283 million – $737,000 = $3.546 million. To cover unexpected costs, a healthy company's free cash flow should be at least enough to exceed the sum of dividend payments and interest payments. A good rule of thumb is to look for companies with a free cash flow about three times greater than the current dividend.

Negative free cash flow doesn't automatically mean the company is in trouble. It may be making huge investments for future earnings growth. However, it's not a good sign for the dividend investor. Companies need to have cash on hand to pay dividends. If they don't have enough cash on hand, they need to take on debt to make the payments or simply stop paying dividends. Borrowing funds to pay dividends isn't sustainable, so free cash flow gives a clear look at how secure the dividend is.

Carrel Industries, Inc.	
Cash Flow Statement	
Period Ending	March 31, 2010
Net Income	**2,613,000**
Operating Activities	
Depreciation	725,000
Adjustments to Net Income	(17,000)
Changes in Accounts Receivables	1,024,000
Changes in Liabilities	(345,000)
Changes in Inventories	512,000
Changes in Other Operating Activities	(229,000)
Net Cash From Operating Activities	**4,283,000**
Investing Activities	
Capital Expenditures	(737,000)
Investments	64,000
Cash Flow From Other Investing Activities	87,000
Net Cash From Investing Activities	**(586,000)**
Financing Activities	
Dividends Paid	(1,215,000)
Sale or Purchase of Stock	(1,090,000)
Net Borrowings	(2,533,000)
Total Cash Flows From Financing Activities	**(4,838,000)**
Exchange Rate Changes	(78,000)
Change in Cash and Cash Equivalents	**($1,219,000)**

Figure 8-3:
Sample
cash flow
statement.

Calculating a Dividend's Relative Strength

Whenever you buy something, you want to make sure you're getting a good value for the price — something that's "worth it." Buying watered-down laundry detergent at the dollar store may seem like a good deal, but if it takes an entire bottle to do a single load of laundry, the expensive stuff may actually cost less. Shopping for stocks is no different. You're looking for a good buy — a stock whose price values it less than other companies with similar profit-making potential.

After you get a handle on the balance sheet, income statement, and cash flow statement (which I cover in the preceding section), you can start to play around with financial ratios. These simple mathematical equations measure the health of the company and its dividend. In the following sections, I introduce the various equations and show you how to use the results of these equations to perform your very own dividend stock analysis.

These equations work particularly well in comparing companies in the same sector. For more about different sectors in which companies commonly pay dividends, check out the chapters in Part III.

Getting a handle on yield

Yield (also known as _dividend yield_) is your dividend's rate of return, and one of the most important numbers to consider. It enables you to compare stocks side-by-side, ensure that a particular stock meets the minimum return requirement for your portfolio, and avoid stocks that have comparatively high dividends (in dollars) but low returns (in percentage).

Don't confuse dividend with dividend yield. The cold, hard cash that lands in your pocket every quarter is the dividend. Yield is the annual percentage return in dividends on your investment.

Yield is a huge consideration for two reasons:

- ✔ It indicates the minimum rate of return you can expect to earn on your shares.

- ✔ It determines whether you can expect this investment to beat inflation. If inflation is running at 3 percent and the yield is only 2.5 percent, you stand to lose ½ percent per year to inflation. (Of course, if the share price rises, too, your return may still beat inflation.)

Use the following guidelines to gauge the relative attractiveness of a stock based on its yield:

- ✔ **Low yield:** Less than the average yield on the S&P 500 Index. The minimum return of low-yield stocks increases your risk because the dividend provides a smaller buffer should the shares drop in price and may fail to keep up with the market or rate of inflation.

  However, don't automatically rule out low-yield stocks. A low-yield stock with consistently rising payouts may turn out to be a better investment than a medium-yield stock with static payouts. If the low-yield dividend grows on a consistent basis, that increases the yield on your original investment, which may soon be higher than the yield of both the market and the stock with the static dividend. In addition, low-yield stocks are often growth companies with the potential for above-average gains in share price.

- ✔ **Medium yield:** Between the S&P 500 yield and up to three percentage points more than the index's yield.

- ✔ **High yield:** More than three percentage points higher than the yield on the S&P 500.

Some fund managers like their dividend stocks to provide a yield double the yield of the S&P 500 index. You can find this yield on the index on Standard & Poor's Web site. Visit www.standardandpoors.com/home/en/us and click Indices, and then under S&P 500, click View Data. Regardless of what some fund managers look for, set your own minimum standards for your portfolio, and if the yield falls short, don't buy the stock.

Avoid "great story" stocks that capture the headlines but pay tiny dividends. Examining a stock's yield is a great way to screen out these poor performers.

In the following sections, I show you how to calculate the figures you need to determine the yield.

Calculating dividend per share

To calculate yield, you must first calculate *dividend per share* — the amount of money you receive each quarter for each share of stock you own. The easiest way to "calculate" this number is to look at the income statement and find the number next to "Dividends per Share," as shown in Figure 8-2 earlier in the chapter. According that income statement, Carrel Industries paid 40 cents in that quarter.

If the number isn't easily available, the calculation is pretty straightforward:

Dividend per Share = Total Dividends ÷ Total Shares

To find the total dividends the company paid, look at the company's cash flow statement under the heading "Financing Activities." In Figure 8-3 earlier in the chapter, Carrel Industries paid $1,251,500 in dividends. Check the income statement to find the total shares (the number of shares outstanding).

In Figure 8-2, you can see that Carrel Industries has 3.1046 million shares outstanding. Now, do the math:

> $1.2515 million in dividends ÷ 3.1046 million shares = $.403 dividend/share

It's a perfect match with the 40 cents listed on the company's income statement.

A small dividend-per-share isn't necessarily bad, nor is a large dividend-per-share necessarily good. The relevant number here is yield — the rate of return on your investment. A small dividend per share on a low-priced stock may be better than a big dividend on high-priced stock.

Computing the indicated dividend per share

Although the dividend per share is important, it represents only the quarterly dividend. To get the annual yield, you need the *indicated dividend,* also called the *annual dividend per share,* because this dividend "indicates" the yield.

The calculation is easy as pie:

> Indicated Dividend = Quarterly Dividend per Share × 4

You may need to adjust the equation if the company pays dividends on a nonstandard schedule. Some companies pay monthly dividends; others, such as many foreign companies, pay every six months. That equation would look like this:

> Indicated Dividend = Biannual Dividend per Share × 2

In the previous section, I show you how to calculate the quarterly dividend per share for Carrel Industries. To calculate the indicated dividend, simply multiply that number by 4:

> $.40 × 4 = $1.60

The indicated dividend stays constant until the company formally changes the payout. For example, a company that pays a dividend of 12 cents a share would have an indicated dividend of 48 cents (4 × 12 cents). If the company raises the dividend to 15 cents a share per quarter, the new indicated dividend would be 60 cents (4 × 15 cents).

Figuring out the yield

Yield is the indicated dividend as a percentage of the share price. You can also look at it as the percentage you receive in dividends of each dollar of stock you own:

Yield = Indicated Dividend ÷ Share Price

The preceding section shows you how to calculate the indicated dividend. To calculate yield, you simply divide the indicated dividend by the current share price — what shares in the company are selling for this instant. Following the example in the preceding two sections, suppose shares of Carrel Industries are selling for $32 a pop:

$1.60 ÷ $32 = .05 or 5 percent

Appreciating how pricing affects yield

High yield alone doesn't qualify a dividend stock as a top pick. (Head to the preceding section for more on yield). You need to know why the yield is high. Two factors affect a stock's yield:

- **Dividends:** Unless the stock's price also jumps, an increase in dividend payments results in an increase in the stock's yield.

- **Share price:** Although the indicated dividend remains fairly constant, the share's price changes every day, which means yield changes every day. Small moves in share price lead to tiny changes in yield. However, a large drop in share price (which isn't something shareholders cheer about) gives yield a big boost because the dividend now equals a greater percentage of the share price. A low share price may present a bargain to buy a good yield, or it may be a signal the company is having problems that may lead to a dividend cut.

Tracking yields is a good way to compare companies, especially in the same sector. If Company A pays a 3-percent yield and Company B pays 9 percent, this discrepancy should raise serious questions. Is Company A paying much less than the industry average, or is Company B paying much more? If Company B's yield is out of whack with its competitors, is it because the share price has recently fallen? If the share price has recently fallen and the yield is three times higher, how safe is the dividend? See Chapter 6 for additional guidance in answering these questions and others.

A case study in yields

During the years 2007 and 2008, Procter & Gamble posted a yield of about 2 percent, qualifying it as a low-yielding stock. Its share price bounced around in a range of $58 to $74, for an average price of $66. In the fourth quarter of 2008, a dividend of $1.60 divided by $66 resulted in a yield of 2.4 percent.

Six months later, at the end of the first quarter of 2009, the share price fell to $47. The new yield equaled 3.4 percent. The one-percentage-point difference between 2.4 and 3.4 percent represented a 42 percent jump in the rate of return.

The actual dividend payout remained the same ($1.60 a year per share), but investors who bought shares at $47 on March 31, 2009, began earning a rate of return 42 percent greater than investors who bought at $66 five months earlier.

Even though its share price fell, pushing up its yield, Procter & Gamble sent a clear signal to investors that business was doing well by continuing its annual dividend increase. The next month, P&G raised its dividend to 44 cents — 10 percent higher than the 40 cents paid out the previous quarter.

Higher payouts increase yield, much like falling share prices do, but in a positive way. The new indicated dividend jumped to $1.76 from $1.60. The yield jumped to 3.7 percent.

Utilizing the price-to-earnings (P/E) ratio

The *price-to-earnings ratio* or *P/E* (sometimes referred to as a *multiple*) indicates how much investors are willing to pay for each dollar of profit they stand to earn per year. For example, if an investor buys a stock with a P/E of 15, he's willing to pay $15 for each dollar of profit, or 15 times the earnings for one share of stock. Another way to look at it is that it will take 15 years to earn back your investment in company profits.

The *P/E ratio* is a good criterion for checking a stock's value relative to the broader market and its competitors. Use the following guidelines to establish your minimum requirement for purchasing a dividend stock:

- **Below the P/E of the S&P 500 Index:** The rule of thumb is to look for stocks below the P/E of the S&P 500 Index, which averages around 18.

- **Below the industry's average P/E:** If your stock has a high P/E, compare it to the P/Es of its competitors and the industry sector as a whole. If a company's P/E is higher than that of its competitors, the stock is probably overvalued.

- **Notable exceptions:** Faster growing industries have higher P/Es, so don't automatically discount a stock with a P/E over 18 — it may still be a good value stock. Many of these growth stocks are smaller than the ones on the S&P 500.

A stock with no P/E means the company posted losses. You want to invest in profitable companies to ensure the stability of the dividend payment. Stocks with P/Es higher than 20 means investors are willing to pay more for $1 of profits because they expect profits to see significant growth. Stocks with P/Es higher than 40 are expected to see very strong growth, but typically that level of P/E means the stock is just overvalued. Stocks with no or excessively high P/Es are speculative buys, not investments.

The following section helps you get the figures you need to determine a stock's P/E ratio.

First things first: Determining earnings per share

Earnings per share, or *EPS* for short, is one of the most important numbers investors use to research companies. Obviously, you want to invest in profitable companies, but is the company that makes a $100 million profit a better buy than a company that makes a profit of just $1 million? Not necessarily. Investors don't care how much the company's total profit is. They want to own the company that gives *them* the most profit, and the best way to gauge that is by looking at profit per share, better known as *earnings per share.*

The easiest way to determine earnings per share is to glance at the company's income statement. In Figure 8-2 earlier in the chapter, Carrel Industries reports 84 cents earnings per share. You may notice that the income statement lists two kinds of earnings per share, basic EPS and diluted EPS:

- **Basic EPS** represents the total shares outstanding, which contains all the stock available to trade at this moment in time.

- **Diluted EPS** represents total shares outstanding plus other company-issued securities that don't start out as shares of company stock but may eventually turn into shares. These items include

  - **Stock options:** Compensation for managers, which can be turned into stock when it hits a target price.

  - **Warrants:** The rights of certain shareholders to buy new shares prior to public offerings.

  - **Convertible preferred stock:** Preferred shares that can be exchanged for common stock after a predetermined date or price.

  - **Convertible debenture:** Debt instruments that have the potential to turn into common stock.

Because these securities can change into common shares at any time, diluted earnings per share accounts for them as part of the total share base. Although these securities likely won't all turn into common stock, a significant number probably will. Many people prefer to look at diluted earnings per share because it provides a worst-case scenario of maximum earnings dilution.

Of course, you don't need to worry about calculating earnings per share if the company already reported earnings. You only need to calculate EPS for the periods not yet reported. Wall Street stock analysts research the rate of growth in the company's revenue and earnings, and then make forecasts for the current quarter or next four quarters. To compare these predictions to the real results 12 months earlier, analysts and investors need to reduce these expected future profits to earnings per shares. You can find future earnings projections for many companies in Wall Street analyst reports. You use this formula when you need to calculate your own net profit projections.

Earnings Per Share = Net Profit ÷ Total Shares Outstanding

You can find the net profit and number of shares outstanding on the company's income statement. Figure 8-2 lists them as $2,613,000 and 3.1046 million shares, respectively. Here's the math:

$2,613,000 ÷ 3.1046 million shares = $.8417 or about 84 cents per share for the quarter

Calculating the P/E ratio

Earnings per share alone isn't very useful for measuring a company's relative profitability. An EPS of $50 on shares selling for $500 is no better than an EPS of 50 cents on shares selling for $5. The P/E ratio provides a better tool for calculating a stock's relative value or how much you're paying for that profit.

A great place to find P/Es is on Yahoo! Finance. Just follow these easy steps:

1. **Fire up your Web browser and go to** `finance.yahoo.com`.

2. **Mouse over the Investing tab and click Industries.**

   A list of Top Industries appears on the left side of the page.

3. **If the desired industry isn't listed, scroll to the bottom of the list, click Complete Industry List, and click the desired industry.**

   Yahoo! Finance displays a page for the selected industry.

4. **Under More on This Industry (upper left), click Industry Browser.**

   Yahoo! Finance displays a spreadsheet for the selected industry, showing metrics that include P/Es for the whole sector, this particular industry, and some of the top companies in this industry.

You can click P/E at the top of the column to sort companies from lowest to highest. When comparing two companies, or a company to its industry, remember the lower P/E, the better value it is.

If you need to calculate a share's P/E ratio, use the following formula:

P/E ratio = Share price ÷ Annual Earnings per Share

Suppose shares of Carrel Industries are selling for $32 each and the annual earnings per share are $3.36 (84 cents per share quarterly × 4 quarters; see the preceding section for more on finding these figures). Its P/E would be

$32 ÷ $3.36 = 9.52

Comparing P/E ratios

The P/E ratio is a great benchmark for comparing any two companies, particularly if they're in the same sector. If the P/E ratio for a business sector averages 15, a company with a P/E of 12 would be undervalued compared to its competitors. A company with a P/E of 20 would be overvalued. In general, you want to buy undervalued companies — companies that are a good value for the profits you're buying. But you need to determine whether the company is undervalued for no good reason or because it's in financial trouble. For additional guidance on how to use the P/E ratio and other data to gauge a dividend stock's comparative value, check out Chapter 6.

The P/E you see in financial newspapers, magazines, and Web sites is the *Trailing P/E,* or *TTM* (Trailing Twelve Months). The *Forward P/E,* or *Estimated P/E,* is based on earnings projections for the next 12 months. Compare the two numbers. If the Forward P/E is considerably smaller than the Trailing P/E, analysts may be expecting to see the company perform considerably better moving forward. Then again, the analysts may just be overly optimistic.

Looking at price-to-sales ratio

The price-to-sales ratio (PSR) is similar to the P/E discussed in the preceding section, but here you're finding out how much you're paying per dollar of company sales. Instead of earnings per share, you use sales per share:

Sales Per Share = Total Sales ÷ Outstanding Shares

If a company generates sales of $20 million and has three million outstanding shares; its sales per share are $6.67:

$20,000,000 ÷ 3,000,000 = $6.67 Sales Per Share

After calculating sales per share, use the following formula to calculate the PSR:

Price to Sales Ratio (PSR) = Share Price ÷ Sales Per Share

Shares of a company selling for $32 each create a PSR of 4.8:

$32 ÷ $6.67 = 4.8

An undervalued stock has a PSR of 2 or less. A PSR of 1 or less may be a real bargain.

Look for stocks that are undervalued across the board. A stock that's under-valued in one area (such as PSR) but fully valued in another (such as P/E) may mean the company is spending too much in expenses.

Calculating the payout ratio

Simply put, the payout ratio tells you how much of the company's profits come back to you as a dividend. You become an investor for the profits, and a dividend investor specifically because you want to pocket some of those profits now. The payout ratio shows you exactly how much of those profits actually land in your pocket.

To calculate the payout ratio, divide the company's dividends per share by the earnings per share (both from the income statement; see the earlier section "Tallying profits and losses with an income statement"):

Payout Ratio = Dividends per Share ÷ Earnings Per Share

In the example shown in Figure 8-2 earlier in the chapter, Carrel Industries reported diluted earnings per share of 84 cents and dividends per share of 40 cents, so the company paid shareholders 48 percent of this quarter's profit in the form of the dividend. The equation goes like this:

$.40 ÷ $.84= 48 percent

Use the following general guidelines to help measure how well various companies' payout ratios stack up:

- **Low:** Anything much lower than 50 percent is cause for investigating further. Don't automatically shun companies with low payout ratios, because they do have room to grow the size of the dividend. Many growth companies have low payout ratios because they continue to reinvest in the business; these companies offer potential for increased dividend payments as well as capital appreciation in stock price. For example, regional banks often pay out between 30 and 50 percent of their profits. But if a company with a low payout ratio isn't growing fast, you know management can pay out more but chooses not to.

- **Traditional:** 50 percent is the traditional payout ratio, meaning the company is paying 50 percent of its profits to the shareholders in the form of dividends.

- **Standard:** 50 to 70 percent is an average range and should not generate any concern. Remember that the range may vary for some industries. Utilities, for example, sometimes pay as high as 80 percent, which is okay for that industry.

- **High:** A higher payout ratio is always better because it means more money in your pocket. However, you don't want to see a payout ratio of

100 percent or higher. A 100 percent payout ratio means nothing is left to invest in the business. A dividend payout that exceeds the quarterly profit is a big cause for alarm and usually indicates an inevitable dividend cut. Also, a high payout ratio leaves little room for error. If most of the earnings are paid out as dividends, a big drop in earnings one quarter may lead to the company taking on debt to make the payments or an immediate dividend cut. Either way, it's a bad sign.

Master Limited Partnerships may have a payout ratio higher than 100 percent of profits, without the need to take on debt, because of their unusual structure. For more on MLPs, head to Chapter 10.

If a company keeps increasing its dividend, but the payout ratio remains below 50 percent, that's a clear sign of strong earnings growth. Procter & Gamble has raised its dividend payment for nearly 60 years while paying out between 40 and 50 percent of its quarterly earnings.

Sizing up management with the return on equity

Return on equity (ROE) measures the return on your investment in the company by showing how well the company invested its investors' money and the company's accumulated profits. Return on equity helps you analyze whether the company's management invests its capital well. To calculate ROE, divide net annual profit by total equity:

ROE = Net Annual Profit ÷ Average Annual Shareholder Equity

To determine net annual profit, total the company's net profits presented in each of its four most recent quarterly income statements (for more on income statements, check out "Tallying profits and losses with an income statement" earlier in this chapter). To determine equity, average the shareholder equity for those same four quarters; you can find that info on the balance sheets for the most recent quarters (head to "Getting a financial snapshot from the balance sheet" earlier in the chapter for information on these documents).

For the previous four quarters, Carrel Industries earned $13.981 million. The average shareholder equity for those same four quarters totaled $65.135 billion. Performing the following calculation, you can see that Carrel Industries produced an approximate 21.5 percent ROE for its investors:

$13.981 million ÷ $65.135 billion = 21.46 percent

After you discover the company's ROE, compare it to others in the same sector. The company with the higher ROE is the more profitable one; try to find companies with an ROE of more than 10 percent. A terrible ROE (say, 0 percent) means the company is mismanaged.

When valuing a stock, ask yourself whether the ROE beat the rate of return the company could have earned just by putting the money into Treasury bonds. Look for companies that post an ROE greater than 10. After you've found that, go to the Yahoo! Finance Industry Browser (see "Utilizing the price-to-earnings (P/E) ratio" earlier in this chapter) to see whether the company's ROE exceeds others in its sector and if so, how many. You want to buy companies with high ROEs that have seen an upward trend over the past five years.

Sneaking a peek at the quick ratio

One of the best indicators of a company's ability to pay dividends moving forward is the *quick ratio,* which looks to see whether a company has enough liquid assets to cover dividends. A company that has paid a dividend sometime in the past is no better than a one-hit wonder. You have no assurance that the company is likely to pay dividends in the future (as in, after you purchase its stock). The dividend investing strategy seeks to find companies that can afford to pay dividends on a regular basis and increase those dividends over time. These criteria became extremely relevant in the wake of the 2008 and 2009 financial crisis. Many companies with a record of increasing their dividends for decades have cut or eliminated their dividends entirely in order to save cash, so finding a good-looking dividend isn't enough anymore. You need to determine whether the company has the resources to continue the dividend payouts.

Because inventories are the least liquid portion of current assets, the quick ratio removes them from the equation. To derive the quick ratio, subtract inventories from current assets; this removal leaves you with the firm's most liquid assets. Then divide the result by current liabilities. (You can find all these numbers on the balance sheet, as shown in Figure 8-1 earlier in the chapter.) Here's the equation:

Quick Ratio = (Current Assets − Inventories) ÷ Current Liabilities

A quick ratio of 1 indicates that the company holds enough liquid assets to cover all of its current liabilities and is unlikely to cut the dividend. Anything less than 1 means the company's going to have to raid the cookie jar for money to pay its shareholders.

In Figure 8-1, Carrel Industries reports total current assets of $22.088 million, inventories of $7.615 million, and current liabilities of $7.996 million. Here's how its quick ratio shakes out:

($22.088 million − $7.615 million) ÷ $7.996 million = 1.8

With a quick ratio of 1.8, Carrel Industries has nearly enough current assets to pay current liabilities twice. With this kind of cushion, you can rest assured the company won't be cutting the dividend.

If you want to get extremely conservative, move beyond the quick ratio and just look at the cash on hand. Pure cash provides the best measure of whether a dividend can be paid because the current assets in the quick ratio may include a lot of accounts receivables from customers who can't pay or aren't required to pay their bills in the time frame that dividends are scheduled to be paid.

Covering the debt covering ratio

Debt isn't necessarily a bad thing, but if a company must continually borrow money just to keep the lights on, that's a sign of trouble. To determine just how manageable a company's debt is, take a look at its *debt covering ratio* to see whether the company generates enough cash from operations to cover current liabilities. To calculate a company's debt covering ratio, plug numbers from its income statement and balance sheet (documents discussed earlier in this chapter) into the following equation:

Debt Covering Ratio = Operating Income ÷ Current Liabilities

The debt covering ratio should equal at least 2. A debt covering ratio below that means the company may not be generating enough to pay both its interest payments and dividends. If this trend continues, the company may soon cut the dividend so it can afford to make its debt payments. You definitely don't want to see a company taking on new debt to pay the dividend.

Valuing the debt-to-equity ratio

An additional ratio to check for the stability of the company in general and the dividend in particular is the *debt-to-equity ratio,* which shows how much debt a company has compared to its equity. A high debt-to-equity ratio shows that the company relies on debt rather than equity to finance its operations and presents a clear warning sign. Although debt offers a good way to get financing to grow the company, too much debt can result in large interest payments, leaving less cash for dividend payouts. Also, if the company doesn't earn enough to cover the dividend, it may take on debt to make its payments, creating an unsustainable state for the business. The equation for the debt-to-equity ratio is

Debt-to-Equity Ratio = Total Liabilities ÷ Shareholders' Equity

You can find these numbers on a company's balance sheet. According to Figure 8-1 earlier in the chapter, Carrel Industries' debt-to-equity ratio comes out to 1.18:

$71,620,000 ÷ $60,775,000 = 1.18

This means the debt is 1.18 times equity. The higher the number, the less stable the company. You want to see a debt-to-equity ratio around 1. Lower is better, but too low means the company may be ignoring growth opportunities to avoid taking on debt.

Working with price-to-book ratio

The price-to-book ratio (PBR) provides one of the best indications in terms of dollars and cents of whether a company is actually worth what investors are willing to pay for it. *Book value* determines what shareholders would get if they were to liquidate the assets. The shareholder equity, or net worth, is calculated by subtracting liabilities from assets (not including intangible assets, such as goodwill). So, book value is net worth minus intangible assets. Suppose a company's book value is $500 million and the total value of the outstanding stock is $600 million. If the company were to liquidate its assets, it wouldn't have enough money to buy back its shares from investors, meaning it's overvalued.

> Book value = Tangible Assets – Liabilities

To calculate PBR, divide the company's market value or market capitalization (share price times number of shares outstanding) by its book value:

> Price-to-Book Ratio (PBR) = Market Value ÷ Book Value

If a company's market value is $12.5 million and the book value is $10 million, the PBR is 125 percent:

> $12,500,000 ÷ $10,000,000 = 125 percent

This PBR means the market values the company 25 percent higher than its book value. You want to see PBR equal to or less than 100 percent, indicating the company is undervalued.

Book value can be misleading because the assets category on the balance sheet reflects the company's cost to acquire an asset, not necessarily the asset's current market value. The greater percentage of total assets made up by current assets, the more accurate book value becomes.

Recognizing a Potentially Good Dividend Stock

Just because a company issues a dividend doesn't make it a good dividend stock. It doesn't even make it a good stock to own regardless of the dividend. Many companies pay a dividend in name only. Although the balance sheets, income statements, and cash flow statements I discuss earlier in this chapter provide valuable insight into a company's liquidity and viability at a particular point in time, you need to look at the bigger picture to really determine whether a dividend stock is likely to be a good investment. Specifically, you need to look at how your prospects measure up in relation to six critical criteria (in the following order of importance):

- Rising dividend payments
- Fiscal strength
- Good value
- Predictable, sustainable cash flow
- Positive shareholder orientation
- Good performance in battered industries

The following sections describe these criteria in greater detail and show you how to use them to assess dividend stocks.

Rising dividend payments

Rising dividend payments are the best form of legally obtainable insider information. By announcing to the public that it plans to increase the company's dividend, management tips its hand on what it really thinks about the future of its business. Essentially, the managers proclaim, "We believe we will earn so much more money next year that we can even give a bit more to the shareholders."

However, rising dividend payments may not be good enough. As a savvy investor, consider companies that have a proven track record for consistently raising dividends in good times and bad. Use the following levels of impressiveness as your guide:

- **Impressive:** Rising dividend payments.
- **More impressive:** A history of consistently raising dividend payments.
- **Even more impressive:** A history of consistently raising dividend payments even during bad economic times.
- **Super impressive:** A history of consistently raising dividend payments in good times and bad, even when the share price is low and yield high. (For more about yield, check out "Getting a handle on yield" earlier in this chapter.)
- **Super-duper impressive:** The company raising its dividend belongs to the financial services industry, a sector of the market that bore the brunt of the pain and punishment inflicted during the 2008 market crash.

Fiscal strength = dividends? Not always

In the midst of the 2008 financial crisis, Royal Caribbean International (RCL) eliminated its dividend. Before the crisis, the cruise line paid out between 35 and 40 percent of its profits in dividends. Although Royal Caribbean didn't participate in any of the financial shenanigans on Wall Street, it had taken on a lot of debt to buy new ships earlier in the year.

When the recession hit, many people lost their jobs, so fewer people went on expensive cruises. When its sales experienced a large drop at the end of 2008, Royal Caribbean experienced a credit crunch. Had business remained brisk, it would have been able to generate enough money to pay off some of the loan and still pay dividends. As a stopgap measure, Royal Caribbean eliminated dividend payments to shore up the company's finances and remain fiscally strong.

The moral of this story is to never judge a company solely by a single criterion. Although a strong history of rising dividend payments is usually a good sign, even well-managed companies can experience a crunch that temporarily prevents them from paying dividends.

Standard & Poor's created an index called the *S&P 500 Dividend Aristocrats Index* to measures the market performance of a select group of companies that consistently raise their dividends. To get into the index, a company must be a constituent of the S&P 500 index and have increased its dividend every year for at least 25 years. In 2010, 41 constituents were listed in the index, down from 52 in 2009 and 60 in 2008. The appendix goes into a deeper examination of the Dividend Aristocrats.

Fiscal strength

Obviously, you want to invest in companies that can flex their fiscal muscle, but determining just how fiscally strong a company is can be quite a challenge, particularly if you don't know what to look for. For investors, one of the best indicators of fiscal strength (or lack thereof) is the amount of debt the company has on its books. Although debt is useful in the purchase of capital expenditures, most dividend companies have seen their growth slow, so their debt levels shouldn't be large. A lot of debt can slow earnings growth and may indicate trouble in the company making its dividend payments. A good way to measure a company's debt is through the debt-to-equity ratio, which I explain in the earlier section "Valuing the debt-to-equity ratio."

Good value

You want to buy a stock below its *intrinsic,* or true, value, as I explain in Chapter 6. You want to know what the company expects business to be like for the next 12 to 18 months and what its cash flow will be. After you determine that, you want to apply a multiple to it, such as the P/E ratio, to get a relative value. The P/E ratio is one good way to determine whether a stock is undervalued or overvalued; flip to "Utilizing the price-to-earnings (P/E) ratio" earlier in the chapter.

Predictable, sustainable cash flow

Strong, sustainable cash flow is perhaps the best sign that a company is healthy. As a dividend investor, you want to put your money in industries, and companies within those industries, that have highly predictable cash flow streams:

- ✓ **Industries:** Banks, railroads, grocery stores, and utilities have a solid reputation for maintaining positive cash flow. Check out the chapters in Part III for more information about good income-generating sectors. Industries with erratic cash flow streams include *cyclical* companies (those more susceptible to the economy's ebbs and flows) and biotechnology firms, which you should avoid.

- ✓ **Companies:** Compare companies within a particular industry to identify the individual companies that perform best in terms of cash flow.

Positive shareholder orientation

A company's shareholder orientation reflects how it treats shareholders — the company's owners. If management appears to be self-serving, maximizing its own pay and bonuses at the expense of the company and its shareholders, be wary. Signs that management places shareholder interests first include the following:

- ✓ **Increasing dividends:** This signal is the best sign of shareholder orientation, because it puts more money in your pocket immediately instead of the company holding onto the cash or investing it in questionable projects.

- ✓ **Paying down debt:** Less debt means greater shareholder equity in the company.

- ✓ **Share buybacks:** Buybacks remove some of the outstanding shares from the market, boosting share value in two ways. First, with fewer shares, each share represents greater ownership in the company. Second, the rules of supply and demand typically kick in to drive up the share price. To find out about buyback plans, check the company's quarterly filings and press releases. News media often report on buyback plans as well.

✔ **High level of ownership among company insiders:** This marker is the best indication that management's interests align with those of its shareholders. When management owns a lot of stock, it has a vested interest in the company's success. Investigate the number of shares each member of the board of directors owns (and I mean actually owns and not just has the option to buy). A bad sign is when directors have options to buy and don't exercise those options, or only exercise options but don't buy shares on their own. You want to see at least 10 percent insider ownership in smaller companies, although that number may be unreasonable for a big conglomerate.

Good performance in battered industries

When an entire sector gets slammed on Wall Street, good stocks in the same industry tend to fall out of favor at the same time. Look for companies that continue to perform well in pummeled industries such as financial services and real estate.

In these situations, companies with good balance sheets that earn profits and continue to increase their dividends can fly under the radar and sell for bargain prices. In addition, many smaller stocks don't receive much, if any, analytical coverage by the big Wall Street firms. They may not be big or sexy enough for most investors, but you can find some of the best investing opportunities among companies that professional investors ignore.

Part III
Exploring Income-Generating Industries

"Oh Martin, you scared me half to death! Next time let me know when you're picking a new stock."

In this part . . .

Some sectors (industries) are better than others at delivering a steady stream of income to shareholders. Companies in the consumer staples sector, for instance, have a better track record for paying dividends than do companies in the biotechnology industry. Likewise, utilities generally trump technology.

The chapters in this part introduce you to the best sectors for dividend investing so that you can focus on individual sectors and diversify your portfolio. For each industry, you discover the types of companies included in that sector, why companies in the sector are more likely to pay dividends, how to size up companies in the sector, and a list of companies you may want to include in your research. This part also introduces you to master limited partnerships (MLPs) and real estate investment trusts (REITs).

Chapter 9

Lighting Up Your Portfolio with Utilities

In This Chapter

▶ Exploring what constitutes a utility

▶ Choosing your utilities wisely

▶ Considering some potentially good prospects

*W*hen people think of income-producing stocks, the industry group that typically comes to mind first is *utilities* — electricity, gas, and water, to name a few. These aren't the most exciting properties to own in the game of *Monopoly,* and they're probably even less exciting in the real world, but that's sort of the point. For dividend investors, utilities are attractive because many offer stability and premium yields — the holy grail of dividends.

In this chapter, I explain what utilities are and why they're generally such great income-producers. I also let you in on some of the factors that influence utilities' success and share a few utility stocks you may want to check out.

Don't follow recommendations, even mine, until you perform your own due diligence. Back in the 1990s, the financial and real estate sectors were attractive, but starting in 2008, that was no longer the case. Individual companies and entire sectors can run into problems, so do the research and analysis I describe in Chapter 8.

Defining Utilities

Utilities are a category of companies that provide the services and power necessary to run buildings and make modern life possible. Given their propensity to pay out 60 to 80 percent of their average annual earnings as dividends, utilities are some of the highest-yielding stocks in the entire stock market. (For more about yield, see Chapter 8.) The following sections give you the lowdown on utility stocks and their benefits.

Knowing which companies qualify

Companies in the utilities sector provide electricity, gas, heat, and water. These capital-intensive industries boast significant ownership of facilities (such as power and water-treatment plants) and infrastructure (such as power lines and pipes) that run overhead and under streets and into homes and businesses. The three main classes of utilities are

- ✔ **Electric companies** are responsible for the generation, transmission, and distribution of electrical power. Integrated utilities provide all these functions under one roof. Generation can involve a variety of sources, including gas, nuclear energy, solar power, and wind power, but the majority of America's electricity comes from burning coal. Transmission and distribution rely on power grids and power lines. Although generation and transmission can come from two separate companies, both fall into the utilities category. Many states have deregulated their electricity markets. See the sidebar "The good and bad of utility growth spurts" later in the chapter to understand what deregulation means to utilities.

- ✔ **Natural gas companies** provide the energy to heat homes and supply cooking gas. They're often aligned with electric companies because gas can be used to produce electricity. Most natural gas companies remain monopolies, which means that these companies almost always earn a profit and pay dividends but also that they can be subjected to heavy regulation. The following section covers the effects of monopolies and regulation on utilities in greater detail.

- ✔ **Water companies** are responsible for distributing fresh water throughout communities, piping it into buildings, and removing sewage. Most water companies are owned or run by the local municipalities. However, water supplies are running scarce in parts of the country and the world. Supplies are expected to tighten, providing earnings growth potential as demand exceeds supply.

You may be wondering about telephone companies. In the old days, when AT&T was the only phone company, it too fell into the utility category, and telephones themselves still qualify as a utility. However, the splintering of AT&T created a telecommunications industry that now encompasses more than just a rotary phone plugged into a wall. The wide variety of telecommunications services and providers has grown into a sector of its own, and I cover it in Chapter 11.

Appreciating utilities' income-generating capabilities

The classic regulated utility makes a great income-generating stock because profits are practically guaranteed. Yet, due to governmental regulations, these earnings experience little to no growth. Limited profit growth significantly lowers the potential for capital appreciation in utilities' stock prices. These companies need another way to give shareholders a return on the equity invested, so they entice investors by promising to pay high yields (through dividends) equal to or above the rate of Treasury bonds. Here are a few reasons utilities traditionally have been good income-producers:

- ✔ **They're monopolies with no competition.** Building power plants and infrastructure requires huge capital investments, and it is neither practical nor desirable to have numerous power grids or sewage systems overlapping each other. The huge capital requirements create a big barrier to other firms entering the business; few companies would commit so much money without some assurance they'd receive a return on their investment. (Recent experiments with deregulation to foster competition among generating plants have shown companies are unwilling to take on this kind of investment without a guaranteed customer base.)

- ✔ **Government-set rates ensure a reasonable profit.** Regulators need to balance the competing interests of shareholders with the needs of consumers. Although customers need rates to remain affordable, the utility must remain profitable to stay in business. To achieve this balance, the government sets what it deems a reasonable profit to provide the company and its investors with a sufficient rate of return. The regulators then add in all the company's expenses to arrive at a necessary level of sales. According to the number of customers and their usages, regulators set a base rate to produce the desired revenues, and thus, profit.

- ✔ **They rarely go out of business.** Utilities have a large captive clientele. Nearly every citizen and business needs to use their services. If a customer doesn't want to get cut off from the utility's services, she has to pay the bill, which means utilities can count on consistent revenues and cash flow. Unless a utility takes on extremely risky ventures, it's almost guaranteed to be profitable.

- ✔ **They typically pay out a large part of their earnings in dividends.** Because all their expenses are factored into the formula for determining the utility's profit, utilities have little need to reinvest profits into the business. With a lot of cash and limited potential for seeing the stock's price rise by a large amount, utilities pay out 60 to 80 percent of their annual earnings to shareholders. The typical return on shareholder equity is between 10 and 12 percent.

✔ **They enjoy such steady and predictable cash flows that they rarely cut dividends.** In fact, profits and cash flow are large enough to allow the companies to hike their dividends on a regular basis. When evaluating their dividend growth, look for consistent increases that keep pace with the rate of inflation.

The good and bad of utility growth spurts

Utilities didn't always suffer from limited growth potential. During the 1950s and 1960s, utilities were actually growth stocks, especially during the 1960s, when many other industries were stagnant. They remained growth stocks in the 1970s as they ambitiously built new nuclear power plants. But in 1979, a partial core meltdown in a nuclear power plant at Three Mile Island in Pennsylvania turned popular opinion against nuclear power. Enormous cost overruns, together with the public's fear of nuclear power, delayed or terminated the opening of many new plants. The electricity industry stagnated.

Utilities experienced a growth spurt with the passage of the Energy Policy Act of 1992. This act deregulated the industry and allowed utilities to enter new businesses, including telecommunications and energy-trading. The utilities tried to re-create themselves as growth businesses and used their cash to invest in telecommunications, real estate, and unregulated foreign utilities. Dividend payments stopped growing. Managers of stable utilities proved to be poor managers of growing technology businesses. Many of these ventures went belly up with the popping of the stock market's technology bubble in 2000. Because many utilities had taken on huge amounts of debt to fund these projects, they were forced to reduce or eliminate their dividends completely.

Deregulation led to more competition in the electricity industry. The expectation was that encouraging new power producers to enter the market would force existing generators to become more efficient and drive prices lower. The competition actually had the opposite effect because the utilities generating electricity never made the investments regulators were counting on. This environment led to the rise of Enron, a utility and energy-trading company. As demand rose, energy suppliers charged more for electricity. During California's 2000–2001 drought and heat wave, the state used so much energy that rates spiked to astronomical levels. The distributors of the electricity were forced to pay more for the electricity than they could legally charge their customers. This situation caused California to experience a series of rolling blackouts, sparking a state of emergency. When news broke that Enron had been manipulating the market to jack up profits, the ensuing backlash sparked Enron's downfall, which became the largest corporate bankruptcy in U.S. history to that point. Eventually, California's huge gas and electric utility, PG&E, was forced to file for bankruptcy.

As investors realized the increased riskiness of this formerly stable industry, they began to treat electric companies like other stocks and sold them off during the bear market from 2000 to 2003. Since then, many of these companies have gotten rid of their nonutility businesses, paid down their debt, and cleaned up their balance sheets, returning them to their more conservative status.

Dimming the lights: The potential pitfalls of utilities

Although utilities produce a lot of cash and are almost guaranteed a profit, not all of them are great investments. Here are few risks to watch out for with utilities:

- **Outside factors in the economy:** Increased competition, as well as the prices and supplies of raw materials (such as coal, natural gas, and water), can affect profits.

- **The tightening of regulation:** Increasing regulation remains the major issue for utilities. Regulators setting the base rate can decide not to allow utilities to pass certain expenses or investment costs on to the consumer. The utility and its shareholders have to bear these costs, cutting into expected profits. Smaller profit means smaller dividends. Utilities also have to deal with local and federal environmental regulations, which can increase the cost of doing business.

- **High debt levels:** Utilities have a lot of debt because of all the capital projects they take on. A company with a lot of debt is very susceptible to the affects of interest rates. Rising interest rates increase the company's costs by making borrowing money more expensive.

Watching utilities beat the market

Although utilities, like most of the stock market, took a beating during the most recent slump, they managed to outperform the broader market over the ten-year period of 1999 to 2008. Table 9-1 shows you that the Dow Jones Utility Average, an index of 15 of the largest U.S. utilities, beat the Dow Jones Industrial Average, the benchmark for the broad market, in cumulative return (18.72 percent versus –4.41 percent) and *annualized* (shorter period computed as if for a whole year) returns (1.73 percent versus –0.45 percent) on both a price return and total return basis. *Price return* measures returns only in capital appreciation, and total return combines capital appreciation with income or interest.

Table 9-1 Utilities Outperform the Broader Market 1999–2008

	Symbol	Price Return 12/31/1998	Price Return 12/31/2008	Cumulative Return 12/31/1998– 12/31/2008	Annualized Return 12/31/1998– 12/31/2008
Dow Jones Industrial Average	DJI	9,181.43	8,776.39	–4.41%	–0.45%
Dow Jones Utility Average	DJU	312.30	370.76	18.72%	1.73%
	Symbol	Total Return 12/31/1998	Total Return 12/31/2008	Cumulative Return 12/31/1998– 12/31/2008	Annualized Return 12/31/1998– 12/31/2008
Dow Jones Industrial Average	DJI	12,670.78	14,945.17	17.95%	1.66%
Dow Jones Utility Average	DJU	628.83	1,072.94	70.63%	5.49%

Source: Dow Jones Indexes

Even more striking is that on a total return basis, which included reinvesting dividends, the Dow Jones Utilities posted a cumulative return of 70.63 percent over the ten-year period versus 17.95 percent for the Dow Jones Industrials. Annualized, that came to 5.49 percent a year for the utilities versus 1.66 percent for the industrials.

Factoring in the financial crisis, utilities still did very well. For the three years ending December 31, 2008, utility mutual funds slipped just 0.2 percent. Comparatively, the three-year annualized return of the S&P 500 was –8.36 percent.

Assessing Utility Companies: What to Look For

So how can you know which utilities *are* good investments? Following is a list of characteristics to examine when evaluating a utility for your dividend portfolio:

- **Dividend performance:** In most cases, you don't realize big returns from share price appreciation, so make sure the utility has been increasing its dividend payouts regularly over the last four to five years. These stocks may be rare; Josh Peters, the editor of Internet newsletter Morningstar DividendInvestor, says dividend cuts among utilities are "downright commonplace relative to banks or energy master limited partnerships."

  Don't worry about cuts that happened at least five years ago if dividends have been growing since then, but make sure you understand the reasons for them. Were they due to poor investments, excessive debt, or poor relations with regulators? Recent cutbacks in dividends are enough to knock them out of a portfolio. If it's a small cut, you may want to stay, but for me a dividend cut is a deal breaker. Who knows when it will come back? If it doesn't, you're left with a stock with low expectations for share price appreciation. Sell these shares and put the cash into a firm with a growing dividend.

- **A focused business:** Utilities with nonutility businesses are riskier than pure utilities. These outside operations have the potential to divert capital away from dividends, hurting yields. When you look at the company's earnings press release or annual report, look for income and investment details broken out by separate units of the corporation. These units may be subsidiaries or company units involved in completely different businesses. As a dividend investor, stick with pure utilities.

- **Regulatory environment:** Some states have tighter regulations than others, and others, such as Texas, are more pro-business. States with laissez-faire attitudes about keeping rates affordable for customers tend to allow utilities to charge higher rates — bad for consumers, but good for shareholders. Florida, Texas, and California are utility-investor-friendly states. Do some research on the Internet to find out which other states fall into this category. Just go to a search engine and type in the type of utility (such as "electric"), the name of the state, and the words "regulatory atmosphere." The results should bring up the kind of information you need.

Although it often gets a negative rap, deregulation isn't necessarily bad. Because deregulation hasn't had its intended effects, utilities in a position to take advantage and charge more when supply is short post higher profits. This action may sound shady to customers, but it's good for shareholders.

✔ **Debt load:** Utilities often carry large amounts of debt because they own significant infrastructure that requires a lot of upkeep and upgrading. Typically, their liabilities are larger than their assets, but debt higher than 60 percent of total capital should be a red flag. These high debt loads make utilities extremely sensitive to fluctuations in interest rates — as interest rates rise and fall, so do the debt payments. Therefore, utilities perform best when interest rates are falling or remain low.

✔ **Very high yields:** Be wary of utilities with yields significantly higher than the sector average. High yields mean the company may be shelling out more than 80 percent of its profits, or the stock has been pushed very low. A low stock price may just be due to a broad bear market, but it may point to fundamental problems in the business. In addition, high dividend payouts may cause regulators to get tougher on the company and lower its rates, which can lead to a dividend cut.

Meeting Some Utilities to Consider

In the good old days, selecting a utility was as simple as buying the best-yielding stock. Not any more. This formerly stable sector has experienced its share of bankruptcies over the past decade. In addition, up through the end of 2007, utilities were seeing huge growth as a group. Then in 2008 and through 2009, a slew of utilities cut their dividends when their capital took a hit from a tight credit environment combined with declining demand.

Although many utilities saw their valuations lowered by the general stock market's downturn, that situation presents an excellent time to start buying utilities, assuming they pass inspection. Prices are low, meaning investors can lock in high yields now. As the stock market rises, share prices will climb to their proper valuations, giving investors the potential for some nice capital gains as well.

Table 9-2 presents a list of income-generating utility stocks you may want to consider. The single criterion necessary to make the list is this: a proven history of regularly raising dividend payments.

Don't approach Table 9-2 as a "buy" list. It includes candidates that I recommend looking at as I write this book, but that can always change. As always, do your own research before making any buying decisions. (See Chapter 8 for details on sizing up potential stock picks, along with information on calculating and comparing yields.)

Table 9-2	Utilities to Consider		
Yield as of 12/31/09	*Name*	*Ticker Symbol*	*Annual Dividend*
6.5%	Integrys Energy Group	TEG	$2.72
6.4%	Pepco Holdings	POM	$1.08
6.0%	Progress Energy	PGN	$2.48
5.7%	Pinnacle West Capital	PNW	$2.10
5.6%	Duke Energy	DUK	$0.96
5.5%	Westar Energy	WR	$1.20
5.3%	Southern	SO	$1.75
5.2%	CenterPoint Energy	CNP	$0.76
5.2%	Consolidated Edison	ED	$2.36
5.0%	SCANA	SCG	$1.88
4.9%	TECO Energy	TE	$0.80
4.7%	AGL Resources	AGL	$1.72
4.7%	FirstEnergy	FE	$2.20
4.6%	Atmos Energy	ATO	$1.34
4.6%	Xcel Energy	XEL	$0.98
4.5%	Dominion Resources	D	$1.75
4.3%	NSTAR	NST	$1.60
4.3%	Exelon	EXC	$2.10
4.3%	PPL	PPL	$1.38
4.0%	Public Service Enterprise Group	PEG	$1.33
3.8%	PG&E	PCG	$1.68
3.7%	Entergy	ETR	$3.00
3.7%	Northeast Utilities	NU	$0.95
3.6%	Edison International	EIX	$1.26

Lighting up utility info on the Internet

For another source of financially solid dividend-paying utilities, check out Google's Stock Screener at www.google.com/finance/stockscreener. For Sector, choose Utilities. In the Div yield (%) box, type the minimum yield you find acceptable. Because you're giving up some price appreciation for yield, you need to seek a yield higher than the rate of inflation — doubling the inflation rate is a good starting point. In addition, you take on more risk by buying an equity than a U.S. Treasury bond,

so you want to earn more than the bond pays. Personally, I think you should try for at least two percentage points higher than the Treasuries. So, if the U.S. bond pays 4 percent, you want the minimum yield on your utility to be 6 percent. Remember, however, not to rely on high dividend yields alone; as I explain in the nearby section "Assessing Utility Companies: What to Look For," too high a yield can signal potential trouble ahead.

Chapter 10

Pumping Up Your Portfolio with Energy Partnerships

In This Chapter

▶ Revving up your portfolio with energy stocks

▶ Taking advantage of master limited partnerships (MLPs)

*E*nergy makes the world go 'round. It provides heat and light; fuels the planting, harvesting, storage, and distribution of food; and powers every form of transportation on the planet. Because of this universality, you may assume that energy stocks are a great place to look for dividends, and in some cases, you'd be right. Yet surprisingly, most energy-related companies don't pay dividends. One reason is their high capital expenditures and unreliable free cash flow. Another is that energy stocks, particularly oil and gas, look and behave a bit like cyclical stocks because oil prices, and hence their profits, rise and fall with the economy. (Head to Chapter 8 for more on cyclical stocks.) When the economy is full steam ahead, demand for oil is great and prices rise. During a recession, however, a decline in demand sends prices tumbling.

Two types of energy stocks do produce dividends: Major integrated oil and gas companies and the energy master limited partnerships, better known as MLPs. Though major oil companies may be an attractive option, MLPs can be a gold mine for dividend investors, offering some the highest yields with not much more risk than companies offering yields half the size. In this chapter, I cover the potential advantages and disadvantages of both options and provide some guidance on choosing the best dividend stocks in this sector.

Exploring Energy Companies

The major integrated oil and gas companies, 11 in all, hold the characteristics of good dividend stocks. They're mature, stable companies, typically with good management, that produce a product necessary to maintain modern civilization. The following sections show you the advantages and disadvantages of these stocks, as well as some to consider.

Appreciating the benefits of energy company investing

The days of cheap oil seem over. Americans use oil in almost every facet of modern life, from heating their homes to driving their cars. All industries need energy, usually oil, to function, and many of the products used today are petroleum-based. As 2008's all-time-high oil price of $147 a barrel shows, when the price of oil goes up, so does the price of nearly everything else. Although the price per barrel has fallen significantly since then, it remains volatile and unlikely to return to previous super-low prices for several reasons:

- **Oil is a nonrenewable energy source.** As people consume oil, less is available, and the law of supply and demand naturally drives up its price.

- **Worldwide demand is increasing.** As China, India, and many other countries become more industrialized, they need more oil and other sources of energy to fuel their growth.

- **Producers aren't interested in offering cheap oil.** The Organization of the Petroleum Exporting Countries, better known as OPEC, says a reasonable price range to make investing in oil infrastructure to meet growing demand worthwhile is in the $60 to $80 per barrel range.

- **Oil production has reached or is nearing its peak.** Unless it occurred already, the world is expected to reach its maximum level of oil extraction sometime in the next decade. After this point, the rate of production goes into a terminal decline. Unless demand drops accordingly, it'll increasingly outstrip supply, sending prices perpetually higher. Check out the nearby sidebar for more on peak oil.

Peak oil: A peek at the future

Peak oil (the point at which the world reaches its maximum rate of oil extraction and production starts to decline) isn't a new concept. According to some theorists, the world has already reached the peak oil point and is now experiencing a decline. Others predict that the world will achieve peak oil within the next decade.

Geologist Marion King Hubbert created and used peak oil models in the early 1960s to correctly forecast the United States hitting its peak in the early 1970s. As supply gets tighter and demand increases, prices are destined to rise significantly unless scientists are able to discover alternative energy sources that can serve the same purpose.

Getting over energy companies' negatives

Although energy companies offer some attractive advantages (see the preceding section), nothing is ever a one way street. They also have some significant negatives you need to consider; these pitfalls seem to affect the entire industry, so no one company should be hurt by them more than another:

✔ **Extreme volatility:** Oil in particular, and commodities in general, are volatile investments. Think about the huge swing in oil prices since 2002. From a low of $18 in 2002, the price tripled in less than three years. It then surged to $147 by the middle of 2008, only to fall back to $40 in early 2009.

The sharp drop in energy prices since 2008 has put a severe strain on energy companies' cash flows as they try to keep paying dividends while maintaining their rate of capital expenditures. The mid-2009 dividend cut by Italian oil company Eni may be a harbinger of more to come.

✔ **Peak oil:** Peak oil theory predicts severe oil shortages by 2030. Although that situation may be a good thing for investors, it also has the potential to radically change the industry. Some companies may do very well while others crumble. (Head to the preceding section and the nearby "Peak oil: A peek at the future" sidebar for more on peak oil.)

✔ **Potential government intervention:** State-owned oil companies hold most of the world's oil and gas reserves, so the government can turn the taps on or off at any time.

✔ **Nationalization:** Many oil-producing countries are fairly poor. As the price of oil increases, they want more of the money, which may strain relations between the governments and the major oil companies. In some cases, countries have gone as far as to nationalize their oil assets, as Venezuela did to Exxon Mobil in 2007. As the price of oil rises, the idea of this nationalization happening in other countries is a real possibility.

✔ **Global unrest:** The people in the poorest oil-producing countries aren't terribly happy with the way the oil companies have polluted their local environments and treated the people in general, and protests commonly disrupt supplies.

✔ **Development of alternative energies:** Alternative energies, such as wind and solar, are expected to feed some of the demand for carbon fuels, including oil and coal. Although this shift would help the broader economy, it would also cause oil prices to fall.

✔ **Bad press:** The oil industry has been responsible for some of the worst environmental disasters and has been accused of being a major villain in global warming. This negativity may reduce demand for the company's stock, which would be bad for investors.

Juicing up your portfolio with energy company stocks

You can't beat 'em, so why not join 'em? With the price of oil and everything else chipping away at your savings, you may as well tap into those record energy profits yourself by investing in energy companies.

Of the 11 major integrated oil and gas companies, only 8 actually pay dividends, and only half provide a yield exceeding the inflation rate. Due to rising oil and gas prices and a corresponding increase in share price, yields aren't quite keeping pace with yields of years past. Table 10-1 gives you the 8 dividend-paying stocks, plus their yields, ticker symbols, and dividends.

Table 10-1	Major Integrated Oil Companies to Consider		
Yield as of 12/31/09	**Name**	**Ticker Symbol**	**Annual Dividend**
5.8%	BP plc	BP	$3.36
5.8%	Royal Dutch Shell	RDS-B	$3.36
5.0%	Total	TOT	$3.23
4.2%	Eni Spa	E	$2.14
3.9%	ConocoPhillips	COP	$2.00
3.7%	Repsol YPF	REP	$0.99
3.5%	Chevron	CVX	$2.72
2.5%	Exxon Mobil	XOM	$1.68

Exploring Master Limited Partnerships

Master limited partnerships or MLPs are securities that trade just like equities, but because MLPs are partnerships, not corporations. They don't sell shares or have shareholders — they sell *units* and refer to investors as *unit holders* or *partners*. The main advantage of this business structure is that the company itself avoids paying taxes, which offers enormous advantages to the dividend investor for maximizing returns. Instead, the tax liability passes directly to the individual partners based proportionally on their unit holdings. Not all companies can claim MLP status. To qualify, a company must receive at least 90 percent of its income from interest, dividends, real estate rents, gain from the sale or disposition of real property, income and gain from commodities or commodity futures, and income and gain from activities related to minerals or natural resources. A huge majority of MLPs are in the energy industry, but energy MLPs aren't tied so much to the price of oil and gas like other energy stocks can be. MLP companies are typically more involved in the extraction, transportation, and storage of oil and gas, so they're less affected by fluctuations in the price of crude oil.

In the following sections, I reveal the pros and cons of investing in MLPs, which should make clear why the pros generally outweigh the cons.

At one time, real estate investment trusts, or REITs, held the majority of high yielding stocks, but the bursting of the housing bubble ended that run. For income investors, MLPs are the new REITs. Chapter 13 gives you more on REITs.

Although MLPs are partnerships, they aren't like energy partnerships of the 1970s and 1980s that were sold as tax shelters and many of which were scams. MLPs are legitimate vehicles that offer real tax savings.

Marking MLP's advantages

MLPs offer a host of advantages that reach beyond the advantages offered by dividend stocks. The primary advantages include the following:

- **Predictable cash flows:** The MLP business structure favors the kinds of companies that create safe, steady cash flow streams — one of the most important characteristics a dividend investor should be looking for.

- **Distributions taxed only once:** One of the big criticisms of dividend investing is that profits are taxed twice, once at the corporate level and again on the investor's income taxes. The partnership structure eliminates one level. Like a mutual fund, the taxable profits pass through the corporate entity directly to the investors, who are responsible for the taxes.

I hear you moaning, "Oh great, I'm still stuck paying taxes on this money." Well, you were paying taxes on your dividends anyway. Because the MLP doesn't pay taxes, you receive a bigger distribution. However, MLP dividends are taxed differently than the maximum 15-percent tax on regular dividends. The following section gives you additional information about tax issues related to MLPs.

- **Huge yields:** In exchange for not being charged taxes, most MLPs are required to pay out all their cash flow to investors. In addition to resulting in huge cash payouts, this setup means management has very little discretion on how much to pay out or whether to cut the dividend.

✔ **Higher returns on equity:** The absence of retained cash means managers are forced to go outside the company to find funding for large capital projects. The scrutiny of outside lenders typically prevents the funding of dubious projects that follow the latest fad.

✔ **Less volatility than regular energy stocks:** Changes in energy prices have little effect on the prices of these stocks.

✔ **Enormous potential for price appreciation:** On top of the high yields, many MLPs are growing by building new assets and acquiring competition. According to the MSN Money Web site, "You can think of MLPs as a pure play on the growth in demand for energy without having to worry about whether crude oil is going to $30 or $100."

Digging into MLP's disadvantages

MLPs aren't without some potential disadvantages:

✔ **Investors have little voice in company decisions.** MLPs have two classes of equity investors: General partners and limited partners. *General partners* are basically company management — they control and run the business. *Limited partners* are like shareholders; they provide the investible capital but have very little say over how it's used.

✔ **Limited partners receive less when distributions are raised.** When the MLP increases distributions, the general partners stand to earn a bigger share of the increase. On the flip side, general partners suffer a bigger decrease when the MLP reduces distributions.

✔ **Partnerships bring greater liability.** Corporations are structured to remove liability from the individual owners, but in a partnership, the partners are liable in most lawsuits. Most of the time, the general partners are fully liable for legal and tax problems. Limited partners do have limited liability in that creditors can demand the return of cash distributions made to the unit holders if the liability in question arose before the distribution was paid, such as in management fraud.

✔ **The tax issues are potentially complex.** Tax issues are the major drawback of MLPs for most investors. Each unit holder must pay his share of the partnership's income taxes, and if you own a large enough stake in the MLP, you may have to file returns in each state in which the partnership does business. In addition, you may not be able to defer taxes by holding units in a retirement account such as an IRA. For more about tax considerations for investing, head to Chapter 20.

Recognizing qualifying companies

In 1986, tax laws changed to promote investment in *midstream* energy assets (infrastructure companies and businesses involved in extracting, processing, transporting, and storing natural resources). These natural resources include crude oil, natural gas, coal, and refined products, such as fuel oil and natural-gas liquids.

Obviously, extracting is the riskiest venture. Oil companies invest a lot of money in pinpointing potential oil reserves, securing rights to the land, drilling the well, and erecting an oil rig. If they drill in the wrong spot, they end up spending a lot of money for nothing more than a big hole in the ground. In addition, as soon as they start pumping the oil, they must contend with the fluctuations in the price of the commodity.

Transportation and storage, however, are two areas in the energy sector that provide a steady cash flow from which to pay unit holders. The following sections explore these two industries in greater depth.

Pipelines

Pipelines transport oil or gas from the well to wherever folks are waiting to process and use it. Due to the nature of the business, pipelines offer investors several unique advantages:

- **Pipelines establish legal regional monopolies.** Because the cost of transporting energy by truck or train can't compete with a pipeline, the only real competition comes from another pipeline following the same route. This situation rarely happens because local municipalities typically grant franchise rights allowing a single distributor to operate in the area. The inability to easily obtain a pipeline right-of-way creates a huge barrier to entry into this market for other companies wanting to compete.

- **Volatile energy prices have little effect.** Pipelines charge oil production companies a fixed fee for the volume of oil or natural gas they actually move. Some of these rates are federally regulated with generous inflation adjustments. Although the current price you can buy or sell oil for may move, the demand for oil fluctuates in a pretty narrow range. Most pipeline arrangements are long-term contracts that guarantee a certain carrying capacity. Some require payment even if the capacity isn't used.

- **Pipelines own long-lasting, high-value physical assets.** These companies hold or are building the hard assets for the U.S. energy infrastructure of the future. According to industry estimates, over the next decade, the sectors for natural gas and for crude oil and refined petroleum products will each need $100 billion in new infrastructure for processing, storage, and transportation, which means there is huge potential for growth in the pipeline industry.

✔ **Pipeline companies are growing organically.** By laying more pipeline themselves or buying other assets, pipeline companies tend to follow a natural growth pattern. By making these acquisitions, the pipelines continue to generate strong cash flow, increasing their distributable cash flow and hence, payments to unit holders.

✔ **Maintenance costs are small.** After the pipeline's installation into the ground, the annual maintenance costs are just a fraction of the operating cash flow.

Terminal and storage facilities

Pipelines are the most popular MLPs, but *terminal and storage facilities* (companies maintain storage tanks near pipeline systems to hold the products until transport) are also attractive. They're not monopolies, but they generate stable cash flows and good returns. Revenues come from fees charged for short-term and long-term storage of the petroleum products.

Energy producers

Although the MLPs were created for hard-asset companies, many energy exploration and production firms have begun to put their assets into MLPs to avoid taxes. Like other MLPs, all their cash flow gets distributed to their unit holders, but because these firms are much more susceptible to the volatile price swings in the commodities they produce, those cash flows aren't always stable. Better-managed firms use a lot of hedges to minimize the effects of fluctuating commodity prices.

These firms buy proven long-life assets that will consistently pump out oil and gas to provide steady cash flow over time. However, wells can run dry. These firms may provide a higher yield than the pipelines, but they also carry more risk in that their income isn't fixed the way that it is for the traditional pipeline firms.

Assessing MLP stocks

Because MLPs aren't your standard, everyday dividend stocks, the same criteria may not apply to the same degree during your evaluation. With MLP stocks, take a close look at the following:

✔ **Coverage ratio:** You want the distribution of cash flow to dividend payout ratio to be higher than 1 (and the higher the better). If you see a coverage ratio of 1.25, the MLP is more likely to increase the dividends, which can push the share price higher.

✔ **Debt:** The typical MLP holds a capital structure of 50 percent debt and 50 percent equity capital. A debt level much higher than that can hurt cash flows and the payout ratio.

✓ **Changes in the tax laws:** Changes that increase the tax burden for the MLP or unit holders may have a huge affect on the yields.

✓ **Changes in the regulatory structure:** In a more tightly regulated environment, profits (and payments to unit holders) may suffer if regulators restrict how much the MLPs may charge.

✓ **Falling demand:** Although some MLPs are somewhat insulated from fluctuating commodity prices, increasing prices or an economic slowdown can hurt long-term demand and ripple through the industry.

✓ **The inability to fund new capital projects or acquisitions:** Because MLPs pass profits to unit holders, they usually need to secure outside financing to fund new projects or acquisitions. If they can't secure financing, growth and profits may stagnate.

✓ **A proliferation of alternative energy sources:** Demand for cleaner or alternative energies coupled with breakthroughs in energy technology may decrease demand for oil and reduce profits for oil companies and related industries.

For more information about MLPs, Alerian Capital Management, the creator of the Alerian MLP Index, has produced an online primer for the sector at www.alerian.com/MLPprimer.pdf. Table 10-2 lists some MLPs you may want to consider. You can also find an exchange-traded note based on the Alerian MLP Index, the J.P.Morgan Alerian MLP Index (AMJ). For more on exchange-traded funds (ETFs) and exchange-traded notes (ETNs) see Chapter 16.

Table 10-2	MLPs to Consider		
Yield as of 12/31/09	**Name**	**Ticker Symbol**	**Annual Dividend**
17.8%	Capital Product Partners	CPLP	$1.64
9.6%	Copano Energy	CPNO	$2.30
9.0%	Linn Energy	LINE	$2.52
8.7%	MarkWest Energy Partners	MWE	$2.56
8.3%	Williams Partners	WPZ	$2.54
8.0%	Energy Transfer Partners	ETP	$3.58
8.0%	Holly Energy Partners	HEP	$3.18
7.0%	Enterprise Products Partners	EPD	$2.21
7.0%	Plains All American Pipeline	PAA	$3.68
6.9%	Kinder Morgan Energy	KMP	$4.20
6.6%	Magellan Midstream Partners	MMP	$2.84
6.2%	JP Morgan Alerian MLP Index ETN	AMJ	$1.77

Passing on royalty trusts

You may have heard of royalty trusts, which are similar to MLPs in that they typically invest in energy sector assets, have high yields, don't pay taxes, and pay out virtually all of their cash flow. Sounds good, right? However, they aren't as popular as they once were, and I recommend passing on them for the following reasons.

Royalty trusts don't offer the steady cash flows that MLPs promise. Unlike MLPs, which hold the hard assets to produce, transport, or store the natural resources, royalty trusts generate income off the sale of the actual commodities, including coal, oil, and natural gas. Because of this difference, the cash flows of royalty trusts fluctuate with the volatile commodity prices, and distributions to investors can fall with the price of the commodity Royalty trusts don't have physical operations or any employees. These trusts are bank-run financing vehicles that receive royalty payments on the resources mined and produced by other firms.

U.S. royalty trusts have a limited lifespan. U.S. trusts can't issue debt or equity to acquire new properties, but they must distribute all the cash generated by their own finite amount of resources. That means when the well runs dry, so does the trust. The financial filings give the date when the trust will be dissolved, but you may have to dig to find it. And even though royalty trusts aren't taxed on a federal basis, states may tax a trust if it has operations in the state. But the biggest reason to avoid the royalty trusts is that they're slated to lose their tax-free status in Canada in 2011. Why should you care about Canada's tax laws? Because most royalty trusts are based in Canada, so this measure will severely cut into dividends.

Chapter 11

Getting Connected with Telecommunications Stocks

. . . .

In This Chapter

▶ Checking out what telecoms have to offer

▶ Looking at important factors in a telecom's health

▶ Introducing a few leaders of the pack

. . . .

*F*or most of the 20th century, the telecommunications industry was the telephone company. That's it, just one company: American Telephone & Telegraph, better known as AT&T or just "Ma Bell." All that changed in 1984 when AT&T divested itself of its local phone companies to settle an eight-year antitrust lawsuit with the U.S. Department of Justice, giving birth to the telecommunications industry.

In this chapter, I introduce you to the members of the telecommunications industry, show you how to evaluate stocks in this sector, and then provide you with a list of major players in the sector you should consider checking out.

Exploring Telecoms

Prior to 1984, AT&T was the largest private company in the world. With few exceptions, AT&T and its subsidiaries monopolized the entire U.S. telephone market. The federal government regulated it as a utility and, like a utility, AT&T consistently paid out dividends, even during the Great Depression. It was one of the famed "widows and orphans" stocks, so called because they were so reliable at generating income. (See the sidebar "Widows and orphans stocks" later in this chapter for more on those stocks.)

As part of the settlement of the antitrust lawsuit, AT&T rid itself of its local telephone service companies (the Regional Bell Operating Companies, better known as the RBOCs or "Baby Bells") and remained a provider of long-distance telephone service. The breakup led to increased competition in the long-distance area of the market with companies such as Sprint and MCI. Later, AT&T spun off its famous research company Bell Labs, renaming it Lucent Technologies, which became a huge player in the telecom equipment world.

As new industries such as cable television and the Internet sprouted up, they wanted to use the existing telephone infrastructure. The Telecommunications Act of 1996 performed a complete overhaul on the 62-year-old Communications Act of 1934 and sparked a wave of innovation that has led to the growth of cellphones, the Internet, the cable industry, fiber optics, and broadband.

Strictly speaking, none of the Baby Bells exist in their original incarnations. After a series of mergers and acquisitions, the current AT&T consists of a recombination of five companies that came out of the 1984 breakup. Verizon, another major telecom, came about from the merger of two Baby Bells.

The following sections spell out what constitutes a telecom and what you should know about the sector as a whole.

Looking at the advantages

Despite the competition, the telecom industry is experiencing huge growth as more people use more of its services. It remains worthy of your interest because many telecom companies currently offer great dividends.

Companies can create steady revenue streams by locking in subscribers to one- or two-year contracts. This allows the telecoms to project their future earnings with more accuracy and provide better profit potential.

Realizing the disadvantages

The rapid pace of technological change and increased competition has made telecom stocks riskier than ever before. Two terms I associate with dividend stocks — *safe earnings* and *reliable cash flows* — no longer apply to telecom stocks because dramatic cost cutting seems to be the common strategy, and customer loyalty appears to be a relic of the past.

In addition, evaluating a telecom investment today demands much more research into the structure of the company's business model and financials than years ago, when nearly every Baby Bell company was a good investment.

Knowing which companies qualify

So many different industries use the modern-day telecommunication industry's infrastructure that the lines defining what is and isn't a form of telecommunications have become very blurry. Some of the subsectors that qualify as telecoms are

- ✔ **Wireless companies:** As people give up their home telephones for cellphones, the wireless phone companies chip away at the classic landline telephone business. With mobile phones capable of browsing the Internet and receiving television signals, wireless companies now offer those services, grabbing advertising dollars that used to go to those other industries.

- ✔ **Cable companies:** Cable companies now offer phone services on the broadband Internet they send over their high-speed video networks.

- ✔ **Classic telephone companies:** Unwilling to sit back and do nothing, traditional phone companies offer bundled packages combining landlines with wireless services such as cellphones, the Internet, and digital TV.

- ✔ **Telecom equipment manufacturers:** Although these companies provide equipment and services to the telecom industry, they share more characteristics with technology companies than they do with the telecoms. Much less stable and with less predictable cash flows, few of these companies offer dividends. Those that do typically have yields small enough that you can ignore them.

Evaluating sector risk

Although the telecom industry features plenty of good companies for dividend investors, the sector isn't risk-free. Prior to investing, consider the following:

- ✔ **Pricing reflects intense competition.** Although companies can offer noticeable differences in service, such as the quality of the calls and networks, for the most part, telecom services all offer nearly the same thing, which means price is often the factor that determines which company a customer uses. Hence, as the cost to provide the service gets cheaper, the firms continue to lower their prices to grab subscribers from their competitors. This shift has led to the growth of the voice-over-Internet providers, who sell telephone service at about half the price of landlines. Lower prices are great if you're a customer buying a phone or new service, but investors hate price cuts because they tend to lower revenues and earnings.

✔ **Survival requires innovation.** Cellphones and smartphones are some of the most sophisticated technology around. They not only provide a way to communicate by voice but also have become mobile entertainment systems and therefore status symbols. Most customers want access to the top-of-the-line, state-of-the-art services and products, and if a company can't provide that, customers quickly go elsewhere. Thus, companies constantly spend huge amounts of money to install and update networks, build new towers, and increase capacity all in the effort to deliver faster and clearer voice, video, and data streams. They usually take on debt to achieve these goals; high debt loads demand a steady cash stream to make interest payments and leave a company highly exposed to interest rate risk.

✔ **Regulators remain a challenge.** The telecom sector is no longer heavily regulated like a utility and has to deal with new competition, but it is still subject to federal regulations. Governments in the United States and elsewhere have a vested interest in making sure the telecommunications industry remains healthy. The U.S. Federal Communications Commission (FCC) and the European Commission in the European Union still need to approve all big mergers and acquisitions in the industry. If the regulators don't like the deal, it doesn't happen.

Assessing Telecom Stocks: What to Look For

Because the nature of the industry has changed dramatically over the last ten years, telecoms are no longer safe stocks for widows and orphans (check out the nearby sidebar for more on so-called widows and orphans stocks). Though they still see steady cash flows from subscriber bases and have boosted dividends, the constantly changing nature of the industry leaves the stability of these businesses much more suspect than in the past. Close analysis of earnings growth, free cash flow, and the payout ratio become absolutely critical; see Chapter 8 for more about analyzing cash flow and payout ratio.

The key factors you want to look at are the company's ability to acquire and keep customers, generate revenue from those customers through a variety of services, keep costs down, and increase profitability, as I explain in the following sections.

Widows and orphans stocks

Historically, *widows and orphans stocks* were shares (typically in utilities) that brokers bought without fear of losing money or cutting their dividend. These stocks were suitable for widows and orphans because they continued to generate income to put bread on the table in good times and bad. The classic dividend story consisted of someone, typically a grandma or great-aunt, who bought a hundred shares of AT&T in the 1930s or 1940s and became rich by holding on for decades as the dividend and share price just kept rising.

For the most part, the term *widows and orphans stock* has outlived its usefulness. Utilities still have their preferred government status, which allows them to operate legally as monopolies, but you don't see many huge, nationwide bulwarks like AT&T anymore.

Subscriber growth

Unlike most other industries, subscriber growth is a crucial metric for valuing a telecom company. Telecom customers are called *subscribers* because many sign up for service for an extended period of time. The more subscribers a company has, the stronger the company's revenue stream and the greater potential for profit growth. By locking in subscribers to one- or two-year contracts, telecoms can project their future earnings with more accuracy.

Because this number is of much interest to investors, telecoms report the change in their subscriber base, either up or down, in their quarterly earnings reports. The formula is pretty simple:

Growth Rate = New Subscribers ÷ Total Subscribers at beginning of period

If the company with 200,000 subscribers at the beginning of the quarter signed 2,800 new subscribers during the quarter, it would post a growth rate of 1.4 percent:

2,800 New Subscribers ÷ 200,000 Total Subscribers = 1.4 percent Growth Rate

You want to see a growth rate rising. A flattening or falling growth rate may mean the company has lost its competitive edge.

Measuring stability of customer base with churn rate

The *churn rate* is a ratio that measures the percentage of subscribers who discontinue their service during a specific time period. Here's the equation:

Churn Rate = Canceled Subscriptions ÷ Total Subscribers at beginning of the period

If 4,200 subscribers out of a possible 200,000 quit, the churn rate is

4,200 ÷ 200,000 = 2.1 percent

Because customers can easily switch providers and take their phone number with them, the providers of landlines and wireless phone services exist in an intensely competitive market where an increase in prices or poor service can have immediate effects. You want to see a low churn rate.

In order to grow, the company's growth rate of new subscribers must exceed the churn rate. A company with a churn rate of 2.1 percent and a 1.4 percent growth rate is losing a third more subscribers than it brings in. This deficit will likely affect revenues and earnings this quarter. If the churn rate keeps rising, the churn is likely the result of poor service and may be the sign to sell.

Lifting the average revenue per user

Average revenue per user (ARPU) is the key indicator of how the actual business of providing telecom services is performing. It measures the average monthly or quarterly revenue generated from each customer. Typically, a company breaks out each revenue stream, such as cellphone service, Internet, and downloads, and calculates total change in dollars. A company can much more easily sell new services to existing clients because it knows exactly where they are and what they like. For instance, if you buy a monthly cellphone service, and the company increases your number of minutes or offers a bundled package of music downloads, game subscriptions, and video streaming, it can increase revenues with minimal costs. Telecoms also try to raise ARPU numbers by targeting customers who want to cut down on the number of bills, encouraging them to buy as many services as they can from one company.

Take a look at which services are driving growth for this company. Companies that rely on outdated services are likely to see falling ARPUs, but a company with a foot firmly planted in popular technology has stronger prospects.

For instance, many providers of telephone services experienced declining revenues in their landline business as subscribers gave up their home phones and exclusively used their mobile phones. On the other end, when Apple, Inc, came out with its highly coveted iPhone, it gave AT&T an exclusive contract for providing the phone's wireless services. Anyone who wanted an iPhone was forced to sign up with AT&T even if they didn't like the service. As more people bought iPhones, AT&T sold more Internet services and applications to subscribers, increasing its ARPU. However, if Apple lets other telecoms serve the iPhone, AT&T's ARPU may fall as subscribers defect.

Watch out when the number of subscribers rises but revenues sink or even remain steady. This situation may indicate that the company cut prices to gain customers without increasing revenue — a key warning sign.

Creating efficiency with consolidation

As telecoms compete by cutting prices, they need to become more efficient to maintain profitability. One way is through *economies of scale,* a situation in which fixed costs are spread over a large group as more goods are produced or services provided. This system actually lowers the average cost of producing each unit and is especially helpful to companies with wide geographic reach, giving a telecom the incentive to buy up competitors. In addition, mergers eliminate competitors, lessening the pricing pressure on a company and maybe even initiating a price hike.

Stepping back to view EBITDA

To expand and maintain their services, telecoms must continually invest in their networks of fiber optics and towers. Don't be surprised to see an otherwise healthy company post a net loss on its income statement if it spends a lot on capital expenditures (CapEx) or the interest payments to fund that CapEx. Companies in the cable and telecom industries typically have high debt levels and huge interest costs, which can make posting a true profit very difficult.

Because high interest expenses and taxes can decimate a company's profits, carefully examine the company's Earnings Before Interest, Taxation, Depreciation and Amortization (EBITDA). *EBITDA* (often pronounced *ee*-bit-dah) provides a way to evaluate the operations of the core business before these costs and CapEx are taken out. Wall Street analysts look at EBITDA because it gives them an objective way to compare the profitability of highly leveraged companies in capital-intensive industries.

To calculate a company's EBITDA for yourself, use the following calculation (get the numbers from the company's quarterly reports as Chapter 8 explains):

EBITDA = Net Income + Interest + Taxes + Depreciation + Amortization

Unlike Net Income, EBITDA has no specific Generally Accepted Accounting Principles (GAAP), which means the numbers you get to figure EBITDA can be much more easily manipulated.

Measuring debt versus equity

Spending to maintain and expand their networks is basic operating procedure at telecoms, and you don't want to ignore these expenditures, especially the amount of debt they take on to finance these new projects. Although debt can be very helpful in growing a business, relying on debt too much to finance operations can produce serious problems — in particular, large interest payments and an inability to weather bad economic conditions.

To assess a company's health in terms of debt and equity, calculate the debt-to-equity ratio:

Debt-to-Equity Ratio = Total Liabilities ÷ Shareholders' Equity

Too much debt can mean less cash for dividends and may even lead to dividend cuts. Lower is better, but too low means the company may be ignoring growth opportunities to avoid taking on debt. You want to see a debt-to-equity ratio around 1. The higher the number, the riskier (and potentially more unstable) the company.

Following the free cash flow

Another very helpful metric for determining the health of a telecom's dividend is *free cash flow* (FCF). The variables for FCF come from the cash flow statement, which looks at the money moving in and out of the company, including capital expenditures. Chapter 8 gives you more info on FCF and the cash flow statement, but for now you can use the following formula to calculate it:

Free Cash Flow = Net Cash from Operating Activities – Capital Expenditures

You want to see free cash flow large enough to cover both the interest payments on the debt and the dividend. In general, after determining the FCF, you want to look at the following two ratios:

- **Interest Ratio = Free Cash Flow ÷ Interest Payments:** You want to see free cash flow at least double the interest payments (a ratio of 2). Too low, and it may affect the dividend's stability. Less than 1, and the company isn't even generating enough cash to cover its interest payments.

- **Payout Ratio = Dividends per Share ÷ Earnings per Share:** For the telecom industry, a payout ratio below 60 percent is ideal because the company still needs to reinvest profits in building and maintaining infrastructure. Be careful if it exceeds a payout ratio of 75 percent because it indicates the company will need to take on much more debt to finance projects.

Meeting Some Telecoms to Consider

As with most sectors, some telecom companies perform better and more reliably than others for dividend investors. Table 11-1 highlights the companies that were leading the pack during the writing of this book.

Table 11-1	Telecommunications Stocks to Consider		
Yield as of 12/31/09	*Name*	*Ticker Symbol*	*Annual Dividend*
12.8%	Frontier Communications	FTR	$1.00
10.8%	Alaska Communications Systems Group	ALSK	$0.86
9.7%	Iowa Telecommunications Services	IWA	$1.62
9.1%	Windstream	WIN	$1.00
8.9%	Consolidated Communications Holdings	CNSL	$1.55
7.7%	Centurytel	CTL	$2.80
7.6%	Qwest Communications Intl.	Q	$0.32
6.7%	Warwick Valley Telephone	WWVY	$0.88
6.3%	BCE	BCE	$1.74
6.0%	AT&T	T	$1.68
5.9%	Hickory Tech	HTCO	$0.52
5.7%	Verizon Communications	VZ	$1.90

Chapter 12

Investing in the Necessities of Life: Consumer Goods

"**B**uy what you know," is the famed investing strategy of Peter Lynch, who managed the Fidelity Magellan Fund to the best returns ever earned by a mutual fund. "During a lifetime of buying cars or cameras, you develop a sense of what's good, what's bad, what sells, and what doesn't. If it's not cars you know about, you know something about something else, and the most important part is, you know it before Wall Street knows it."

Lynch's strategy tells the investor to identify the products she really likes as well as the favorites of her friends and family. Warren Buffett, considered by many to be the best investor in the world, follows a similar strategy. He says if you can't explain what the company does or why you want to own it, you shouldn't buy it.

As an individual and a consumer, what you know best is what you use most — everyday household and personal products such as food, beverages, washing machines, automobiles, sporting goods, and electronics (as well as many other items). Wall Street classifies these as *consumer goods*. In this chapter, I explain the different types of companies that produce consumer goods and how to identify which ones are likely to provide the steady cash flow and earnings required to maintain a decent dividend.

Discovering the Consumer Goods Sector

When it comes to human beings, you can count on one thing — they consume stuff. People need all sorts of products to live, including food, beverages, personal hygiene and cleaning products, and even technically nonessential items that some people can't live without, such as coffee, cigarettes, and booze. In addition, people *want* all sorts of stuff to feel comfortable and make their lives more enjoyable — electronics, appliances, new cars, restaurant meals, vacations, and more.

The good thing for consumer goods investors is that consumers always use up what they buy and need more. In the following sections, I introduce the two types of consumer goods companies, reveal why companies of the second type are typically better for dividend investors, and then explain what makes these companies potentially such good picks.

Recognizing a consumer goods company

Any company that manufactures or distributes products that people use falls into the consumer goods category, but this category includes two subcategories: consumer cyclicals and consumer staples. In the following sections, I show you how to distinguish between the two.

Consumer cyclicals

Consumer cyclicals owe their name to the fact that demand for these products waxes and wanes, typically in lock step with the economy. Products in this category fall into two categories: durable and nondurable goods.

- **Durable goods** are physical goods that should last for years, such as cars, electronics, hardware, and appliances.

- **Nondurable goods** represent services and less-tangible items, such as anything related to entertainment or travel, including movies, concerts, air travel, hotels, and restaurants.

The share prices of cyclical stocks correlate to the movement of the business cycle and consumer sentiment regarding the economy. During a boom, these companies see strong sales and profits as retail and leisure spending increases. People have plenty of disposable income or are confident enough to borrow the money to pay for these creature comforts. When times aren't so good, consumers tighten their budgets, and these products are the first items to get squeezed out, because they aren't necessary. On top of being poor buy-and-hold stocks, cyclicals make poor dividend stocks because the volatility of their earnings leads to unreliable cash flow, which can lead to dividend cuts.

Investing in cyclicals is essentially a strategy of market timing. Most of the advice in this chapter focuses on consumer staples, but if you really want to try cyclicals, here are a few tips:

- **Sell when you see signs of economic trouble.** Cyclicals are among the first to fall and experience deep declines in share price when the economy turns sour.

✔ Buy cyclicals at the end of recessions when the economy begins to pick up.

✔ Remember that falling interest rates help the performance of cyclicals; rising interest rates hurt it.

✔ Focus on the price-to-book ratio more than the price-to-earnings (P/E) ratio. Buy when the price is discounted to the price-to-book value. A stock selling at several times book value may be overvalued. I explain price-to-book ratio and P/E in Chapter 8.

✔ Look for insiders buying stock without the use of options.

✔ Look for a strong cash position.

The first industries to come out of a recession include petrochemicals, cement, pulp, and paper. During an economic recovery, it's very hard to determine on a day-to-day basis where you are in the cycle, but watch for this pattern: As the recovery builds steam, the second group to experience some movement will be cyclical technology stocks, such as semiconductors. Pulling up the rear of the economic cycle will be consumer companies such as automakers, airlines, and firms dealing with clothing, entertainment, or travel.

Consumer staples

Consumer staples are noncyclical — no matter what part of the business cycle the market is in, demand for these products doesn't slow down. Consumer staples have a low correlation to the gyrations of the stock market because people need to buy these items to carry on their everyday lives. (Utilities, which I discuss in Chapter 9, are another classic noncyclical stock.)

Because consumer staples are must-have products compared to the want-to-have nature of cyclicals, they exhibit most of the essential characteristics for a dividend stock:

✔ Mature companies

✔ Effective management

✔ Stability

✔ Steady stream of income

✔ Predictable cash flow

Most consumer staples fall under the heading of *consumables,* also referred to as *consumer-packaged goods* (CPG). These packaged products get consumed quickly and need to be replaced on a steady schedule. Even during a recession, people need to eat, bathe, and brush their teeth every day. Consumers' constant need for consumables provides these companies with steady sales and predictable cash flow, which translates into a stock that doesn't fall much during market corrections and is great to own during economic downturns.

Not only do consumer staples have limited volatility in share price, but they also have less risk than the general market and provide nice-sized yields. Although high yield often means little capital appreciation, some staples have the potential to grow two to three times the rate of inflation. Typically, consumer staples post middle-range yields higher than the S&P 500 average.

Many investors find these companies too boring to invest in because the flip side of low risk of loss is that they don't see big gains when the stock market surges. This low correlation of share prices to the swings in the markets puts consumer staples in the category of *defensive stocks,* so named because they defend the portfolio from the market's fluctuations. Defensive stocks provide steady earnings and predictable cash flows that allow a company to maintain the dividend during bad times and increase it when conditions improve.

The low correlation of defensive stocks to the movements of the broader market means their share prices may rise while the market falls or plateaus.

Understanding what influences a consumer staple's income

With a steady demand for their products in good times and bad and a lot of competition, companies in the consumer staples industry have a difficult time increasing profits and dividend payments through rising demand or increasing prices. However, they do produce steady earnings growth. They just need to be more creative in differentiating their products from their competitors. For foods and beverages, taste is a great way to stand out from rivals, but what about soap and shampoo? Here the companies rely on branding, advertising, marketing and good-old cost- and price-cutting to attract attention to their products. The following sections discuss these strategies.

Brand strength

Branding is a strategy companies use to create differences between products that are very similar in quality. Strictly speaking, brand is the name and packaging of the product. But the concept of brand is essentially a feeling about the qualities the consumer associates with the product.

Sometimes brands have qualities, such as taste, that truly differentiate them from competitors. Heinz Ketchup and Hunts Catsup are both a type of sweetened tomato sauce, yet their recipes are distinct enough that a person who likes the taste of one may not like the taste of the other. Coke versus Pepsi is another good example.

However, some brands are more a feeling or perception than any real difference, so companies use advertising and promotions to build and boost their brands. Is one laundry detergent really better than any other, or do consumers merely think it's better because of the way it's been marketed? Companies hope their marketing strategies will keep customers coming back to their products out of *brand loyalty.*

Because brand strength relies so much on how consumers *feel* about the brand, it may be tough to pin down, but you can gauge brand strength by looking at a company's market share. *Market share* indicates the percentage of the market the brand owns:

Market Share = Product's Revenue ÷ Total Revenue from Sales of All Products in the Same Market

Market share provides a good indicator for how well a product is doing against its competitors. For instance, if Laundry Detergent A posts sales of $6 million a year and the total market is $200 million, Detergent A's market share is 3 percent. If Laundry Detergent B posts sales of $10 million, Detergent B owns 5 percent of the market, indicating that more consumers prefer Detergent B to Detergent A.

Unfortunately, market share is a tricky number and isn't easy to find. Not all companies break out the sales of individual markets, so getting a feel for how much money is being spent in any broad market may be difficult. The easiest way to get a market share for a company or a product is from a Wall Street analyst's report. However, you typically need to be a client of the firm. Information Resources, Inc. (us.infores.com) and NPD Market Research (www.npd.com) both measure market share, but you may have to pay for copies of their reports. You can check industry publications, AdWeek magazine, or articles on Yahoo! Finance and Google Finance, which may include market share estimates.

Head down to your local or college library and ask the librarian whether the library subscribes to any market share publications or databases, such as Market Share Reporter or Consumer USA. You may be able to use these powerful (and pricey) research tools for free.

Cutting costs

One way to boost profits and lift share prices is to reduce the cost of business, especially with the materials needed to make the products. Most of the materials to create consumer goods are commodities — wherever you buy them, the quality is pretty much the same. Companies can reduce their costs of materials by switching suppliers, merging with or buying suppliers, buying larger quantities for discounts, and leveraging the *economies of scale* (the spreading of fixed costs over a large group) that come from good management.

Tobacco: The new utility

Tobacco is a classic consumer good — consumers use it up very quickly and buy more to replenish their supplies. In addition, tobacco companies have a little thing called nicotine to keep you buying their cigarettes. However, certain factors cause tobacco companies to act more like utilities than consumer staples. In the late 1990s, the tobacco industry settled a huge lawsuit with the U.S. attorneys general from 46 states. As part of the agreement, the tobacco companies agreed to pay in perpetuity (like forever) the health care costs of people who get sick from smoking. The tobacco settlement currently funds a lot of state programs. However, the states didn't get the money upfront — the tobacco companies continue to pay it out. Therefore, the states have a vested interest in keeping the tobacco companies healthy enough to continue payments. Although you may not see much earnings growth in this sector, the tobacco companies are expected to perform like bonds or utility stocks. People buy them for their consistently high yield. (Flip to Chapter 9 for the lowdown on utilities.)

Reducing prices

When looking at consumer staples, make sure their pricing is stable or growing. You don't want a company that may have to lower prices to keep up with the competition or raise prices because of rising material costs; both situations cut into profit margins. However, don't write off a price cut right away. Because the products a staple sells are very similar to its rival, one company may lower prices as a way to boost profits and expand market share by grabbing new customers.

Watching for the Signs of a Good Consumer Staples Stock

Consumer staples include a lot of companies producing very similar products. But just because these are mature companies doesn't mean they don't need to keep growing sales and profits at least as fast as the country's general population. As you evaluate companies in this sector, look for management that's successful at maintaining or lowering the costs of goods sold while increasing sales and revenue.

A key sign of growth at a consumer staple is an operating margin that continues to rise. The operating margin measures the efficiency of a company's pricing strategy by seeing the profits before interest and taxes are paid. The *operating margin* is the percentage of revenue that remains from the sale of a product after subtracting the variable costs of producing that product, including the cost of wages and raw materials:

Operating Margin = Operating Income ÷ Net Sales

Operating margins vary from industry to industry, but in general, look for operating margins in the mid-to-high teens. A company can raise its margins in numerous ways. Here are two of the most commonly used methods

> ✔ **Add new benefits to an existing product (increasing its value) and raise the price.** Because the company doesn't have to spend so much on developing an entirely new product, it can boost its profit without significantly increasing the cost of producing the product.

> ✔ **Add a new product line.** If the company can launch a new product line by using, for the most part, the personnel and equipment it already has, it can do so cost-effectively.

When evaluating operating margins, determine whether the sales growth is from more sales or fewer sales at higher prices. You want to avoid a situation in which the company is raising prices as sales and market share decline.

Also check how much the company spends on research and development and on sales and promotions. Did it boost margins but cut its budgets for research and advertising, or did it become more cost efficient, leading it to continue to invest in R&D, ads, and promotions?

In addition to carefully evaluating a company's operating margin, look for the following positive signs:

> ✔ **Innovation:** The launch of new products creates new revenue streams and gives the company a competitive edge until rivals begin to enter the new market.

> ✔ **A high barrier to entering the market:** The *barrier to entering a market* indicates how easily competing firms and products can enter the market. A low barrier means this entry is pretty easy; because most consumer products are easy to replicate, these markets have low barriers to entry and most brands have a lot in common with their competitors. Look for companies whose products have a barrier to others entering the same market.

> ✔ **Access to international markets:** Selling products to international markets gives a company the ability to continue growing sales even if the local market is in a downturn.

> ✔ **Better treatment at stores:** Although evaluating how effectively a company gets its products to its customers is difficult, you can gain insight into the company's relationships with its retailers by doing your own field research. The more powerful brands get better treatment and more

attention at a retailer because of a strong brand–retailer relationship, which is a sign of competitive strength. Usually, the powerful products sit at the front of aisles, or on shelves at eye level.

Considering Some Consumer Goods Companies

As with most sectors, some consumer goods companies tend to excel and perform more reliably than others for dividend investors. Table 12-1 highlights the companies that were leading the pack during the writing of this book. The list includes tobacco companies, as well as a few cyclical stocks such as Rocky Mountain Chocolate Factory, VF, Mattel, and Hasbro.

Table 12-1	Consumer Goods Companies to Consider		
Yield as of 12/31/09	*Name*	*Ticker Symbol*	*Annual Dividend*
11.4%	Vector Group	VGR	$1.60
6.9%	Altria Group	MO	$1.36
6.8%	Reynolds American	RAI	$3.60
5.6%	United-Guardian	UG	$0.64
5.5%	Superior Uniform Group	SGC	$0.54
5.0%	CCA Industries	CAW	$0.28
5.0%	Lorillard	LO	$4.00
4.9%	Rocky Mountain Chocolate Factory	RMCF	$0.40
4.8%	Philip Morris International	PM	$2.32
4.2%	Diageo	DEO	$2.89
4.1%	Universal	UVV	$1.88
3.8%	Mattel	MAT	$0.75
3.8%	Kimberly-Clark	KMB	$2.40
3.6%	Sara Lee	SLE	$0.44
3.5%	ConAgra Foods	CAG	$0.80
3.3%	Campbell Soup Co.	CPB	$1.10
3.3%	Clorox	CLX	$2.00

Yield as of 12/31/09	Name	Ticker Symbol	Annual Dividend
3.3%	Golden Enterprises	GLDC	$0.13
3.3%	VF	VFC	$2.40
3.3%	The Hershey Co	HSY	$1.19
3.0%	PepsiCo	PEP	$1.80
3.0%	Tasty Baking	TSTY	$0.20
2.9%	Procter & Gamble	PG	$1.76
2.8%	General Mills	GIS	$1.96
2.8%	Kellogg Co.	K	$1.50
2.5%	Hasbro	HAS	$0.80

Chapter 13

Exploring REITs and Financials

In This Chapter

▶ Reaping dividends from real estate investment trusts (REITs)

▶ Gauging the dividend potential of the banking industry

▶ Checking out some notable REITs and financials

*R*EITs and financials comprise a short list of what many experts deem the has-beens of dividend stock investing. The popping of the housing bubble over 2006 and 2007 blew away the REITs. The ensuing financial crisis shook the foundation of the financial industry, including many large banks, and led to widespread dividend cuts in both industries. Some banks cut their dividend payouts by as much as 99 percent!

Amid the carnage remains a small but strong group of dividend providers in both industries. These survivors have managed to weather the storm and, as a result, may potentially capitalize on the crises as their competitors fall out of contention. For instance, a REIT's ability to continue paying a stable dividend in the wake of the bursting housing bubble says something about the resilience of its properties and its management's expertise. Such a company may be well positioned to take advantage of any recovery in the real estate market. Of course, a REIT that pays a sizeable dividend and has a solid cash flow isn't a sure thing, but it's certainly worthy of consideration.

This chapter explores some hard-hit industries traditionally considered fertile ground for dividend investors and provides guidance on how to identify the top picks in each sector.

The REIT Stuff: Getting a Handle on REIT Basics

Real estate investment trusts, or REITs, provide a way for investors to receive capital appreciation and income from real estate without having to actually purchase and maintain property. It's like being an owner/landlord without all the hassles and responsibilities that typically accompany those roles. True to their name, REITs are trusts, not corporations. Like any trust, a REIT has beneficiaries — the shareholders.

To be considered a REIT, these trusts must follow the requirements of the Real Estate Investment Trust Act of 1960. This law states that if the trusts follow certain criteria, they're exempt from paying corporate income tax and capital gains taxes. The main criterion? The trust needs to pay out at least 90 percent of its annual profit to shareholders. This huge payout typically results in high yields. I discuss the other criteria in "Knowing which companies qualify" later in this chapter.

REITs trade like stocks but in some ways are more like mutual funds. Like stocks, shares of a REIT

- ✔ Trade publicly on a stock exchange and are bought and sold through a stockbroker.
- ✔ Are sold in an initial public offering (IPO).
- ✔ Are very liquid. You can buy and sell them anytime the stock market is open for business.
- ✔ Have the same trading options as stocks, including short sales and limit orders.
- ✔ Pay dividends to investors.
- ✔ Are subject to SEC regulations and carry the same SEC reporting requirements as stocks.

Like a mutual fund, a REIT is

- ✔ An investment company that manages investment assets instead of selling goods and services. A REIT buys, rents, leases, manages, develops, and sells buildings — commercial, industrial, or residential developments. The REIT is typically a landlord, generating revenue from rents, property leases, and fees. REITS may also earn interest from mortgages they own. In addition, the underlying assets can increase in property value.
- ✔ A pool of money accumulated from many investors looking for a diversified real estate investment portfolio.
- ✔ A portfolio run by a professional manager.
- ✔ A portfolio that holds assets that it can sell off if it needs to be liquidated.
- ✔ A tax entity that helps investors avoid double-taxation. Trusts, like mutual funds, don't pay taxes. The tax expense is passed onto, and becomes a liability of, the shareholder.

In the following sections, I reveal some of the advantages and disadvantages of investing in REITs and explain which companies qualify as REITs.

Investigating the advantages and disadvantages

When you buy a REIT, you're becoming more of a real estate investor than a dividend stock investor. This move carries some advantages and disadvantages, which I discuss in the following sections.

Advantages

A REIT offers several advantages to both stock and real estate investors:

- ✔ **REITs must pay out at least 90 percent of their income as dividends.** This requirement is the number one reason why investors buy REITs. Management can raise the payout to more than 90 percent but, by law, can't lower it below 90 percent. In other words, management can't decide to slash the dividend payment.

- ✔ **Large payouts result in higher-than-average yields.** For dividend investors, high yield is a primary consideration.

- ✔ **REITs help diversify an investment portfolio.** Because real estate values don't generally correlate to stock prices, stock prices and real estate values can move together or in completely opposite directions. Unless a real estate slump triggers a financial crisis or vice versa, a portfolio that contains both stock and real estate holdings may provide some protection over slumps that affect only one or the other.

- ✔ **REITs help diversify a real estate portfolio.** Money pooled from many investors allows the trust to purchase more buildings than an individual would be able to buy alone. If you buy real estate on your own, you may lock up all your money in one building. A REIT gives you a piece of many different properties; that way, one underperforming building won't ruin your portfolio. This setup allows small investors to have a diversified real estate portfolio with a minimal investment. Though diversified in terms of holding many properties, most REITS focus on one area of the real estate market, such as commercial offices or residential apartment buildings, and are usually in one geographic region.

- ✔ **You can own real estate without the costs and hassles associated with real estate investing.** You don't have to find and research properties — the REIT's managers do that for you. You don't need to come up with a down payment and closing costs or worry about making monthly mortgage payments and maintaining properties. You can jump into the real estate market with a purchase as small as one share of stock.

- ✔ **REITs own physical assets with a value all their own that can appreciate over time.** As an investor, you own tangible assets that tend to rise in value over the long term.

- ✔ **REITs are more liquid than typical real estate investments.** Instead of selling the property to cash out, you simply sell your shares.

Disadvantages

Because REITs allow you to invest in real estate, they carry risks associated with real estate investing as well as stock investing, including the following:

- Falling occupancy rates and increasing vacancies hurt revenues.
- Share prices can drop when property values fall.
- Share prices can fall with the broader stock market based on supply and demand of shares.
- High dividend payouts for REITs force management to take on debt to expand real estate holdings.
- Rising interest rates hurt profitability.
- Not all REIT dividends quality for 15-percent tax rates. Some are taxed as ordinary income.

Prior to investing in a REIT, consult a tax advisor to determine the net effect on your tax bill.

Knowing which companies qualify

Just because you own a real estate stock doesn't mean it's a REIT. When you're looking at REITs, determine whether the trust receives the tax-free benefit. To avoid paying corporate income tax and capital gains taxes, the company must follow certain rules. The biggest rules address the REIT's assets and profits:

- At least 75 percent of the REIT's annual gross income must come from real-estate related income, such as rents.
- At least 75 percent of the REIT's total assets must be in real estate investments, such as property or loans secured by property.
- Shareholders must receive a minimum of 90 percent of the REIT's taxable income. The REIT pays taxes on any income it retains.

After a company agrees to satisfy all those requirements, management can focus on one of three areas: property, mortgages, or a hybrid of the two, as I explain in the following sections.

Property REITs

Property REITs follow a classic landlord scenario. They make their money by leasing properties and collecting rent. Success hinges on management's ability to secure properties in high-rent districts and manage them effectively. It's all about location, location, location.

Mortgage REITs

Mortgage REITs operate more like banks than landlords. These companies make, own, and manage loans for the purchase of real estate. Instead of earning revenues from rent, the REIT earns interest on its loans. Often the loans are funded by money the REIT borrowed. With increased levels of interest-rate risk and credit risk, mortgage REITs are riskier than property REITs, and dividends are less stable. Many of these companies faced financial distress during the 2008–2009 financial crisis. Their dividends fell with their falling profits.

Hybrid REITs

As you may guess, a hybrid REIT is a cross between a property and a mortgage REIT. Hybrids buy, own, and manage both properties and loans, which can provide some protection against fluctuations in the real estate markets. As properties become costlier to purchase and own, the mortgage side often declines while demand for rentals rises.

Evaluating REITs

Because REITs aren't your average, everyday dividend stocks, using the criteria from Chapter 8 to evaluate them makes little sense. The following sections show you various ways you can get an idea of a REIT's condition before investing.

Assessing REITs

Determining the value of real estate assets requires a unique set of criteria. When shopping for REITs, examine the following factors:

- **Geography:** A property's value and rent-generating potential are both closely linked to the property's location. Look for REITs that invest in areas with growing populations and thriving economies. Typically, areas located in the Sun Belt rather than the Rust Belt tend to be better bets, but keep in mind that every area of the country and even an area within a town or city has hot and cold spots. For example, after the popping of the housing bubble, many areas of the Sun Belt are no longer good investments. Carefully research an area before buying a REIT that invests heavily in that area.

- **Property type:** Office and industrial properties charge higher rents, but tend to suffer more in a recession as occupancy rates decline when companies go out of business. Residential and retail buildings tend to charge lower rents, but are more resistant to tough economic times.

✔ **Diversification:** Is the trust well diversified? Many REITs focus on just one sector of the market — commercial, industrial, or residential — or just one local market. Because not all real estate markets move together, diversification is a good thing.

✔ **Occupancy trends:** An increasing occupancy rate is a good sign. In real estate, high vacancy rates can wipe out profits. Find out the vacancy rate for the properties the REIT holds and determine the direction the vacancy rate is moving — up or down. Although a vacancy rate of more than 10 percent may affect a REITs ability to pay dividends, the trend is more important than the actual figure. Beware if vacancies are on the rise.

✔ **Tenant concentration:** Determine whether the bulk of the REIT's income comes from just one type of tenant or industry or a wider range. If the REIT invests only in gas stations or only in strip malls, its profits may be tied too closely with the health of a particular industry or location. Research not only the REIT and type of real estate it owns but also the tenant's industry. If that industry is stable and growing, investing in a REIT that serves this particular industry may be a good thing. If the industry or geographical area is suffering, the REIT may be a dud.

✔ **Management:** The reputation, strength, and skill of the company's managers are just as important, if not more so, than the type of building. Check for managers that have an excellent track record for picking properties with high potential for capital appreciation, purchasing them at bargain prices, and then managing the properties for maximum profitability. The managers who performed well during the real estate meltdown were those who thought about the possibility of the 100-year flood and moved to higher ground.

✔ **Credit rating:** Because most property is bought with borrowed money, make sure the REIT has an excellent credit rating, so it can borrow money at competitive interest rates.

✔ **Lease duration:** Ask management about the average lease duration of its holdings. Single-year leases give landlords the ability to raise rents regularly, but they also provide tenants with an easy out. Multiyear leases lock in tenants and provide a predictable revenue stream on which you can base expectations of steady dividend payments.

✔ **Funds from operations:** Perhaps the most important factor to consider is the REIT's funds from operations (FFO), which provides an indication of how much money the REIT has available to fund dividend payments. (See the following section for more about this key figure.)

Calculating funds from operations (FFO)

As I explain in Chapters 9 and 11, net income isn't always the be-all and end-all of an entity's success, especially when looking at the entity's ability to pay dividends. Earnings per share and the P/E ratio don't give the most accurate representation of a REIT's value because the net income calculation deducts depreciation. Deducting for depreciation misrepresents the REIT's value because it takes part of the property's value out of income producing assets, even as the property continues to rise in value and produce income. A better number for evaluating the REIT's overall performance and ability to pay dividends is called *funds from operations* (FFO), which indicates how much cash is available for paying dividends:

FFO = Net Income + Depreciation – Gains from One-Time Sales

FFO is similar to net cash flow (NCF) from operating activities as explained in Chapter 8. Both NCF and FFO add back in depreciation and amortization because these are non-cash charges. In FFO, this add-back means the REIT has a predictable pile of tax-free cash sitting in its vault equal to the value of the depreciation and amortization, ready to pay out as dividends over the coming years.

However, there's one key difference: NCF, which deals with the actual movement of cash during the quarter, includes one-time gains and losses, but FFO doesn't. With FFO, analysts just want to see the amount of sustainable dividend-paying cash that comes strictly from operations.

Most REITs report their FFOs in press releases along with their quarterly earnings, as shown in Table 13-1. Table 13-1 is part of the earnings report of a company called Big Edifice Realty and shows you how to figure out FFO and adjusted FFO from the net income; you may then use those numbers to determine the FFO per share, the adjusted FFO per share, and the payout ratio the company's dividend represents.

Why discount depreciation?

The government generally allows companies to claim deductions for assets that tend to physically wear down over time. For example, if a company purchases a high-end computer server for $250,000, the government may allow the company to deduct the cost of that server over the course of several years (typically five to ten). According to Barron's *Dictionary of Business Terms* (San Val), "The purpose of charging depreciation against equipment is to distinguish the portion of income that is a return of capital. This generates a tax-free stream of income equal to the portion of the asset that has been used up."

The government typically allows for depreciation of real estate, too, based on the fact that real estate wears out just like everything else — a computer, a desk, a chair, you name it. However, unlike other assets that typically decline in value as they wear out, real estate often rises in value over time. So, although the REIT deducts for depreciation to save on taxes, it needs to account for the true market value of its holdings. When calculating the FFO, the REIT adds back in the amount it deducted for depreciation, giving a clearer indication of the true value of the properties it holds

Most analysts value REITs by their FFO per share:

FFO per Share = FFO ÷ Total Shares Outstanding

In Table 13-1, the REIT's net income is $26.497 million, or 29 cents per share. After adding depreciation with adjustments back in ($22,922), and then subtracting the gains from the sale of real estate ($2,239), FFO comes in much higher, at $47.18 million or 52 cents per share.

To obtain an accurate indication of a REIT's performance, always calculate the dividend payout ratio using the FFO, not net income.

The REIT paid out dividends of 42.6 cents a share. Comparing that to net income, the payout ratio comes in at an astounding 147 percent. It's ridiculously huge and unsustainable, and it violates all the rules about dividend payouts. The REIT, however, has a stash of cash sitting in its depreciation vault. Add that cash back in when determining the FFO, and the payout ratio is 82 percent of FFO. Lower is better, and a payout ratio of 85 percent or less gives the REIT a bigger cushion to fall back on.

For a REIT to achieve tax-exempt status, it needs to pay out at least 90 percent of its taxable income, not FFO (no requirement dictates how much of the FFO must be paid to shareholders). Because FFO is typically much higher than taxable income, the dividend payout is usually a smaller percentage.

Table 13-1	Big Edifice Realty FFO		
June 30, 2009	**Net Income**	**FFO**	**Adjusted FFO**
Net income after preferred dividends	$26,497,000	$26,497,000	$26,497,000
Add in depreciation and Amortization		$22,961,000	$22,961,000
Depreciations adjustments		($39,000)	($58,000)
Subtract income from sale of real estate held for investment		($2,239,000)	($2,222,000)
Subtract capital expenditures			($593,000)
Totals	$26,497,000	$47,180,000	$46,587,000
Common stock outstanding	91,000,000 shares	91,000,000 shares	91,000,000 shares
Amount per share	29 cents	52 cents	51 cents
Payout ratio on dividend of 42.6 cents a share	147%	82%	84%

Calculating adjusted funds from operations (AFFO)

Some analysts think that the cash available for dividend payouts should take into account the cost of maintaining the buildings. If you own a home, you know buildings demand constant upkeep, such as painting and new fixtures. Analysts subtract the capital expenditures for maintaining the properties (on the cash flow statement in Chapter 8) to arrive at a more conservative measurement, *adjusted funds from operations* (AFFO):

$$AFFO = FFO - Capital\ Expenditures$$

FFO and AFFO are *non-GAAP earnings,* which means the numbers don't adhere to Generally Accepted Accounting Principles (GAAP) — the authoritative standards by which revenue, net income, and balance sheet components must be presented in filings with the SEC. Many companies don't like GAAP earnings, because they feel the standards are too strict and fail to provide an accurate measure of the company's performance. To counteract this perceived discrepancy, companies often provide their own numbers alongside the required GAAP earnings — an alternative non-GAAP earnings measurement, such as EBITDA (discussed in Chapter 11) or FFO.

First Industrial's FFO fudging

First Industrial Realty (FR), a Chicago-based REIT, provides a great example of why gains from sales of buildings shouldn't be part of the FFO equation. Because FFO isn't a GAAP earnings measurement but rather a suggested formula by the industry trade group, the National Association of Real Estate Investment Trusts (NAREIT), First Industrial didn't feel bound by NAREIT's "suggestion" that FFO exclude gains and losses from the one-time sale of real estate property.

Instead of just a landlord, First Industrial acted as an asset manager, buying and selling properties, similar to the manager of a mutual fund holding stocks. Basically, they were flipping properties. Because this flipping was a big part of the REIT's main business, First Industrial felt these capital gains should be part of its FFO. It left them in instead of subtracting them out like most other REITs. However, these transactions were still one-time events and not a recurring revenue stream on which to base dividend predictability. The typical investor who figured that FFO showed reliable cash flow was caught unaware when First Industrial could no longer do what it called "capital recycling."

In October 2008, at the height of the financial crisis, First Industrial warned the stock market that the credit crunch and liquidity crisis in the capital markets had caused real estate transactions to dry up and prices to plunge. With income from property sales in freefall, First Industrial's FFO plummeted. For the third-quarter of 2008, the REIT's FFO fell 42 percent to $32.8 million (66 cents per share) from $57.2 million ($1.13 per share) in the third quarter of 2007. Net income fell further, plunging 86 percent to $4 million (9 cents per share) versus $29.3 million (66 cents per share), in the year-earlier quarter. In a little over a month, First

(continued)

(continued)

Industrial's share price sank to $5.98 from $31.00, and its quarterly dividend tumbled 65 percent to 25 cents per share from 72 cents.

Although First Industrial explained its unique formula for FFO in its earnings releases, investors who just looked at the FFO number but failed to read footnotes missed it. After the debacle, First Industrial agreed to follow the NAREIT standards for FFO, but the damage had been done. The moral of the story is that you need to make sure the REIT's FFO is based on a recurring source of income.

Accounting for debt

Typically, a payout ratio below 85 percent of FFO and a recurring revenue stream should give you a good indication of the dividend's stability. However, because most of a REIT's cash is paid to shareholders as dividends, little equity remains for buying properties. Thus, most REITs have high debt levels and maximize shareholder returns through leverage. In addition to the other debt ratios mentioned in Chapter 8, look at the REIT's debt-to-capital ratio.

The *debt-to-capital ratio* adds together all forms of debt (long-term and short-term) and then divides by total capital, which equals total debt plus shareholder equity (preferred stock and common stock).

Debt-to-Capital Ratio = Total Debt ÷ Total Capital

Josh Peters, editor of the *Morningstar DividendInvestor* monthly newsletter, says the debt-to-capital ratio should be less than 65 percent on a market value basis and equal to or less than 80 percent of an FFO basis. In an interview after the financial crisis, Peters told me that investors need to look not just at the total amount of debt but also when the debt comes due: Will the REIT meet its obligations on an ongoing basis or will it need to borrow money when the credit markets are difficult? Typically, a REIT pays off a loan coming due with a new loan. But when no one was lending during the 2008–2009 credit crunch, REITs saw their short-term debts come due at a time when they weren't able to secure new loans. Desperate to pay off their debt with the funds from operations, many REITs slashed their dividends, which is why dividend investors want to keep an especially close eye on this factor.

Valuing a REIT

Valuing a REIT is similar to valuing a corporation (see Chapter 8), but you use FFO per share rather than earnings per share and a P/FFO ratio rather than the P/E ratio.

FFO/share measures the company's performance from year to year and allows you to compare the performance of two companies. To calculate a company's FFO and FFO/share, see "Calculating funds from operations (FFO)" earlier in this chapter.

The P/E ratio (covered in Chapter 8) gives you a *multiple* (how much an investor pays for $1 of profit) with which to compare two companies' relative valuations. Because FFO is the main metric among REITs, use the P/FFO ratio to calculate the multiple:

P/FFO Multiple = Price per Share ÷ FFO per Share

The lower the multiple, the cheaper the stock compared to FFO. The preferred multiple varies depending on property type — commercial, residential, or industrial — and on the local real estate market. To get the multiple levels for each category, read some Wall Street research from analysts. As a rule of thumb, look for REITs with a P/FFO ratio below 10.

If you're focusing on the dividend yield much more than capital appreciation, making sure the company has a recurring cash stream for predictable payouts should be enough. If you want capital appreciation, look at growth levels, as explained in the following section.

Growth among the REITs

If you're looking for capital appreciation in addition to dividends, look for the following signs of growth:

- ✔ Rent increases
- ✔ Rising occupancy rates
- ✔ Success in buying bargain properties, upgrading them, and renting them out
- ✔ The growth rate at which the company acquires new properties

To compare your REIT or REIT fund to the broader REIT market, check out the two benchmarks for the market: the MSCI U.S. REIT Index and the Dow Jones U.S. REIT Index. They each track about two-thirds of the domestic REIT market.

Meeting some REITs to consider

Although REITs took a beating in the fiscal crisis of 2008 and 2009, some managed to survive and continue to pay handsome dividends. Table 13-2 highlights some REITs you may want to consider. In addition, many ETFs and mutual funds focus solely on REITs. The Vanguard REIT ETF (VNQ) tracks the benchmark MSCI U.S. REIT Index. For more on REIT ETFs, head to Chapter 16.

Table 13-2	REITs to Consider		
Yield as of 12/31/09	*Name*	*Ticker Symbol*	*Annual Dividend*
17.3%	Annaly Capital Management, Inc.	NLY	$3.00
7.7%	Investors Real Estate Trust	IRET	$0.69
7.5%	Universal Health Realty Income Trust	UHT	$2.40
7.4%	Entertainment Properties Trust	EPR	$2.60
7.1%	National Retail Properties, Inc.	NNN	$1.50
6.7%	Macerich Co.	MAC	$2.40
6.6%	Reality Income Corp.	O	$1.72
6.4%	First Potomac Realty Trust	FPO	$0.80
6.4%	Urstadt Biddle Properties Inc.	UBA	$0.97
6.3%	Washington Real Estate Inv. Trust	WRE	$1.73
6.1%	Health Care REIT	HCN	$2.72
5.9%	Liberty Property Trust	LRY	$1.90
5.6%	Home Properties Inc.	HME	$2.68
5.6%	Duke Realty Corp.	DRE	$0.68
5.4%	EastGroup Properties Inc.	EGP	$2.08
5.3%	Regency Centers Corp.	REG	$1.85
5.1%	Mid-America Apt. Communities Inc.	MAA	$2.46
5.0%	Sovran Self Storage Inc.	SSS	$1.80
4.9%	Essex Property Trust Inc.	ESS	$4.12
4.7%	Ventas Inc.	VTR	$2.05
4.3%	Corporate Office Properties Trust Inc.	OFC	$1.57
4.0%	Vornado Realty Trust	VNO	$2.60

Banking on Dividends from Banks

Banks have always paid dividends, but for most of the 1990s they posted yields below 3 percent. Then, in the first decade of the new century, banks became great stocks for dividend investors by offering a great package of total return with fast earnings growth and rising payout ratios.

Then in the fiscal crisis of 2008, the entire banking industry blew up. Many banks went out of business and of those that survived, many either cut their dividends or eliminated them entirely. J.P. Morgan Chase, the strongest of the bunch, cut its dividend by 87 percent in early 2009.

In the aftermath of the bank bailouts, with dividends and balance sheets decimated, the banking sector as a whole isn't promising. However, the banks that do come back will be much stronger. Many that dramatically cut their dividends during the liquidity crisis of late 2008 and early 2009 have stabilized and begun to post profits as of the writing of this book. Some experts think the banks that survive will eventually try to bring their dividends up to former levels quickly.

Not every bank filled its loan portfolio with loans to subprime lenders and credit default swaps. Many banks maintained a conservative business strategy. They not only survived but also came out much stronger and were able to grab market share by buying competitors. These survivors are the banks you want to put your money in. They shouldn't be too hard to find — they're the ones still paying a decent dividend. Funny how that worked out.

In the following sections, I take you shopping for dividend-paying financials and show you how to improve your odds in picking a winner.

Sizing up the 2008 financial crisis aftermath

There's no way to sugarcoat it. The banks screwed up. When the technology bubble popped in 2000, dividend stocks came out smelling like roses. The high-flying growth stocks of the technology sector barely paid dividends. Meanwhile, the mature, stable, and well-managed financial companies saw their dividends exit the crash of 2000 practically unscathed. Even at the end of 2008, after the U.S. government had bailed it out, the financial industry still had the most dividend paying companies in the S&P 500 with 71. It continued to pay the largest portion of the index's dividends: 20.5 percent of the total payout.

Unfortunately, the banks got careless or greedy, depending on which story you want to believe. They relaxed their underwriting standards and helped to inflate the mother of all housing bubbles. By the end of 2009, more than a year after the bubble burst, five banks stopped paying dividends, accounting for half the dividend suspensions that year. J.P. Morgan chopped 87 percent off its dividend, to pay just a nickel per fiscal quarter. The sector's total payout fell 56 percent, to comprise just 9.0 percent of the S&P 500's total dividend. The sector's average yield, 4.44 percent at the end of 2008, fell 73 percent to 1.22 percent by the end of 2009. Banking, one of the strongest and most consistent payers of dividends suddenly became one of the worst.

So where does the banking sector sit today? It's really a mixed bag. Conservative banks that avoided making risky loans survived and even thrived as their competitors crashed. Some banks that managed to hold on, with or without government bailout money, may still crumble sometime in the future. As a dividend investor, you can still profit from financials. You just need to be more careful in choosing the right institutions.

Investigating the pros and cons

If you're waffling about whether to invest in banks, I can give you plenty more to waffle about. In the following sections, I reveal the pros and cons to consider before deciding to invest a portion of your portfolio in banks.

Pros

In terms of stability and reliability, banks actually have a lot going for them:

- **Plentiful supply of cheap money:** Banks have a constant source of cheap funds: depositors. Most other lending institutions need to form partnerships or sell equity or debt to investors to raise the money they lend. These companies pay a premium for that money by giving away part of the company or paying interest. Not banks. Customers just hand them cash, practically for free, relying on the bank to keep their money safe and liquid. And talk about cheap money! Most checking accounts pay 0 percent interest. At the end of 2009, banks paid a measly 0.05 percent annual interest on a savings account while the U.S. Treasury was paying around 0.35 percent for a 52-week Treasury bill — seven times more! With that much of a spread, banks are hard-pressed *not* to make a profit.

- **Customer stability:** When customers choose a bank, they tend to stay put because the time, money, and hassle of changing banks typically outweigh the benefits. As soon as customers receive their checks and ATM cards and set up direct deposit and electronic bill pay, they've made a significant investment of time and are reluctant to do it all over again with another bank.

- **Stiff regulation:** Banks are a heavily regulated industry, and after the banking fiascos of 2008 and 2009, regulators are becoming even stricter in monitoring banks and enforcing regulations, which benefits investors in two ways. First, it enhances customer stability by increasing customer confidence in making deposits. Second, it helps stabilize the banking industry, so your investment is safer.

- **Economies of scale:** Size matters. A huge company can force suppliers to give it better, cheaper goods than competitors; it then spreads the fixed costs over a greater number of stores. By lowering its cost of doing business so much, it can still make huge profit margins while charging less than its competition. Big banks with many branches have economies of scale by spreading costs over a large network of branches.

Cons

Don't assume that investing in banks is 100 percent risk-free. Investors who owned stock in Washington Mutual learned this lesson the hard way in September 2008, when the FDIC seized Washington Mutual — a bank that held a loan portfolio with $307 billion in assets. WaMu was the largest bank failure in U.S. history. Depositors got their money back. Shareholders lost everything.

Another risk of investing in banks is, well, risk. Banks act as financial interme-diaries between the people who need the money and the people who have it. As banks manage the money that flows through them, they assume two types of risk, interest rate risk and credit risk:

✔ **Interest rate risk:** Banks may pinch pennies, but sometimes they can get pinched, too. More precisely, their *net interest spread* (the differ-ence between the rate they charge on their assets and the rate they pay to their liabilities) can feel the pinch when the interest they collect on loans dips, the interest they pay on deposits rises, or both.

   • Most deposits and CDs have short-term maturities, so a sudden rise in interest rates forces the bank to pay more for deposits. Unless the bank can charge more on loans, the spread tightens.

   • When interest rates rise, more people may deposit more money in the bank while fewer people take out loans.

   • Banks can also get their money tied up in bonds — a loan with a fixed interest rate. If interest rates rise, the bond's coupon loses value compared to competing investments.

   To offset a tightening of the spread, the bank may institute more fees and charges to make up the missing revenue.

   The *yield curve* determines the amount of interest rate risk. It's a graph that examines bonds with the same credit quality by plotting out their yields over a range of maturities from shortest to longest. Banks like when short-term rates are low and the curve makes a steep upward move to the longer maturities, because they pay depositors short-term rates while charging borrowers long-term rates. This wide spread increases profitability. When long-term yields aren't much higher than short-term yields, the yield curve is much flatter, cutting into profits.

   Depending on which assets the bank holds, net interest income can be very sensitive to changes in interest rates. Deposit accounts with short-term maturities may pay variable interest rates, which fluctuate up and down. Meanwhile, many liabilities have a fixed rate, although adjustable-rate mortgages do see rate increases.

✔ **Credit risk:** *Credit risk* is the likelihood that a bank will lose part or all of the principal, as well as the interest, in the event a borrower defaults on the loan. Poor management of credit risk was a major contributor to the fiscal crisis of 2008. Rising interest rates can hurt adjustable-rate loans because they increase the interest payments the borrowers must pay, potentially causing them to miss payments and turning these into problem loans. Banks hold cash in allowances to absorb these potential losses, but if their reserves fall short, they can get into a serious credit crunch of their own.

Financial services perform best in low interest-rate environments. When interest rates decline, banks pay depositors less interest as revenue from mortgages and loans increases. In addition, a drop in interest rates usually sparks a boost in business development, leading to more borrowing to finance new projects.

Watch out for super-low interest rates. In late 2009, interest rates in the U.S. were at historic lows. The *federal funds rate* (the rate banks charge each other for overnight loans), sat between 0 and 0.25 percent. Interest rates had nowhere to go but up, and when interest rates rise, banks and other dividend investments, including utilities, may feel the pinch.

Figuring out which companies qualify

The financial services sector (financials, for short), includes commercial banks, savings & loans, mortgage companies, investment banks, stockbrokers, asset managers, mutual fund companies, credit services, and insurance companies. As demonstrated during the crash of 2008, these financials can generally be divided into two groups:

- **Risky investments:** Investment banks, brokerages, asset managers, and mutual fund companies are very volatile, following the fortunes of Wall Street.

- **Conservative propositions:** Commercial banks, regional banks, and insurance companies are more stable, and when you're talking dividend investing, you're looking for stability.

Looking at banks' income-generating capabilities

Banks are pretty simple operations. They take money from depositors and then lend it to borrowers. Much more than manufacturers or service providers, a bank's profitability is intimately linked to its balance sheet. Its assets consist of all of its loans: personal, commercial, and mortgages, and whatever securities it holds and collects interest from. The liabilities are customer deposits on which it pays interest. This situation opens banks up to unique risks not seen in other industries.

Banks want the rate they receive on loans to be much higher than the rate they pay savings accounts. If the bank charges 6 percent for loans and pays only 1 percent on interest, the net interest spread is 5 percentage points. If the net interest spread turns negative, the bank is paying more out to depositors than it's collecting in interest on loans — a recipe for losing money.

Profits come from the difference in the actual interest revenue the bank's assets generate and the interest expense it pays out on its liabilities. This profit is called the *net interest income.* The net interest income must be large enough to cover all the bank's operating costs in order to post a profit and pay dividends. See "Net interest income" later in this chapter to determine this number for a particular bank.

Assessing banks

When banks go belly up, investors can lose everything, so if you're considering investing in a certain bank, take a close look at its financials. Some of the financials are the same as those I explain for other sectors in Chapter 8, but with banks, you have to look at a few additional numbers. The following sections highlight the most important numbers to consider.

The main factor contributing to a bank losing money is bad loans, so check the quality of the bank's assets (its loans) carefully.

Eliminating the riskiest candidates

When evaluating banks, eliminate the riskiest of the bunch by looking for the following red flags:

- ✔ **Bailout recipients:** Cut banks that received bailout money from the U.S. government right off your list. Let the government take the risk.

- ✔ **Dividend cuts:** Unless the bank has increased its dividend after making a cut, avoid it. Over 2009, many companies that cut or eliminated their dividends continued to perform poorly, and that's not just a recent phenomenon. According to Ned Davis Research, stocks that cut or eliminated their dividends have significantly underperformed the S&P 500 over the past 40 years.

Dividends are sacred cows. Management typically wants to do everything it can to avoid a cut. But after it's gone down that road, there's nothing to stop it from cutting the dividend again. In addition, a cut dividend means the managers have proven themselves to be fiscally irresponsible, poor managers of risk, and not looking out for shareholders. Make sure the management that brought the bank low has been dismissed before you put money into it.

Just because a bank survived so far doesn't mean a dividend cut isn't in its future. As a second wave of foreclosures begins to hit the economy at the writing of this book (this time from commercial real estate rather than residential), analysts are mixed on whether banks have hit their bottom and the days of dividend cuts are over. In addition, interest rates have nowhere to go but up, and that's sure to eat into bank profits.

If you choose to invest in banks, stay on top of the foreclosure statistics for both commercial and residential real-estate. Foreclosure is a very volatile area of the economy these days.

Focusing on banks that make the cut

Avoiding all financials may negatively affect your portfolio as the sector moves toward recovery. Though many of the largest banks no longer pay a dividend, a significant number of regional banks have been paying dividends for years and look like value plays. The share prices have been beaten down, but the financial reports look great, and the yield is still fairly high — between 6 and 9 percent. Three banks that fall into this category are New York Community Bancorp (NYB), United Bankshares (UBSI), and Capitol Federal Financial (CFFN).

Canada's five major banks also provide a good way to get financial exposure. Toronto-Dominion Bank (TD), Bank of Montreal (BMO), Royal Bank of Canada (RY), Canadian Imperial Bank of Commerce (CIBC), and Bank of Nova Scotia (BNS) appear to have escaped the crisis no worse for wear. They continue to pay decent yields and haven't experienced any cuts.

The insurance sector is another financial group that has a history of dependable dividend growth and still pays decent yields. And although AIG remains the insurance industry's poster child for bad behavior during the meltdown, many insurance companies did what they were supposed to do and managed their risk and cash flow very well to come out very strong. The Chubb (CB) and Aflac (AFL) are two companies paying decent yields.

Checking the return on equity

Return on equity (ROE) determines the shareholders' rate of return. (For a full explanation, including the formula, see Chapter 8.) Scratch any bank off your list that doesn't have an ROE of at least 15 percent.

Calculating the net interest income

Net interest income is the difference between what the bank earns collecting interest from borrowers minus what it pays out in interest to depositors. Check the bank's most recent balance sheet to see the interest earned off of its total assets (loans, leases, and other debt instruments) and the interest paid on its total liabilities (deposit). Then do the math:

> Net Interest Income = Interest Earned on Assets − Interest Paid on Liabilities

The net interest income must be sufficient to cover all the bank's operating costs *and* pay dividends. If the bank can't cover the dividend payments, scratch it off your list.

Assessing the equity/asset ratio

The equity/asset ratio tells you the bank's cushion in the event that its assets begin to lose value. Obtain the two values you need (shareholder equity and asset values) from the bank's most recent balance sheet. Then, do the math:

Equity/Asset Ratio = Shareholders' Equity ÷ Total Assets

The higher the number here, the better. Conservative lenders can get away with a ratio of 5 percent. However, if you're looking at smaller banks or riskier lenders, the ratio should be more than 8 percent.

Evaluating the charge-off ratio

Charge-offs are bad loans — the ones the bank expects to lose money on. This number is typically hidden somewhere in a quarterly report's footnotes. You want to see a low charge-off ratio — less than 1 percent. You also want to look for consistent results to make sure the year you're looking at isn't a fluke either way — positive or negative.

Investigating nonperforming assets

Isn't that a great name? *Nonperforming assets* makes it sound like they're on a break . . . and, well, they are. They're loans the borrowers have stopped making payments on. Nonperforming assets become bad loans when they go into default. This statistic is also typically found in the footnotes of the earnings reports, right near the charge-off ratio. Growth in this category is a bad sign.

Looking into the efficiency ratio

The efficiency ratio measures how well the bank keeps down its operating costs, also known as overhead. Rising costs cut into profits. To measure a bank's efficiency, perform any one (or all) of the following four formulas; you can find the values you need on the company's annual report or 10-K:

Noninterest Expenses ÷ (Total Revenue – Interest Expense)

Noninterest Expenses ÷ Net Interest Income before Provision for Loan Losses

Noninterest Expenses ÷ Revenue

Operating Expenses ÷ (Fee Income + Tax Equivalent Net Interest Income)

Look for banks with an efficiency ratio of 50 percent or lower — the lower, the better. As operating costs eat up more of the profit, the efficiency ratio rises.

Checking out the payout ratio

The *payout ratio* is the percentage of profits being used to pay the dividend. For a full explanation, complete with the necessary formula, check out Chapter 8.

Bank payout ratios typically reside around 50 percent. If the ratio rises, is it because the bank has no opportunities to invest the money and grow the company, or is it having a bad year? Neither of these is a good sign, but don't base your decision solely on payout ratio; do more investigating.

Considering some potential banks

The mortgage meltdown may have scorched the financials landscape, but several banks escaped the fire or managed to rise from the ashes. Table 13-3 mentions some of the most notable, but remember: You still have to do your homework and research a company before buying stock in it.

Table 13-3	Financial Companies to Consider		
Yield as of 12/31/09	Name	Ticker Symbol	Annual Dividend
6.9%	New York Community Bancorp Inc.	NYB	$1.00
6.0%	United Bankshares Inc.	UBSI	$1.20
6.4%	Capitol Federal Financial	CFFN	$2.00
6.5%	United Bancshares Inc.	UBOH	$0.60
4.2%	Astoria Financial Corp.	AF	$0.52
5.4%	Canadian Imperial Bank of Commerce	CM	$3.48
4.1%	Trustmark Corp.	TRMK	$0.92
4.2%	Bank of Nova Scotia	BNS	$1.96
3.4%	Cullen/Frost Bankers Inc.	CFR	$1.72
3.6%	Royal Bank of Canada	RY	$2.00
3.9%	Toronto-Dominion Bank	TD	$2.44
2.5%	Westamerica Bancorporation	WABC	$1.40
2.4%	BB&T Corp.	BBT	$0.60

Part IV

Checking Out Dividend Investment Vehicles

The 5th Wave   By Rich Tennant

"I read about investing in a company called Unihandle Ohio, but I'm uneasy about a stock that's listed on the NASDAQ as UhOh."

In this part . . .

Buying shares in a company is sort of like buying cereal. You can purchase one big box of a particular cereal or an assortment. In the world of investing, you have even more options — dividend reinvestment plans (DRIPs), direct purchase programs (DPPs), mutual funds, exchange-traded funds (ETFs), and foreign dividend funds, to name the most popular of the lot.

Don't let the acronyms and investor jargon scare you off. In this part, I explain each of these options in turn, and in plain English; discuss their pros and cons; and show you how to implement them in your dividend investment strategy.

Chapter 14

Compounding Your Returns with Dividend Reinvestment Plans

....

....

Drip, drip, drip . . . Water from a leaky faucet may not seem like much, but at the end of the year, it's likely to account for more than 30 gallons. Likewise, dividends reinvested in a company through a DRIP or DRP (dividend reinvestment plan) can form a surprisingly large pool of investment capital over time. As your shares earn dividends, you pour them back into your investment to buy more shares, which earn more dividends to buy even more shares to earn even bigger dividends — well, you get the idea. If you drip some additional investment capital into the mix, your pool fills even faster.

Companies that offer DRIPs usually run the programs themselves or through an affordable transfer agent and often charge no or minimal transaction fees. In addition, they may even offer a discount so that investors enrolled in the program can pick up shares for less than the current market rate and reinvest dividends without incurring transaction fees. All these benefits and more encourage investors to leave their money in a company for the long haul and continue to invest even more, which is usually good for both the company and the investors.

In this chapter, I bring you up to speed on DRIPs and other direct investing strategies, such as direct stock purchase plans (DSPs). I explain their many advantages, tell you how to enroll in a DRIP, and explain how to calculate your cost basis to take into account the different prices you paid for shares when reinvesting your dividends.

Understanding the Nature of DRIPs and DIPs

A DRIP is one type of *direct investment plan* (DIP). Instead of buying shares on the stock market, you purchase shares directly from the company on a regular basis. Dividends automatically go toward purchasing additional shares, and in many plans you can buy additional shares outside of the dividend-funded purchase, either as a one-time purchase or on a regular basis.

If you need some of that dividend money, many plans offer the option of reinvesting only a portion of your dividends and letting you take the remaining dividends as cash.

Investing through DRIPs is old school — the way investing was intended to be. When you invest through a DRIP, you and the company make a long-term commitment to one another. Every dollar you invest and reinvest is a vote of confidence in the company and its management. To earn your vote, the company is motivated to remain profitable and grow, and with money from you and other investors, it has the capital to do just that.

Don't let the fact that a company has a DRIP or a DIP be the reason you invest in it. Research the company's fundamentals first, as I explain in Chapter 8. Only after identifying companies you want to invest in should you concern yourself with whether the companies offer DRIPs or DIPs.

Recognizing the many names for DIPs

When DRIPs were created more than a half century ago, the main criteria for joining the plan was that you needed to already be a shareholder in the company. Sometimes this rule required owning as little as one share, but you had to buy it through a stockbroker, and all you could do was reinvest the dividends.

As DRIPs became popular in the 1960s, some of these plans evolved to allow investors to purchase their initial shares directly from the company, cutting out the middleman (the broker) entirely. These other plans go under a variety of names, but they all refer to essentially the same thing:

- Direct purchase plans (DPPs)
- Direct stock purchase plans (DSPs)
- Direct enrollment stock purchase plans (DESPs)
- No-load stock purchase plans

Understanding the difference between DRIPs and DSPs

DRIPs and DSPs are kissin' cousins, not identical twins. Both DRIPs and DSPs allow you to reinvest dividends and purchase additional shares of stock. The big difference between the two is that DRIPs still mandate buying your first share through a stockbroker and then enrolling in the plan by submitting an application and the stock certificate. DSPs allow you to enroll in the plan when you buy your first share of stock.

At first glance, DSPs seem like the better deal: hassle-free, without the restrictions imposed on DRIPs. However, DRIPs comprise most of the low- or no-fee plans, whereas many DSPs carry significant fees and even commissions. For more about costs, head to "Looking Out for Fees" later in this chapter.

Managing the plans

Companies vary in how they administer their direct investment plans. Some administer the plans themselves, whereas others work through a transfer agent:

- ✔ **Company:** Some companies have the internal resources to manage their own DRIPs. You may not need to enroll in a DRIP to buy company stock, but you do have to enroll to have your dividends reinvested.

- ✔ **Transfer agent:** A *transfer agent* is a financial institution that specializes in recordkeeping for entities with many small investors, such as publicly-traded companies and mutual funds. Transfer agents record every transaction in the account — deposits and withdrawals. They also produce and send investor mailings and issue stock certificates.

Tracing the roots of DRIPs

Companies originally established DRIPs to enable their employees to invest in the company through stock purchase plans. These companies soon realized that they could expand the program to investors, and because the plans were already in place, they could cost-effectively handle the expansion.

Companies knew that if investors reinvested their dividends, the companies could sell new shares and raise new capital without having to go through the lengthy and expensive regulatory process of a full-blown secondary stock offering. They could sell shares directly to investors for less cost than having to hire an investment bank to underwrite the new shares.

Companies with large capital needs, such as utilities, financials, and real estate companies, realized this strategy was so advantageous to them that they encouraged investors to reinvest

(continued)

(continued)

their dividends by offering discounts of as much as 5 percent off the share price.

The only rule was that participants were required to own at least one share of the company's stock to participate in the program. This rule is still in place for many DRIPs today to restrict participation to employees and investors who are serious about making a long-term commitment to the company. Some DRIPs may waive this rule and let investors buy shares through a direct enrollment plan.

Weighing the Pros and Cons of DRIPs

Prior to investing in anything, examine the potential advantages and drawbacks so that you know what you're getting yourself into before you get into it. With DRIPs, the advantages tend to carry more weight than the disadvantages for long-term dividend investors, but they make little sense for investors who have a high turnover in their portfolios or need to keep their assets more liquid. The following sections explain why.

Perusing the potential advantages

For dividend stock investors who are looking to build wealth over the long haul, few (if any) investment programs can compete with the many advantages DRIPs offer. The following sections reveal and explain the many benefits. Hopefully, after reading through this long list, you'll decide PDQ that DRIPs are A-OK!

Getting started on a shoestring budget

DRIPs are very similar to mutual funds in that they're good for investors starting out with very little capital. With a minimal investment, you can purchase stock in small quantities with low or no fees.

The one big difference is that mutual funds provide you with a portfolio that's diversified to some degree. With DRIP purchases, you own the stock of just one company. Sure, you can diversify your portfolio by enrolling in a number of DRIPs, but it's more costly and complicated than buying mutual fund shares.

One major benefit of DRIPs over mutual funds is that with DRIPs, you don't get stuck paying another investor's tax bill. As I explain in Chapter 20, you have to be careful about your timing when you're buying mutual funds so that you don't end up paying taxes on profits that someone else collected.

Investing at your own pace

Although all DRIPs require a minimum investment to join the plan, you generally have the luxury of investing at your own pace. On top of reinvesting dividends on a regular schedule, these plans offer you the ability to buy more shares through the plan, often with no commissions. This enables you to make additional investments — regularly or only when you have some extra money to invest.

Here's what you can expect:

- ✔ For most plans, the minimum investment can be as little as a single share.

- ✔ Some DPPs have a minimum investment requirement between $250 and $1,000.

- ✔ You may be able to buy additional shares commission-free through optional cash purchase plans (OCPs). Many of these plans allow you to invest as little as $10 at a time, although most set the minimum between $25 and $50 with a maximum close to $10,000. Check the fee structure before investing.

Some companies may even let you set up automatic debits from your bank account to purchase shares on a regular basis. This setup is a perfect way to take advantage of dollar cost averaging (which I cover in Chapter 18) and follow the old rule of personal financial management — pay yourself first.

Saving on broker commissions

DRIPs eliminate the middleman (the broker who charges a commission to process every transaction) because you purchase stock directly from the company that issues it, saving you a ton of money in transaction costs. Compared to a mutual fund, you avoid the load charged every time you make an investment and the hefty management fees deducted from the fund's assets.

The less you shell out in broker commissions, the more money you have to invest.

When the plan reinvests your dividends, you may save even more. In addition to charging no transaction fee, about 100 companies offer a discount on shares purchased with the dividend reinvestment — typically from 1 to 10 percent of the current market price.

If you purchase stock through a brokerage, it may also allow you to reinvest your dividends at no cost, but this arrangement isn't a bona-fide DRIP. These programs lack one main advantage DRIPs — they don't allow you to purchase additional shares directly through the company. As a result, you have to pay a commission to buy additional shares. Ouch!

Taking the emotion out of stock investing

Investing can get emotional. When the market is going well, euphoria drives Wall Street into a buying frenzy, with investors screaming "Buy! Buy! Buy!" In the midst of dramatic economic downturns, fear drives the herd. Those same investors who were once yelling "Buy! Buy! Buy!" are now frantically trying to "Sell! Sell! Sell!"

When you buy a DRIP and commit to investing on a regular schedule, the market's movements have little effect on how you invest. In good times and bad, you calmly and coolly acquire shares, building wealth slowly and more surely.

Compounding growth one drip at a time

In Chapter 3, I tell the story of two investors — Party Pete and Frugal Frank, who each own 100 shares of ABC Inc. at $20 per share. Party Pete spends all of his dividends as he receives them, while Frugal Frank reinvests his by purchasing more shares. At the end of three years, Party Pete sees a total return on his investment of $1,100, while Frugal Frank cashes out a profit of $1,327 — 21 percent higher than the party guy! Investing in a DRIP basically turns you into a Frugal Frank automatically. You don't receive a dividend check tempting you to cash it out and fly to Aruba or use it to pay bills. Every penny in dividends is automatically reinvested for you to purchase additional shares of the company. These additional shares produce dividends, too. By allowing the dividends to be reinvested, you tap into the power of compounding growth without ever having to think about it.

Purchasing fractional ownership

When you purchase stock through a broker, you can't buy a half or a third of a share. With most DRIPs, as with mutual funds, you can. Suppose you earn $100 in dividends, and shares cost $35. Instead of buying only two shares for $70 and having the extra $30 sitting on the sidelines, you can buy 2.86 shares and put all that money to work for you immediately. (Head to Chapter 15 for more on fractional ownership of mutual funds.)

When the next dividend distribution rolls around, you get a fraction of the dividend based on the fractional share you own. If the quarterly dividend per share is 50 cents, you earn $1.43 for those 2.86 shares you purchased: 50 cents each for the two whole shares and then 43 cents for the 0.86 shares. ($.50 × 0.86 = $.43).

Dollar cost averaging without lifting a finger

DRIPs are a perfect way to implement a *dollar cost averaging* strategy — investing a fixed (or in the case of DRIPs, a semifixed) amount of money regularly over time. (For more about dollar cost averaging, check out Chapter 18.) You don't even have to lift a finger because the plan automatically reinvests your dividends for you, purchasing shares on a regular basis regardless of current market conditions or share price.

Looking at the downside

After ticking off the many benefits of DRIPs, you may be tempted to dump your broker and deal direct. Not so fast. As with most things in the world of investing, DRIPs have a flip side — some potential negatives to counterbalance all those positives. Before breaking up with your broker, consider the potential drawbacks highlighted in the following sections.

Buying on the company's schedule regardless of price

When you reinvest dividends, you get a bargain because you buy the new shares right after prices drop due to the dividend payout, giving you more stock for your dividend dollars. However, you may lose out when the time comes to make other stock purchases. You have no control over the price you pay for optional cash purchases, which occur on the company's schedule, not yours. A company may choose to sell OCP shares once a week, once a month, or even once a quarter. (It's always the same day, such as the 15th of the month.) If the stock happens to hit an all-time high that day, well, that's your price.

When you're buying and selling shares directly through a company, you can't issue any of the stop or limit orders I describe in Chapter 19. Of course, if you're investing for the long term, this limitation shouldn't be a huge issue.

Losing liquidity

When you buy and sell stocks through a broker, you can cash out at any time. Just pick up the phone and tell your broker to sell, or log in to your online brokerage account and issue a sell order. The trade occurs within minutes, and in a matter of hours or days you can have the money in your checking or savings account.

When buying and selling shares directly through a company, you relinquish that liquidity. You must contact the company or the plan's transfer agent; obtain, complete, and submit the necessary forms for closing out the DRIP; and then wait for your request to be approved. This process can take a few weeks and may be an available option only once a quarter. You may also incur some fees for closing the account.

Looking out for fees

Although DRIPs are cheap and commission-free, only about half the DRIPs are totally fee-free. As money gets tight, more companies try to quietly slip in fees. As for DSPs, most charge fees, some on every transaction. To protect yourself, read the prospectus to find out what all the fees in the plan are and whether any terms seem unreasonable. Some companies charge $5 for an investment of as little as $25 — that's a 20-percent load on your OCP! ("Investing at your own pace" earlier in this chapter gives you more information on OCPs.)

Check the plan's prospectus (included with the application packet) for any of the following fees:

✔ Set up fees to establish the account may run as high as $25.

✔ Termination fees to close the account may run anywhere from $5 to $25.

✔ Commissions (yes, commissions) in DSPs can be in one or more of the following forms:

  • A flat fee between $2 and $25

  • A percentage of the amount invested, like a load

  • A per-share charge, which can range from a penny to 15 cents a share

A company may nickel and dime you to the point at which you're kicking yourself for not paying your broker $10 for the transaction.

Don't let fees automatically scare you off. If you really like the stock, a direct purchase may still be the more cost-effective way to buy shares.

Paying taxes in a DRIP

Even though you don't receive a check for all those reinvested dividends, the IRS considers them taxable income. Plan for the following (and check out Chapter 20 for more on potential tax issues and qualified dividends):

✔ Dividends earned from new shares purchased through a reinvestment plan the previous quarter are taxed as *qualified* dividends — as in qualified for a lower tax rate.

✔ Dividends from new shares purchased through an OCP must meet the holding period requirements to qualify for the lower tax rate.

Keeping detailed records

For all their benefits, DRIPs provide you with one big fat pain in the neck — recordkeeping. Though you may get a neat printout from the company's transfer agent showing all your trades and tallying which dividends and capital gains qualify for reduced tax rates, you may not. Either way, you alone are responsible for keeping track of each purchase, including the date, number of shares purchased, and price paid, so you know exactly how much you owe in taxes when you sell your shares.

Invest in a good spreadsheet program for your computer or purchase a program specifically for managing DRIP accounts, as I suggest later in this chapter in the section "Calculating the Cost Basis of Shares Acquired through DRIPs."

Enrolling in a DRIP

To enroll in a DRIP, you can't just download an enrollment form, complete it, and then send your form along with a check to the company you want to invest in. No, that would be far too easy (and logical). Before you can do anything, you typically must acquire at least one share and then submit a copy of your share along with an application or enrollment form to request acceptance into the program. The following sections step you through the process.

Prior to enrolling in a DRIP, contact the company's Investor Relations department and request information about the program. The company should be able to supply you with a prospectus that sets out all the details of the plan, including how to enroll, the minimum number of shares required to open an account, how often you can make additional investments, how much you can invest at any one time, how to sell shares, and any fees or other charges you may incur.

Scoring your first share

Enrolling in a DRIP is like being caught up in a chicken-and-egg dilemma: You can't enroll unless you own at least one share of stock in the company, and you can't buy shares unless you're enrolled. This setup is a throwback to the times when DRIPs were created as a way for employees to invest in their company. The company would issue shares to the employee, who could then enroll in the DRIP to have any dividends reinvested. Fortunately, a couple of options are available for clearing this hurdle:

- ✔ About half the DRIPs allow you to purchase your first share through the company DPP.

- ✔ The rest require you to purchase that first share through a regular stockbroker, which means opening an account, meeting the broker's trading requirements, and making a minimum deposit (usually around $1,000).

You've acquired a share. Great, but you're still not done. Now you need to become the *shareholder of record* (the person holding possession of the shares according to the company's records). Even though you usually legally own the shares when you buy stock, the actual shareholder of record is the brokerage firm. This designation keeps your shares safe and simplifies the process of selling shares, lending them out for short sales, or using them to create ETFs (discussed in Chapter 16.) This arrangement usually makes life easier for you as well.

To become the shareholder of record, you must take physical delivery of the shares. Ask the brokerage to send you the actual certificate (and know that the brokerage may charge a fee for this service).

Obtaining an application

After you get a stock certificate in your name, you're ready for the next step in the process — obtaining a copy of the DRIP enrollment application from the company or its transfer agent. If you don't have contact information for the transfer agent, visit the company's Web site. Poke around the site to find the Investor Relations area or call the company and ask to speak with someone in Investor Relations who may be able to send you the application you need or at least put you in touch with the transfer agent. Tell the person you speak with that you need a DRIP application or enrollment form.

Submitting the paperwork

After receiving the DRIP application or enrollment form, complete it, make a copy of it and the stock certificate, and mail both originals (certified mail with confirmation request) to the transfer agent as instructed. The transfer agent processes the paperwork and notifies you when you've been approved to participate in the DRIP (which you will be, assuming you follow the application rules).

When you receive notice of approval, contact Investor Relations or the transfer agent and ask when you can start purchasing additional shares. With some programs, you can begin buying shares immediately. In others, you must wait until you've received your first dividend payment.

Calculating the Cost Basis of Shares Acquired through DRIPs

One of the main challenges of managing DRIPs is calculating the *cost basis* (how much money you pay for your shares) of your investment for tax purposes. As you make additional investments in a company and reinvest your dividends, you pay a different price for each batch of shares you purchase, so your cost basis can vary among the shares you own and changes with each transaction. Unfortunately, you can't simply use an average cost basis when calculating the taxes you own on shares you sell, so you need to keep track of each purchase to know the cost basis of each share.

For tax purposes, keep track of the following information:

- ✔ Total amount of money spent and total number of shares acquired with each purchase.

- ✔ Dividends paid, even if they're reinvested, because dividends are taxed separately.

- ✔ Any discounts the company provides when you purchase shares. This discount qualifies as an additional dividend.

- ✔ Total amount of money and total number of shares acquired with each dividend reinvestment.

- ✔ Any commissions you paid to purchase shares, which can help offset taxes due on dividend payments.

- ✔ Total amount of money received when selling shares and the total number of shares sold.

When selling shares, follow a *first in, first out* (FIFO) strategy in determining your capital gains. In other words, the first shares you purchase are the first shares you sell. This method increases your holding period so that you're more likely to qualify for the lower long-term capital gains tax rate. (Flip to Chapter 20 for details on taxation concerns.)

Keeping track of all the details can be quite a chore. I recommend using a good personal finance program (or an accountant) to keep detailed records and perform all the necessary calculations. Most personal finance programs, including certain versions of Quicken and MS Money, include features for managing investments. You may also consider using a specialized program such as DRIP Wizard (www.dripwizard.com).

Squeezing Out More Information about DRIPs

When you're ready to get serious about direct investing and reinvesting and have a craving for information about specific companies that offer these plans, check out the following resources:

- ✔ The Moneypaper at www.directinvesting.com (see the nearby sidebar)

- ✔ The Direct Purchase Plan Clearinghouse at www.enrolldirect.com

- ✔ Direct Investment at www.wall-street.com/direct.html

- ✔ DRIP Central at www.dripcentral.com

Because transfer companies commonly manage plans for multiple companies, they're also good sources of information about specific plans. Two of the larger transfer companies are

- ✔ First Share at www.firstshare.com
- ✔ One Share at www.oneshare.com

Checking out Moneypaper

The Moneypaper is a company that specializes in teaching investors about direct investment plans. A subscription to its monthly financial newsletter, *Moneypaper,* costs about $153, but it offers deals all over the Internet to first-time subscribers. Your subscription also gives you access to Moneypaper's Web site (www.directinvesting.com), which lists all the companies that offer DRIPs. Moneypaper also publishes a bimonthly newsletter called *DirectInvesting,* which follows six portfolios, and an annual book entitled *The Moneypaper's Guide to Direct Investment Plans.*

The Moneypaper offers a unique service to help investors sign up for DRIPs. Its affiliate broker, Temper of the Times Investor Services, acts as your stockbroker. Temper buys one share of the company for you, registers you immediately as the shareholder of record, sends the stock certificate to the transfer agent, signs you up for the DRIP, and opens the account for you. The fee for this service ranges from $15 to $50, but it sure takes the hassles out of getting started.

To keep transaction costs down, Temper gathers orders from investors throughout the month, closes the offering on the last day of the month, and orders the stock on the 10th of the following month.

Chapter 15

Diversifying Your Dividends through Mutual Funds

In This Chapter

▶ Getting up to speed on mutual funds

▶ Understanding the costs of mutual fund investing

▶ Choosing dividend mutual funds

▶ Checking out some dividend mutual funds worth looking at

---

*N*o doubt about it, building and managing a successful dividend stock portfolio requires a fair amount of expertise and a whole lot of work. For people who want to follow a dividend stock strategy but don't have the time, skill, or interest in building a portfolio, mutual funds and ETFs (exchange-traded funds) provide a solution.

This chapter describes how mutual funds work and how you can use them to build a diverse portfolio that takes advantage of the dividend stock strategy. To focus on ETFs, skip to Chapter 16.

Taking a Refresher Course on Mutual Funds

Mutual funds are investment companies that pool money from many investors to buy securities and create a portfolio more diverse than most investors would be able to assemble on their own. Each investor shares in the fund's profit or loss according to the number of shares they own. The fund brings in more investing money by selling shares of the portfolio to the public. As an open-end investment company (see the nearby sidebar), the mutual fund can sell as many shares as people want to buy, using the money to purchase additional assets.

The following sections bring you quickly up to speed on the basics of mutual funds so that you can determine whether you want them to play a role in your dividend investment strategy.

Recognizing different types of investment companies

Not all investment companies are created equal. Before buying shares in an investment company, recognize the differences among the three main types of companies:

✔ **Open-end investment companies** accept investors at all times and have no restrictions on the number of shares they sell. When investors want their money, they redeem their shares by selling them back to the investment company (fund) at the going rate. The fund then pulls these shares out of circulation. Mutual funds and ETFs are both open-end funds.

✔ **Closed-end investment companies** issue a fixed number of shares in an initial public offering (IPO) just as public companies issue stock. You buy these shares on the stock exchange from other investors, not from the fund company.

✔ **Unit Investment Trusts** are similar to open-end companies in that they can sell an unlimited number of shares to meet investor demand. Unlike open-end funds, however, UITs have no manager or board of directors to change the UIT's components after it launches. So, the UIT is pretty much a static portfolio for its limited lifetime. Because no manager is in charge, a UIT can't reinvest the dividends earned in the portfolio.

Remember: Investment companies are highly regulated entities that must register with the SEC. They're organized under the Investment Company Act of 1940, better known as the 1940 Act. Hedge funds are private, unregulated investment pools.

Open-end and closed-end funds fall into the category of managed investment companies; UITs are unmanaged. In a managed fund, the manager can adjust the portfolio, but the unmanaged UIT is a static portfolio. Another difference is that managed funds come with a higher price tag to cover compensation for their managers. For more about the costs of investing specifically through mutual funds, check out "A Necessary Evil: Paying Someone to Manage Your Mutual Fund Investments" later in this chapter.

Examining the pros and cons of mutual funds

Owning shares of a mutual fund is a trade-off. Mutual funds provide investors with an easier way to build and manage a diversified portfolio, but investors relinquish control over which stocks the portfolio holds. That's the biggie. The following sections provide a more detailed list of the trade-offs you can expect.

Advantages

Mutual funds offer a host of benefits that essentially boil down to simplicity and diversity. Mutual funds

✔ Are easy to buy and sell

✔ Offer a diversified portfolio with a minimal investment

✔ Are run by a professional portfolio manager who does all the research and decides which securities to buy

✔ Work well with the dollar cost averaging strategy (discussed later in this chapter and Chapter 18)

✔ Require little work from investors

✔ Are regulated by the SEC

✔ Reinvest dividends

✔ Keep track of all the bookkeeping involved

✔ Allow for redemptions over the phone

✔ Permit the purchase of fractional shares

A *fractional share* is a part of a share. If you plan to invest $100 a month to buy shares of a favorite stock selling for $75 a share, you can only buy one share because stocks sell in whole units. You then have $25 sitting around until you come up with another $50. However, if you invest with a mutual fund, the fund invests the entire $100. If one share of the mutual fund sells for $75, the fund sells you 1⅓ shares of the fund.

Disadvantages

Many of the disadvantages of mutual funds are simply the flip side of the advantages — you willingly relinquish control over which equities are included in the portfolio because you don't have the time, energy, or inclination to do the research yourself. However, before you invest in a mutual fund, be aware of the following drawbacks:

✔ Mutual funds charge management fees.

✔ All taxes are passed on to and paid by the shareholders.

✔ Some charge big commissions.

✔ Shares don't trade like stocks — they have only one price during the day.

✔ The actions of other investors in the fund affect the amount of capital gains taxes you pay.

✔ Mutual funds may incur other costs, such as transaction fees for the stocks it buys and sells.

Diversifying on the cheap

In Chapter 4, I encourage you to diversify your investments to mitigate your risks. In other words, don't put all your golden goose eggs in one basket. One of the biggest challenges to creating a diverse portfolio is coming up with enough money to purchase a wide variety of stocks. In addition, paying sales commissions on all those transactions, tracking so many different stocks, and handling the bookkeeping related to them can cost additional time and money and make your head spin.

The solution? Mutual funds, which offer instant diversification — and you may even save commission.

Suppose you have only $2,000 to invest. One option is to purchase 80 shares of a small pharmaceutical company at 25 bucks a pop. Unfortunately, this option leaves you with a very concentrated portfolio. If the company's blockbuster drug fails to earn FDA approval, you stand to lose a good chunk of your investment. Another option is to purchase 10 shares of 20 different companies for $10 apiece. This strategy gives you some diversity, but the transaction fees take a bite out of that $2,000. A third option is to purchase $2,000 worth of shares in a mutual fund with 500 different stocks in its portfolio. Option three gives you a far more diversified portfolio than the other two options, without the added cost of commissions (though you likely pay management fees). Even with a management fee, this route is still usually less than paying commissions.

Investment companies have become the main savings vehicle for most Americans because they provide a quick and easy way to build and maintain a diversified portfolio with a minimal investment.

Reaping the benefits of dollar cost averaging

Dollar cost averaging is a method of systematically investing in anything over a long time period to achieve a reasonable average price for the asset. Mutual funds are great vehicles for following a dollar cost averaging strategy for a couple of reasons:

✔ You can buy a little at a time without having to pay a broker for every purchase.

✔ You can buy fractional shares. In a no-load fund (where you pay no commission), the ability to buy fractional shares means every single dollar you invest goes into the fund and goes to work immediately instead of sitting in cash waiting for enough to buy a full share.

For more about dollar cost averaging, check out Chapter 18.

Understanding how funds pay dividends

Funds are required to distribute any income in excess of their expenses. If the dividend yield is 1 percent of the fund's assets, and the expense ratio (operating expenses) is 1 percent of the fund's assets, the fund uses the dividend to pay the expenses, and investors receive no income. On the other hand, if the dividend yield is 3 percent of the fund's assets, the fund uses 1 percent to pay the expenses and then distributes the remaining 2 percent as dividends. If the mutual fund is focused on producing income, it will pay a dividend.

Mutual funds receive dividends much the same way as individual investors do. The companies whose shares the fund holds mail checks to the fund for the dividend amount. At the end of either every month or every fiscal quarter, the fund adds up all the dividends received from its holdings and divides by the total number of shares to determine the amount of dividends per fund share.

If the fund pays out too much "income," some of it can be classified as a return on capital, which falls under capital gains for tax purposes. See "Getting stuck paying taxes" later in this chapter for more about how returns on mutual fund investments are taxed.

A Necessary Evil: Paying Someone to Manage Your Mutual Fund Investments

When you invest in a mutual fund, you're hiring a professional — the individual running the fund — to manage your investments. Unfortunately, this person doesn't work for free. Managing a diversified portfolio that earns reasonable returns requires some expertise, time, and effort — all of which you pay for either in fees or commissions.

Some fund managers earn their keep, and many don't; all charge fees that can put a serious dent in the money you have available to invest, and they may perform no better than a standard S&P 500 Index fund that charges next to nothing. When investing in mutual funds, you really need to look at the costs to maximize the net return on your investment. In the following sections, I explain key factors to consider.

You can never guarantee the returns your fund will produce; however, you can always know what the fees will be. Your goal is to find a fund that produces the most consistent, and hopefully largest, return for the smallest amount of expenses. (Be aware that annual reports from mutual funds typically show the performance of the fund prior to deducting expenses and loads.)

Avoid funds with high expense ratios and loads. These costs can significantly reduce your capital gains.

Analyzing a fund's management style

Choosing a mutual fund is often a matter of choosing a management style, investment theme, or even a specific fund manager. All mutual funds follow an investing theme, such as buying the stocks of large U.S. companies or the bonds of emerging market economies. Some funds and their managers are very proactive in managing the portfolio — they may buy and sell shares daily to maximize the funds' returns. Others are more passive — building a solid portfolio and adjusting its holdings only occasionally, if at all.

In *actively managed funds* the manager has the freedom to buy and sell whatever stock or bond she wants, whenever she wants, as long as she stays within the investing theme. Almost every mutual fund that follows a dividend-based or income-focused strategy is actively managed, but many don't charge a load (see the following section).

With a *passively managed fund,* the manager receives not just a theme but typically also an index to track, such as the S&P 500 Index or the Russell 2000 Index. He doesn't have the freedom to buy and sell whatever stocks he wants — he's locked into the index. Because the portfolio must perform in line with the index, he buys only the index components or a close approximation. Index funds are classic examples of passively managed mutual funds.

Accounting for expense ratios

Every fund is required to state its *expense ratio* or annual operating expenses. The expense ratio breaks down into three parts: management fees, 12b-1 costs, and other expenses.

- ✓ **Management fees:** Managers of active funds must hire research staffs to scope out new investments on a continual basis. They also need to keep on top of all market developments to buy and sell securities at the best time to maximize profits. On top of that, the managers need to manage all the other functions that a mutual fund performs, including accounting, record keeping, administration, and distribution, to name a few.

  Management fees for passively managed funds are significantly lower than management fees for actively managed funds because managers of passive funds don't have the added expenses of research or stock selection.

- ✓ **12b-1 fees:** This special marketing fee (named after a section of the 1940 Act) pays for promotion and advertising of the fund. Some people think it's a hidden commission, but it basically goes to pay brokers to keep selling these funds. The fee is typically 0.25 percent, but can go as high as 1 percent.

- ✓ **Operating expenses:** This all-encompassing category covers all the other costs necessary to run the fund, paying for the fund's administrator, custodian, transfer agent, accountant, index provider, and distributor.

Should I hire a financial advisor?

You meet two kinds of mutual fund investors: those who use a financial advisor and those who don't. If you're buying and selling individual dividend stocks on your own, consulting a financial advisor can be beneficial, especially when you're first starting out. If you're simply buying shares in a mutual fund, hiring a financial advisor may only add another expense. By reading this chapter, you should have the knowledge you need to research and choose mutual funds that meet your investment needs. Pick a mutual fund with a good manager and you already have a financial guru on your side.

Financial advisors who give advice on how to steer through the financial waters work under many titles. They can be called stockbrokers, certified financial planners (CFP), or registered investment advisors (RIA). Each one has different characteristics. The best choice is usually a CFP or RIA who takes a percentage of your assets to run your portfolio for you. Much like the fund manager who takes a percentage of the funds assets, this arrangement aligns the investment advisor's interest to yours. When you make money, he makes money, so it gives him incentive to perform well for you.

The average expense ratio for an actively managed fund is about 1.3 percent of the fund's total assets, and the management fees typically account for the lion's share of that figure. The nice thing about paying a percentage rather than a set fee is that the fund manager's interests are more aligned with yours. If your assets increase in value, she makes more money. If your assets decrease in value, she makes less money. Paying a management fee isn't necessarily a bad thing as long as the return you receive justifies the fees.

Paying for the privilege with loads

Because mutual funds don't trade on the stock exchange, brokers can't charge a typical commission, so they charge a special commission called a *load,* which is another cost on top of the expense ratio. There are three different kinds of loads: front-end load, back-end load, and no load.

- ✔ **Front-end load:** The front-end load is a percentage of your investment taken off the top and paid to the broker at the front end of the investment — the moment you buy shares. For instance, if you buy $100 worth of shares in a fund with a 5-percent load, you pay the broker $5 and invest $95 in the fund. You immediately invest less than you wanted to, which decreases your returns going forward. Typically, the shares that charge a front-end load are called *Class A shares.*

- ✔ **Back-end load:** In the back-end load, the broker takes his percentage when you sell your shares rather than when you buy them. If you sell $1,000 worth of fund shares, the fund with a 5-percent back-end load pays the broker $50 and leaves you with $950. Because the object is to have more money coming out of the fund than going in, the broker stands to make more with a back-load fund than with a front-load fund. However, the percentage of a back-end load gets smaller every year until it disappears five to ten years after the investment, so if you're in the fund for the very long term, you can avoid paying a back-end load when you sell. *Class B shares* typically charge a back-end load.

✔ **No load:** No-load funds charge no load when you buy or sell your shares. Because you research the fund and fill out the forms to purchase it, you essentially pay yourself the broker's load, which, of course, you invest into the fund. Invest $1,000, and all of that money goes toward the purchase of shares. When you sell, you keep all the money, except for any taxes you owe on your gains. To maximize your profits, I recommend you buy only no-load funds.

The load goes to the financial advisor or stockbroker who sells you the fund, not the actual mutual fund or its managers.

Many funds with loads also sell their funds through 401(k) retirement plans as *Class C shares.* Because a 401(k) plan is a closed system with limited choices, the fund companies don't charge investors a load to invest within the 401(k). However, they do typically charge a higher expense ratio.

Because mutual funds' annual reports often show performance without accounting for load and expense deductions, a no-load fund with a small expense ratio may actually provide a bigger return on your investment than a fund with a high load and expense ratio that performs better.

You can sometimes buy a loaded fund without paying a load if you join a mutual fund supermarket at a company like Charles Schwab.

If you use a financial advisor, make sure you're hiring a *fiduciary* — someone legally responsible for making investments in your best interests. A stockbroker isn't required to be a fiduciary. He needs to make appropriate investments for your risk level, but he doesn't have to present you with the most affordable choice. If two similar funds are available and one pays him a 5-percent load, the broker can sell you the one that costs you more and earns him more money. For more information on hiring a financial advisor check out Chapter 19.

Investing in Dividend-Focused Mutual Funds

Mutual funds abound, and many of them focus more on capital appreciation than on dividends and income, so you have to be selective. In the following sections, I explain how to dig up information on mutual funds, identify dividend-focused funds, and understand how share prices are calculated. In addition, I reveal how mutual funds pay out dividends and detail some of the tax implications related to these payouts.

Finding information on mutual funds

Most of the Web sites I mention in Chapter 7 offer information on mutual funds as well as individual companies. For information that's more focused on mutual funds, check out the following resources:

- ✔ **Morningstar:** This company's main focus is the evaluation and rating of mutual funds. The Morningstar Web site (www.morningstar.com) offers tons of information about performance, fees, and management. You can often find analyst reports on specific funds.

- ✔ **Lipper:** Lipper features an extensive rating system for mutual funds called the Lipper Leaders. It classifies funds in five areas: total return, consistent return, preservation of capital, tax efficiency, and expenses. Funds that do well in the majority of categories are called Lipper Leaders. Go to www. lipperleaders.com to get to the Lipper Research Center.

- ✔ **Charles Schwab:** In addition to selling its own mutual funds, Schwab runs what it calls a mutual fund supermarket — a platform that allows you to buy and sell thousands of funds with no loads or transaction fees. It also offers load funds. In addition, it contains research reports and screens to help you make more informed decisions.

For additional information about a fund, visit the fund company's Web site, where you can usually find gobs of information on the funds, as well as an online prospectus and application forms.

Spotting dividend-focused mutual funds

When shopping for dividend-focused mutual funds, don't let the names of the funds confuse you. Some mutual funds that advertise themselves as dividend funds hold plenty of growth stocks, and many mutual funds that do deal exclusively in dividend stocks don't even have the word *dividend* in their name. What's a dividend investor to do?

The first step is to screen for dividend funds. You can do so using any of the online tools presented in the preceding section. For example, the Lipper Leaders Web site enables you to screen for Equity Income Funds.

Another strategy is to look for funds that have any of the following words in their names: *total return, income,* or *value.* Some income funds or blend funds can also hold bonds, generating income from both stocks and bonds, but searching for income or value funds should screen out most of the funds that have nothing to do with dividends.

When researching funds, carefully examine their holdings to determine what portion of the portfolio is comprised of companies that pay dividends. In the fund's prospectus, read its investment objective to determine what kind of strategy you're getting into. Look for mutual funds that have a yield greater than the yield on the S&P 500 Index. Any funds that fall short of this benchmark don't really qualify as dividend funds. Even among funds that focus on dividends, you can find significant differences in strategy and goals, as exemplified in the following list:

✔ Al Frank Dividend Value Fund (VALDX) is an actively-managed fund, but even though at least 80 percent of the portfolio is made up of dividend-paying stocks, it seeks total return from capital appreciation, and to a lesser extent, dividend income.

✔ Aston/River Road Dividend All Cap Value Fund (ARDEX) also invests at least 80 percent of its capital in dividend-paying stocks, but it focuses on providing high income through dividends. Long-term capital appreciation is a secondary concern.

✔ Alpine Dynamic Dividend Fund (ADVDX) focuses on yield much more than total return. It buys high-yielding stocks, holds onto them long enough to get the low tax rate, and then sells them for other high-yielding stocks. This strategy clearly works; as you can see in Table 15-1 at the end of this chapter, this fund posted one of the highest yields for 2009. However, as I point out in Chapter 8, high-yielding stocks can sometimes have problems, which can negatively affect total return.

✔ Hennessy Total Return Fund (HDOGX) uses a strategy in which it seeks a return by allocating 75 percent of the portfolio to the Dogs of the Dow dividend strategy (which I explain in Chapter 18), and 25 percent of the portfolio to U.S. Treasury bills.

✔ RNC Genter Dividend Income Fund (GDIIX) eliminates stocks with a yield below 2.5 percent and tries to capture twice the yield of the S&P 500.

✔ Hodges Equity Income Fund (HDPEX) focuses on total return and long-term capital appreciation by holding companies with a growth and income focus that consistently raise their dividend.

As with dividend stocks, you want to look for funds that raise their dividend distribution, because they invest in companies that consistently increase their payouts. A fund that has a rising dividend is making good investment choices from the payout perspective. And just like dividend stocks, you want the dividend fund to have regular payouts and less volatility than growth funds.

Understanding a fund's share price

Shares of mutual funds are sold and priced differently than shares of stock. Shares of stock trade on the stock exchange between investors. The market drives the price, which can rise or fall throughout the day according to investor demand. On the other hand, you buy mutual fund shares directly from the fund.

To determine the mutual fund's share price the fund company first calculates its *net asset value* (NAV). When the market closes, the fund obtains the end-of-day price for every equity held in the portfolio and multiplies each separate value by the number of shares the fund holds of that particular equity to determine its value. It then adds up the values of all equities in the portfolio and subtracts any liabilities to determine the NAV:

NAV = Total Value of All Equities – Liabilities

If the fund has $30 million in stocks and liabilities of $3 million, the NAV would be $27 million:

$30 million – $3 million = $27 million

To calculate the share price or NAV per share, the fund divides the NAV by the total number of shares sold to investors. Continuing from the previous example, if the fund sold 900,000 shares to investors, the NAV per share would be $30:

$27 million ÷ 900,000 shares = $30/share

Although you must place an order to buy or sell shares of a mutual fund when the stock market is open, you don't know what price you will pay. That's because the fund needs the closing price of every equity before it can calculate the NAV, and it can't get that until after the market's 4 p.m. close.

Reinvesting mutual fund dividends

When you first invest in a mutual fund that holds shares in companies that pay dividends, you need to specify what you want to do with the dividends. Typically, you have three choices — leave the cash in the account, receive the dividend as a check, or reinvest the dividend and buy new shares at the current NAV:

✔ **Leave the cash in an account:** If you choose to leave the cash in the account, it just sits there until you tell the fund manager what to do with it — buy more shares of the same fund, buy shares of another fund in the same fund family, or withdraw the cash. In some cases, the money earns interest.

> ✔ **Get a check:** Much like a dividend-paying company, the fund cuts you a check when it announces its dividend payout. Some pay on a monthly basis and some on a quarterly basis. This setup allows you do whatever you want with the dividend. You can use it to go on vacation or buy a completely different investment.
>
> ✔ **Reinvest the dividend:** Mutual funds make reinvesting the dividend very easy. They simply use the dividends to buy more fund shares and send you a statement to show you how much you bought. For most funds, reinvesting the dividend is the default option and the best choice for long-term growth and income.

An added benefit of reinvesting is that the share prices fall after their ex-dividend dates (see Chapter 2 for more on the significance of this date). This drop lowers the fund's NAV, and because the fund doesn't receive the dividends until after the ex-dividend date, it reinvests them for you at the lower NAV.

Getting stuck paying taxes

Dividends from mutual funds are taxed just like dividends from stocks; those that don't qualify for the 15-percent tax rate are taxed at your ordinary income tax rate. However, mutual funds don't pay taxes — mutual fund investors do. Mutual funds are called *pass-through vehicles* because the tax liability passes through the fund to the shareholder. In addition, because actively managed mutual funds buy and sell shares on a regular basis, they earn significant capital gains. At the end of the year, the fund sends you a tax form telling you how much of these capital gains are short-term gains and how much are long-term gains. *Short-term gains* (on securities held for less than a year) are taxed at your ordinary tax rate, and long-term gains are taxed at 15 percent or less. For a detailed explanation of which dividends qualify for lower tax rates, head to Chapter 20.

Good funds manage their payouts so that most dividends qualify for the lower tax rate. Part of your research should look at how much of the dividends that the fund pays out qualify for the lower tax rate and what percentage of dividends don't. Obviously, you want a fund that pays out a very high percentage of dividends that qualify for the lower tax rate.

Spotting a good pick: A checklist

Typically, if you buy an actively managed fund, you're paying the fund manager to produce returns that beat his market benchmark. For large U.S. equity funds, that benchmark is the S&P 500; for small U.S. equity funds, it's the Russell 2000. For a dividend fund, you're obviously more concerned with making income, so you give up some potential for capital appreciation from non-dividend paying stocks in exchange for immediate income and less volatility.

In other words, as a dividend investor, you shouldn't expect the fund's return from capital appreciation to beat an index that holds growth stocks. However, you do want to see less volatility in the NAV and that the fund's total return with dividend income comes close to the index.

Now that you know now to evaluate mutual funds, look for funds that meet or exceed the following criteria:

✔ **No load:** The amount of money you lose to loads can significantly decrease your portfolio and its potential for capital gains. (Flip to the earlier section "Paying for the privilege with loads" for more on these expenses.) I include funds with loads in Table 15-1 (at the end of this chapter) for investors who decide to use financial advisors who don't sell no-load funds.

✔ **Expense ratio below 2 percent:** Expense ratio fees also eat into your capital appreciation, as I discuss in the earlier section "Accounting for expense ratios." Make sure the dividend yield exceeds the expense ratio so that your income covers your costs and then some. That way you at least capture all the fund's capital appreciation, even though you're spending some of your dividends. The higher the fees, the less likely the returns you receive from the fund will actually beat the market. I would never buy a fund that charges an expense ratio higher than 2 percent. Lower is better, and Table 15-1 contains quite a few under 1 percent. However, sometimes paying a little higher fee for consistently better performance is worth the price.

✔ **Fund's 12-month yield exceeds the 12-month yield of the benchmark index:** If the fund's 12-month yield doesn't beat the index, you're better off buying the index fund. From December 1936 through March 2009, the average yield for the S&P 500 Index was 3.814 percent. At the end of 2009, the S&P 500's 12-month dividend yield was 2.01 percent versus the 3.14 percent yield for December 2008. The yield is based on the cash dividends paid over the prior four quarters and the closing quarterly price.

✔ **Minimum returns:** Remember that share prices fluctuate, so dividend investors are willing to give up big gains in capital appreciation in return for steady dividend payouts higher than the benchmark index's yield. Don't be afraid to look at funds with a total return that is 1 or 2 percentage points lower than the index.

✔ **Established:** Don't buy new funds. You want a fund with a track record — the longer the better. You want to be able to see how the fund performs in a variety of market conditions. Be wary of anything with less than a three-year record. If you know an experienced manager who is starting her own fund, you may invest a little bit, but consider this investment very risky until she builds a record.

✔ **Five-year-plus history of consistently increasing dividend payments:** After all the other criteria, this one really boils it all down. Plenty of no-load funds have decent yields, but as with dividend stocks, you want your dividends to grow. A five-year record shows that the manager knows how to consistently pick stocks that have growing dividends.

Meeting Some Premier Dividend Mutual Funds

When you make a commitment to investing in dividend stocks, you automatically screen out more than half of the mutual funds. You can further narrow your list by focusing on the top performers. Table 15-1 lists the highest yielding U.S. funds with minimum investments of no more than $10,000; I've listed them in descending order by their annual yields (as of December 31, 2009).

Though not all of these funds use the S&P 500 Index as their benchmark, here are the S&P results for a comparison: The yield was 2.01 percent, the one-year return was 26.46 percent, the three-year return was –5.62 percent, and the five-year return was 0.42 percent.

Table 15-1		U.S. Mutual Funds with Highest Yields through 12/31/2009							
Fund Name	Ticker Symbol	Category	12-mth Yield	1-yr Return	3-yr Return	5-yr Return	Front Load	Expense Ratio	Minimum Initial Purchase
Pimco Fundamental Index Plus	PIXAX	Large Blend	58.06	56.60	–1.96	NA	3.75	1.19	1,000
Metropolitan West AlphaTrak 500	MWATX	Large Blend	41.22	39.68	–12.43	–3.77	0.0	0.22	5,000
Alpine Dynamic Dividend	ADVDX	Large Blend	21.10	25.65	–12.03	–2.20	0.00	1.18	1,000

Fund Name	Ticker Symbol	Category	12-mth Yield	1-yr Return	3-yr Return	5-yr Return	Front Load	Expense Ratio	Minimum Initial Purchase
ING Strat Allocation Growth Port I	ISAGX	Large Blend	9.82	25.38	−5.60	0.22	0.00	0.33	0
Eaton Vance Enhanced Equity Option Inc A	EEEAX	Large Blend	8.03	18.64	NA	NA	5.75	1.50	1,000
Eaton Vance Dividend Income A	EDIAX	Large Value	7.03	10.44	−7.53	NA	5.75	1.33	1,000
Eaton Vance Tax-Managed Dividend Inc A	EADIX	Large Value	5.81	20.73	−5.31	1.35	5.75	1.21	1,000
Putnam Asset Allocation: Growth A	PAEAX	Large Blend	4.37	36.88	−4.32	2.51	5.75	1.22	500
ING Retirement Growth Class Instl	IIRGX	Large Blend	4.34	26.61	−5.77	NA	0.00	0.16	0
Wasatch Strategic Income	WASIX	Mid-Cap Value	4.29	38.03	−7.02	NA	0.00	0.95	2,000
Rochdale Dividend & Income	RIMHX	Mid-Cap Value	4.22	19.21	−2.76	2.68	5.75	1.35	1,000
RiverSource Dividend Opportunity A	INUTX	Large Value	4.20	28.71	−4.58	2.84	5.75	1.03	2,000
ING Fidelity VIP Mid Cap Adv	VPFAX	Mid-Cap Growth	4.08	38.89	−1.46	4.67	0.00	0.55	2,000
AIM Moderate Growth Allocation A	AAMGX	Large Blend	3.93	30.53	−3.97	NA	5.50	0.37	1,000

(continued)

Table 15-1 *(continued)*

Fund Name	Ticker Symbol	Category	12-mth Yield	1-yr Return	3-yr Return	5-yr Return	Front Load	Expense Ratio	Minimum Initial Purchase
ING Corporate Leaders Trust Series B	LEXCX	Large Value	3.82	12.15	−4.19	3.09	0.00	0.51	1,000
Eaton Vance Dividend Builder A	EVTMX	Large Blend	3.76	12.88	−4.69	6.00	5.75	1.05	1,000
Marisco Flexible Capital	MFCFX	Large Growth	3.65	51.09	4.47	NA	0.00	0.75	2,500
Industry Leaders D	ILFDX	Large Blend	3.63	25.08	−4.16	1.84	0.00	0.76	10,000
Federated Strategic Value A	SVAAX	Large Value	3.51	11.64	−8.37	NA	5.50	1.04	1,500
MFS Blended Research Core Equity	MUSEX	Large Blend	3.36	25.24	−4.71	2.01	0.00	0.60	0
RiverSource Disciplined Equity A	AQEAX	Large Blend	3.26	21.42	−7.83	−0.64	5.75	0.95	2,000
Oppenheimer Equity Income A	OAEIX	Large Value	3.23	42.21	−2.05	3.12	5.75	1.36	1,000
SunAmerica Focused Dividend Strategy A	FDSAX	Large Value	3.11	47.83	1.00	3.67	5.75	0.94	500
Fifth Third LifeModel Moderately Aggressive A	LMAAX	Large Blend	3.08	21.70	−4.41	0.76	5.00	0.33	1,000

Fund Name	Ticker Symbol	Category	12-mth Yield	1-yr Return	3-yr Return	5-yr Return	Front Load	Expense Ratio	Minimum Initial Purchase
Vanguard Equity Income	VEIPX	Large Value	3.05	17.10	−5.36	1.31	0.00	0.36	3,000
JHT Lifestyle Growth Series 1	JELGX	Large Blend	3.01	33.30	−3.14	2.30	0.00	0.12	0
ING Opportunity	IIVOX	Large Blend	2.93	15.10	−8.61	−1.06	0.00	0.71	0
CSI Equity Investor	CSIIX	Large Blend	2.93	20.32	−4.22	1.65	0.00	0.99	1,000
American Funds American Mutual A	AMRMX	Large Value	2.89	25.43	−3.21	2.04	5.75	0.66	250
Federated Equity Income A	LEIFX	Large Value	2.88	15.71	−5.96	1.11	5.50	1.13	1,500
American Funds Washington Mutual A	AWSHX	Large Value	2.86	18.98	−6.11	0.23	5.75	0.65	250
Consulting Group Large Cap Value Equity	TLVUX	Large Value	2.81	22.70	−8.96	−0.47	0.00	0.71	100
RiverSource 120/20 Contrarian Equity A	RCEAX	Large Blend	2.81	42.73	NA	NA	5.75	1.50	10,000
ING Index Plus LargeCap Port 1	IPLIX	Large Blend	2.79	23.20	−6.69	−0.38	0.00	0.47	0
Franklin Equity Income A	FISEX	Large Value	2.79	26.42	−7.62	−1.09	5.75	1.04	1,000

(continued)

Table 15-1 *(continued)*

Fund Name	Ticker Symbol	Category	12-mth Yield	1-yr Return	3-yr Return	5-yr Return	Front Load	Expense Ratio	Minimum Initial Purchase
RNG Genter Dividend Income	GDIIX	Large Value	2.48	19.55	NA	NA	0.00	1.25	2,500
Aston/ River Road Dividend All Cap Val N	ARDEX	Mid-Cap Value	2.08	21.33	−4.52	NA	0.00	1.21	2,500
Al Frank Dividend Value Fund	VALDX	Large Value	1.11	24.41	−6.50	0.30	0.00	1.98	1,000

Courtesy of Morningstar, Inc., 2010

Chapter 16

Tapping the Best of Both Worlds with Exchange-Traded Funds

....

In This Chapter

▶ Introducing exchange-traded funds (ETFs)

▶ Counting the many blessings of ETFs

▶ Following the dividend flow (and accompanying tax issues)

▶ Getting up to speed on fundamental indexing

▶ Checking out some potential picks

....

*E*xchange-traded funds, better known as ETFs, are the mutual funds for the 21st century. They're investment companies similar to mutual funds but have some significant differences and advantages. (For the lowdown on investment companies and mutual funds, check out Chapter 15.)

This chapter provides everything you need to know to begin investing intelligently in ETFs, including what they are and where to find additional information about specific funds.

Understanding the ETF Difference

The easiest way to think about ETFs is as mutual *funds* that *trade* on an *exchange* like stocks — hence, the name. They're a fairly new concept made possible by the wonders of modern technology: computers. Seventy years ago, when the Investment Company Act of 1940 gave birth to the modern mutual fund, computers weren't around in the financial industry. As a result, a fund manager had to wait until the market's close to price the stocks in each portfolio and determine its net asset value (NAV). This method is still the modus operandi for mutual funds, as I explain in Chapter 15, but ETFs play by different rules.

Although the ETF determines its true NAV this same way every evening, during the trading day ETFs can move away from the NAV. ETFs trade like stocks based on the demand for shares, so their prices fluctuate throughout the 9:30-a.m.-to-4-p.m. session.

Behind the scenes with ETFs

A lot of the ETF's benefits come from the unique way the fund acquires the basket of securities it holds in its portfolio. Unlike mutual fund investors, ETF investors don't buy or sell their shares directly with the fund, but rather with other investors on the stock exchange. To get to the stock exchange, ETF shares go through a *creation process* with a select, small group of broker-dealers or specialists known as the *authorized participants,* or *APs.* That's because ETFs only sell shares in lots of 50,000 called *creation units.*

Basically, the AP and the ETF make a cashless trade. In order for the AP to get ETF shares, it must gather together a basket of securities that match the index the ETF tracks. To do this, the AP either buys the shares on the stock market or pulls them from its massive inventory of securities. For example, if the ETF tracks the S&P 500, the AP assembles a basket of 50,000 shares of each of the 500 companies in the

S&P 500, in the proper weighting. Then instead of paying cash, the AP exchanges its basket of securities for the ETF's creation unit. This even trade of stocks for ETF shares is called an *in-kind trade* and bypasses stockbrokers, avoiding commissions. Even more important, the cashless in-kind trade creates no taxable events, so the ETF almost never incurs capital gains. Thus, ETF investors rarely pay the capital gains taxes inflicted on mutual fund investors. For more on capital gains, see "Achieving Greater Tax Efficiency" later in the chapter.

After the AP makes the in-kind trade, it takes the 50,000 newly minted ETF shares and sells them on the secondary market to investors large and small. If demand for ETF shares is great enough, the AP can form additional baskets of stock to trade for ETF creation units so that it has more ETF shares to sell. If demand drops, the AP can redeem a basket of ETF shares for a basket consisting of the original 50,000 shares.

ETFs come in two varieties: *open-end investment companies* (funds) or *unit investment trusts* (UITs). The main difference between them is that open-end funds have fund managers and UITs don't. However, neither type has restrictions on how many shares it can sell; ETFs can sell as many shares as needed to fill investor demand. And when investors want to sell, they redeem the shares back to the ETF, taking the shares out of circulation.

Taking a Look at the Benefits and Pitfalls of ETFs

Investors typically react to new options in one of two ways: Overly bold investors jump on board immediately, and cautious investors carefully weigh the pros and cons. When you understand the many benefits of ETFs over their mutual fund counterparts, however, you may become bolder. In the following sections, I introduce you to the many benefits and a few drawbacks of ETFs.

Comparing advantages with mutual funds

Although ETFs differ from mutual funds, they offer many of the same advantages, including the following:

- ✔ You can own part of a diversified portfolio with the minimal investment of just one share — no large, upfront investment required.
- ✔ ETFs are easy to buy and sell.
- ✔ Most ETFs are run by professional managers.
- ✔ Your workload as an investor is minimal.
- ✔ ETFs are regulated by the SEC.
- ✔ ETFs are good for asset allocation and focusing investment dollars on a particular industry, asset class, or segment of the market.

Unlike mutual funds, ETFs don't keep track of all the bookkeeping involved. Instead, your brokerage firm takes care of this service. Also, ETFs don't allow redemptions over the phone.

In addition, ETFs offer solutions to some of the disadvantages of owning mutual funds. Compared to mutual funds, ETFs offer

- ✔ Greater flexibility
- ✔ Lower fees
- ✔ Increased tax efficiency
- ✔ Greater transparency
- ✔ The ability to invest in a variety of asset classes, such as commodities and currencies. (In this chapter, I deal exclusively with equity — that is, stock — ETFs.)

I discuss these advantages in more detail in "Taking a Closer Look at Some Unique ETF Advantages" later in the chapter.

Recognizing a few drawbacks

ETFs offer several advantages over mutual funds, but they also have a few drawbacks that mutual funds don't:

- ✔ You can't buy fractional shares of an ETF.
- ✔ You must buy shares through a stockbroker and pay a commission.
- ✔ ETFs may not be cost effective for a dollar-cost averaging strategy in a taxable account. (For more on dollar-cost averaging, see Chapter 18.)

Along came a Spyder

The Standard & Poor's Depositary Receipt holds all 500 stocks in the Standard & Poor's 500 Index. Because of its initials, SPDR, it received the nickname Spyder, spelled that way because of its ticker symbol: (SPY). Launched on the American Sock Exchange on January 29, 1993, the Spyder was the first ETF created in the United States. On its second day of trading, the Spyder's trading volume fell more than 50 percent to just 480,500 shares. Yet by the end of 2009, it was the single largest stock/fund on the U.S. stock market, with an average daily volume around 170 million shares and a total of $72.26 billion in *assets under management* (or AUM, the amount of money invested in the fund).

Taking a Closer Look at Some Unique ETF Advantages

In "Comparing advantage notes with mutual funds" earlier in this chapter, I touch on some ways ETFs go above and beyond mutual funds in the benefits department. Because a short list just can't do all those extra advantages justice, I break them down here so you can get an idea of exactly what ETFs have to offer you.

Gaining flexibility

Without a doubt, the biggest improvement the ETF holds over the mutual fund is its ability to trade on the stock exchange. With a mutual fund, you issue a buy or sell order during the stock market's trading session, but your order won't be filled until market close. If the market happens to crash after you initiate a sale, you may end up selling at the lowest price of the day. If the market rallies after you decide to buy, you probably end up paying the highest price of the day. However, you can buy and sell ETFs just like shares of stock anytime during the day.

Time flexibility isn't the only aspect giving ETFs the win here; you also have more trading options. The ETF investor can use all the trading tools available to the dividend-stock investor. An ETF investor can

 ✔ Trade with market orders

 ✔ Place limit orders

 ✔ Place stop loss orders

✔ Sell ETF shares short

✔ Borrow against ETF shares

✔ Purchase ETF shares on margin

You can't use any of these trading orders with a mutual fund. For more about the various ways you can issue buy and sell orders, check out Chapter 19; to get the skinny on mutual funds, head to Chapter 15.

Reducing your cost of ownership

Almost every equity ETF is an *index fund* — a passively managed fund. Because index funds have low management costs, ETFs typically charge an *expense ratio* (amount of annual operating expenses) lower than almost all actively-managed mutual funds. In addition, they usually charge less than comparable index-based mutual fund.

For the most part, the ETF holds what's in the index. It has a manager, but the manager doesn't have the freedom to buy and sell what he wants as many mutual fund managers do. He needs the fund's performance to closely match the return of the index the fund is tracking, and the easiest way to do so is to hold all the stocks in the index.

An ETF manager may decide to buy options or futures to approximate the index's return without holding every component if the index is huge or holds a lot of small and/or illiquid stocks. If a big fund kept buying these shares, it would influence the movement of the share prices.

The following sections can help you set reasonable expectations about costs and fees associated with ETFs.

Investigating the expense ratio

The three components of the mutual fund expense ratio are management fee, 12b-1 fee, and other expenses. Chapter 15 explains how these expenses apply to mutual funds; here's how ETFs stack up:

✔ **Management fee:** The ETF pays a management fee, but it's smaller than comparable index funds and dramatically smaller than actively-managed funds. An ETF's manager doesn't need to spend money on hiring a research staff to pick stocks because the ETF's tracking index already dictates its composition.

✔ **12b-1 fee:** ETFs don't charge a 12b-1 fee — at least not yet — which saves about .25 to 1 percent of a fund's assets. However, rumors abound that some ETFs want to start charging a fee. (For more about 12b-1 fees, check out Chapter 15.)

> ✔ **Other expenses:** Other ETF expenses include the index licensing fee, compensation for the board of directors, custodial fees, and accounting fees.

Mutual funds tend to be high maintenance, at least when compared to ETFs. Because of this difference, ETFs avoid many of the costs and fees that mutual funds incur, including the following:

> ✔ Recordkeeping costs (known as *transfer agent compensation*). This amount is usually a significant cost.
>
> ✔ Fund administrator compensation.
>
> ✔ *Bid-ask spreads* (the difference between the price buyers are willing to pay and the price sellers are willing to accept) inside the mutual fund every time it buys or sells stock. (However, a bid-ask spread may exist when the investor buys the ETF.)

Examining transaction fees

In a battle over low transaction fees, ETFs win hands-down. Because they acquire shares through in-kind exchanges, they avoid having to pay broker commissions altogether. Mutual funds, on the other hand, pay broker fees whenever they buy securities in response to increasing demand for mutual fund shares or they buy or sell securities to adjust the portfolio.

Achieving greater tax efficiency

The ETF's tax efficiency comes from avoiding capital gains taxes inside the fund. Because ETFs don't buy or sell the securities held in their portfolios, they don't incur capital gains or need to pay capital gains taxes like mutual funds do. Capital gains taxes can add up quickly and come right out of your mutual fund returns. Because it's more tax efficient, the ETF leaves more money in your hands.

Of course, you still pay taxes when you buy and sell your ETF shares, but you maintain control of the tax strategy and timing. You can hold the shares a short period of time or for years. Just like shares in a company stock, you can take a capital gain or capital loss when it best suits your strategy. The mutual fund investor pays this same capital gains tax on the shares held in his fund account, in addition to the taxes from the capital gains on the stocks sold within the fund itself.

Increasing transparency

When dealing with fund managers, transparency is key. This fact is especially true as I write this in the aftermath of all the hedge funds that blew up during the 2008–2009 fiscal crisis because they held toxic assets such as credit default swaps and other risky instruments. Hedge funds aren't required to report their holdings to their shareholders; That's why the transparency you get with ETFs is so crucial. The ability to see what the fund holds provides certain advantages, including the following:

- ✔ **You know exactly what you own and what you don't.** If your fund is missing something you want as part of your portfolio, you can fill the gap with another fund or individual stock.

- ✔ **You can avoid doubling up on stocks you already own through your funds.** If you didn't know the composition of each fund, you could end up assembling a portfolio overly weighted with stocks from a certain sector. For example, if you owned Spyder, Invesco PowerShares QQQ (QQQQ), a large-cap growth fund, and a technology fund, you'd have a portfolio heavily weighted in the tech sector.

- ✔ **By seeing what the fund holds, you can avoid owning what you don't like.** Had the hedge fund investors mentioned earlier seen the huge amount of very risky investments their funds held, they may have tried to get out a lot sooner.

The *creation unit* (the 50,000 ETF shares traded to the AP) forces a transparency not required by the mutual fund. Because the AP (a broker or specialist called the *authorized participant*) needs to buy all the securities in the ETF to make an in-kind trade, the AP needs an updated list of stocks in the fund, so the ETF needs to publish this list daily. Check out the "Behind the scenes with ETFs" sidebar earlier in the chapter for more on creation units and APs.

Mutual funds, on the other hand, are required to publish their portfolios only at the end of each quarter and have 60 days to release the information. Considering how much stock turnover can happen in an actively managed fund, the odds are pretty good that the end-of-quarter report is a poor reflection of the fund's current composition.

Offering a variety of asset classes

With all the benefits I list in the preceding sections, the ETF has spawned an industry that seeks to offer a variety of products tracking alternative assets previously out of the realm of the individual investor. These exchange-traded products offer commodities and currencies through a variety of investment vehicles. Although they're regulated by the SEC and are close cousins of the ETF, these exchange-traded products have different structures and are taxed differently than ETFs. In this chapter, I only deal with stock ETFs regulated by the 1940 Act (covered earlier in the chapter). For information on these other exchange-traded products, flip to "Digging Up More Information on ETFs" later in this chapter.

Comparing loads against commissions

You buy ETFs through a broker, which translates into paying commissions. When comparing mutual funds that charge a front-end or back-end *load* (special commission taken on either the purchase or sale of shares) to ETFs, paying broker commissions may cost you less. The percentage of your purchase you pay for a mutual fund load stays the same regardless of the dollar amount of your share purchase, but the percentage you pay in commissions decreases as the dollar amount of your ETF purchase rises. Investing $100 in a mutual fund with a front-end load of 5 percent costs you $5, while purchasing $100 worth of shares in an ETF may cost you a $10 commission (10 percent). Invest $10,000, however, and your 5 percent load rises to $500 while your ETF commission remains at $10, just 0.1 percent of your investment.

ETFs don't always win the load/commission battle with mutual funds, however. With a *no-load mutual fund,* you pay no commission. The advantage here clearly goes to the no-load mutual fund, but you can significantly reduce the commissions you pay by purchasing through a discount broker (for about $10 per trade) and buying in bulk — the bigger the purchase, the less of a percentage you pay in commissions.

If you're following a dollar-cost averaging strategy of making small purchases regularly, the commissions you pay on the purchase of ETFs can negatively affect your overall returns significantly.

Getting the Lowdown on Dividends from ETFs

Like mutual funds, ETFs maintain their tax-free status by distributing their dividends back to investors, usually on a quarterly basis. Typically, the fund sends dividend payments to the investor's brokerage account, but you may be able to reinvest the dividends.

In the following sections, you discover two methods for reinvesting dividends in an ETF and gather some insight into how the dividends you receive are taxed.

When researching a dividend fund's holdings, determine how much of the fund actually holds dividend stocks. A fund that markets itself as a dividend fund isn't required to hold only dividend stocks. Check the fact sheet on the ETF's Web site to see which sector of the market the ETF's index tracks and what percentage of the portfolio holds dividend stocks. Typically, a dividend fund holds more than 80 percent in dividend stocks. Names other than "Dividend" that indicate the fund may be following a dividend strategy include "total return," "income," and "value."

Reinvesting dividends

As with any dividend investment, reinvesting your dividend payments is a key component of growing your assets. With ETFs, dividends can be reinvested at the fund level or the investor level, as I explain in the following sections.

Fund level

If the ETF is an open-end investment company, (see "Understanding the ETF Difference" earlier in the chapter), it can reinvest the dividends it receives from the stocks in its portfolio to buy more stocks. This strategy avoids the problem of *cash drag* (having a fund not fully invested in the market because the fund holds cash) on the portfolio and can help boost returns a little bit. Then when the fund needs cash to distribute dividends to the shareholders, it sells the shares, which may incur a capital gain.

ETFs structured as UITs don't have a manager or board of directors, so no one is available to reinvest the dividends. The cash sits in the ETF's account creating a cash drag until the quarterly dividend distribution. If the market rises, the stocks in the portfolio appreciate, but the cash doesn't generate interest, so it drags down the portfolio's total return.

The number of ETFs organized as UITs is pretty small, but this group includes some of the largest ETFs. In addition to the Spyder, others include the Dow Diamonds (DIA), which tracks the Dow Jones Industrial Average; the PowerShares QQQ (QQQQ), which follows the technology-heavy NASDAQ 100 Index; and the MidCap SPDR (MDY), which tracks the S&P MidCap 400 Index, a benchmark for midsized companies.

An open-end ETF that tracks the S&P 500 but doesn't have the cash drag of the Spyder is the iShares S&P 500 Index (IVV).

Shareholder level

Unlike a mutual fund, an ETF can't reinvest dividends for you. The ETF distributes the cash dividend to the investor's brokerage firm, typically at the end of each quarter. Some brokerage firms offer ETF investors the service of automatic dividend reinvestment for free, but some don't. If your broker doesn't offer this service, you have to pay another commission to reinvest your dividend by purchasing new shares.

Paying taxes on ETF dividends

Paying taxes on dividends is always a drag, but the ETF may be able to give you a break through its accounting practices. Qualifying dividends are eligible for a 15-percent tax rate, just like dividends you may receive from mutual funds and stocks. Most fund managers can manage the dividend payouts so that a larger portion qualifies for the lower tax rate. For more on taxes, see Chapter 20.

When researching ETFs, check the portion of dividend payouts that qualifies for the 15-percent tax rate. Look for ETFs that tend to pay out a very high percentage in qualified dividends.

Shaking WisdomTree's Family of Dividend Funds

Investors who want a pure dividend fund need to become acquainted with WisdomTree Investments. This New York firm has created a line of indexes comprised only of dividend stocks and launched a family of ETFs to track these indexes. These funds are the only ETFs comprised entirely of dividend stocks. The firm's benchmark is the WisdomTree Dividend Index, which holds every dividend-paying stock in the United States with a *market capitalization* (share price times total number of shares outstanding) greater than $100 million. The stocks also need to meet certain liquidity requirements. Currently, the index comprises 1,110 stocks, and every WisdomTree U.S. stock ETF is based on this index or an offshoot of it.

Dividend weighting is a form of fundamental indexing, which I explain in the nearby sidebar "Wrapping your brain around fundamental indexing." In dividend weighting, a company's index weighting is based on the actual dollar value of its annual dividend rather than its price. To get the total dollar value of the dividend paid to shareholders, WisdomTree takes a company's dividend per share and multiplies it by the number of common shares outstanding. It compares this amount to the total dividend stream of all the companies in the index. The larger the dividend, the heavier the weighting. So a small company paying a big dividend can have a greater weighting than a large company paying a small dividend.

For instance, the total dollar amount of dividends paid in the United States is around $220 billion. AT&T, with a 6-percent yield, currently pays out about $10 billion in dividends per year. To get AT&T's weighting, you divide its dividend by the total market dividends:

$10 billion ÷ $220 billion = 4.5 percent

Wrapping your brain around fundamental indexing

Fundamental indexing came to prominence in 2005 when the *Financial Analysts Journal* published a paper called "Fundamental Indexation." The paper was the brainchild of Robert Arnott, the chairman of Research Affiliates, a research-intensive asset management firm in Pasadena, California.

Most indexes are weighted to reflect the fact that large companies have more influence over the value of the index than smaller companies. The premier weighting system is called *market-cap weighting* because it's based on a company's market capitalization. Market capitalization is the basis of the S&P 500 and most market benchmarks.

Some experts, however, consider market-cap weighting unreliable because it can give too much weight to a company with an inflated share price and too little weight to a company with under-priced shares. Proponents of *fundamental indexing* claim that fundamental metrics (such as revenues, profits, book value, and gross dividends) are a more reliable measurement of value because they provide a more accurate indication of a company's market position. Arnott devised an index called the Research Affiliates Fundamental Index, or RAFI for short. It took four fundamental components — revenues, profits, book value, and gross dividends — combined them, and then averaged them to determine a company's value in the economy.

You can find RAFI in many investment circles:

- ✔ Charles Schwab sells mutual funds based on the RAFI.

- ✔ Invesco PowerShares sells ETFs based on the RAFI.

- ✔ The PowerShares FTSE RAFI US 1000 Portfolio ETF (PRF) tracks the 1,000 largest U.S. stocks as measured by the RAFI.

- ✔ The PowerShares US 1500 Small-Mid Portfolio ETF (PRFZ) tracks the small-cap and mid-cap markets with the RAFI. PowerShares also sells six international ETFs based on the RAFI formula.

Dividends make up one-fourth of the RAFI formula, but the RAFI isn't focused on dividends, nor are the RAFI ETFs dividend-based funds. The RAFI seeks to measure the broader economy, so it includes a significant number of growth stocks that don't pay dividends. The RAFI holds about as many dividend stocks as the market-cap indexes, between 70 percent and 80 percent. This is approximately the average percentage held by dividend-based mutual funds.

This gives AT&T a weighting of 4.5 percent in the index. As mentioned in Chapter 8, high yields can be a sign that a stock is undervalued. By focusing the index on the high-yielding companies, the index gives greater weight to companies with more potential for capital appreciation.

WisdomTree offers 34 dividend-weighted ETFs that cover the U.S., international, and emerging markets. The international and emerging market ETFs are based on the WisdomTree Global Index, which contains about 4,000 securities (more international companies pay dividends). The total returns for WisdomTree ETFs include dividend and capital appreciation.

WisdomTree has created subindexes for different regions called the equity income indexes. These offer the top 30 percent of the index as measured by yield. You can find out more about WisdomTree and its ETFs by visiting www. wisdomtree.com.

Digging Up More Information on ETFs

To explain the universe of exchange-traded products effectively would require an entire book in itself. In fact, I wrote a book on the topic. It's entitled *ETFs for the Long Run: What They Are, How They Work, and Simple Strategies for Successful Long-Term Investing* (Wiley). If the idea of reading yet another book on investing doesn't appeal to you, you can find plenty of information about ETFs online. Use the resources in Chapter 7 as a start. If you're considering a specific ETF, visit the company's Web site, where you can find a prospectus and fact sheet laying out the fund's performance, expenses, index components, and sector allocations.

Mutual fund research sites also offer substantial information and reports on ETFs. Check out Morningstar at www.morningstar.com and Lipper at www. lipperweb.com.

The top ETF Web sites include the following:

- ✔ **IndexUniverse.com (indexuniverse.com):** This site is the main news source for the ETF industry and is home to the *Journal of Indexes* magazine. The company also published the *ETF Report*.

- ✔ **ETF Guide (etfguide.com):** This independent Web site focuses on education and includes a subscription-based area where you can find ETF portfolios.

- ✔ **ExchangeTradedFunds.com (exchangetradedfunds.com):** The company that manages this site sponsors the Global ETF Awards. It's one of the few sites that offer information on the entire global ETF industry, not just the United States. It also offers a lot of resources.

If you're interested in what the ETF bloggers have to say, visit the following blogs:

✔ My ETF blog at `www.ETFsForTheLongRun.com`

✔ ETF Expert at `www.etfexpert.com/etf_expert`

✔ ETFTrends.com at `www.etftrends.com`

✔ FT Alphaville (from the *Financial Times*) at `ftalphaville.ft.com`

You can also see my stories on ETFs at TheStreet.com and SmartMoney.com:

```
www.thestreet.com/author/1111789/LawrenceCarrel/
articles.html?page=1&perPage=100
```

```
www.smartmoney.com/search/?searchtype=author&searchterm
=Lawrence%20Carrel
```

Meeting Some Other Dividend Based ETFs

Although most ETFs serve as index funds, these indexes can track very narrowly focused slices of the market. They can vary a great deal in terms of yield, year-to-date return, and expense ratio. Table 16-1 from Morningstar highlights the top-performing ETFs during the writing of this book.

Table 16-1		Top U.S. ETFs by 12-Month Yield through 12/31/2009				
Fund Name	**Ticker Symbol**	**Category**	**12-month Yield**	**1-Year Return**	**3-Year Return**	**Expense Ratio**
WisdomTree International Real Estate	DRW	Global Real Estate	9.41	46.53	NA	0.58
PowerShares Financial Preferred	PGF	Preferred Stock	8.82	40.68	−5.41	0.68
iShares FTSE NAREIT Mort Plus Cp Idx	REM	Real Estate	8.15	11.59	NA	0.48
PowerShares Preferred	PGX	Preferred Stock	8.08	19.35	NA	0.50

(continued)

Table 16-1 *(continued)*

Fund Name	Ticker Symbol	Category	12-month Yield	1-Year Return	3-Year Return	Expense Ratio
iShares S&P U.S. Preferred Stock Index	PFF	Preferred Stock	7.87	39.28	NA	0.48
iShares FTSE EPRA/ NAREIT Dev RE ex-US	IFGL	Global Real Estate	7.14	44.23	NA	0.48
First Trust FTSE EPRA/ NAREIT Glb Real Estate	FFR	Global Real Estate	5.97	35.01	NA	0.60
Claymore/Zacks Multi-Asset Income	CVY	Mid-Cap Value	5.32	50.59	−6.16	0.65
iShares S&P DEV ex-US Property Index	WPS	Global Real Estate	5.15	42.10	NA	0.48
iShares FTSE EPRA/ NAREIT Dev Asia Index	IFAS	Global Real Estate	5.05	43.25	NA	0.48
PowerShares NASDAQ-100 Buy Write	PQBW	Long-Short	5.04	44.11	NA	0.75
WisdomTree Global Equity Income	DEW	World Stock	4.90	34.01	−7.50	0.58
PowerShares Dynamic Utilities	PUI	Utilities	4.86	3.35	−4.15	0.63
WisdomTree International Utilities	DBU	Utilities	4.84	3.74	−3.75	0.58
SPDR Dow Jones International Real Estate	RWX	Global Real Estate	4.79	38.66	−14.22	0.59
WisdomTree Middle East Dividend	GULF	Diversified Emerging Markets	4.65	7.74	NA	0.88
iShares FTSE NAREIT Retail Cp Idx	RTL	Real Estate	4.65	25.24	NA	0.48
PowerShares High Yield Dividend Achievers	PEY	Mid-Cap Value	4.54	3.74	−18.45	0.60
iShares MSCI Austria Investable Market Index	EWO	Europe Stock	4.50	61.33	−15.35	0.55
PowerShares FTSE RAFI Asia Pacific ex-Japan	PAF	Pacific/Asia ex-Japan Stocks	4.47	76.75	NA	0.80

Fund Name	Ticker Symbol	Category	12-month Yield	1-Year Return	3-Year Return	Expense Ratio
WisdomTree DEFA	DWM	Foreign Large Blend	4.46	31.38	−5.25	0.48
Vanguard REIT Index ETF	VNQ	Real Estate	4.40	29.73	−11.94	0.11
WisdomTree International Communications	DGG	Communications	4.34	13.19	−2.03	0.58
SPDR Dow Jones Global Real Estate	RWO	Global Real Estate	4.33	34.13	NA	0.50
iShares MSCI Spain Index	EWP	Europe Stock	4.22	37.83	0.92	0.56
iShares Dow Jones US Real Estate	IYR	Real Estate	4.20	30.16	−13.85	0.48
Utilities Select Sector SPDR	XLU	Utilities	4.10	11.42	−2.00	0.22
iShares S&P Global Telecommunications	IXP	Communications	4.04	14.41	−1.10	0.48

Courtesy of Morningstar, Inc., 2010

Chapter 17

Going Global with Foreign Dividends

In This Chapter

▶ Scoping out the advantages and disadvantages of global dividend investing

▶ Knowing how to invest globally from the U.S.

▶ Dealing with currency exchange issues

▶ Recognizing potential tax ramifications

Any advisor worth her salt will tell you that to truly diversify your portfolio you need to invest outside the United States. Just as you should never invest all your money in one company, one industry, or one asset class, you shouldn't invest in only one country, either. Investing exclusively in one country ties you too closely to that country's economy. If that economy flounders, your entire portfolio flounders, too.

Another way to look at it is this: You live and work in the U.S. and get paid in U.S. dollars. If the U.S. economy crashes, you already stand to lose a great deal financially. Diversifying your investments outside the U.S. provides protection and growth potential for at least some of the money you have working for you.

One beautiful thing about dividends is that they aren't limited to the U.S. You can go global with dividends, investing in both mature, developed economies and emerging, fast-growing economies. But before you shift all your investments to Brazil, China, or India, read this chapter so you're aware of all the potential landmines.

Weighing the Pros and Cons of Investing in Global Dividends

In the global economy, opportunities abound, but wherever you find opportunity, risk is right around the corner. In the following sections, I reveal the pros and cons of investing in global dividends so that you can make an educated decision about whether to invest globally and how much of your portfolio to allocate to foreign investments.

In terms of market capitalization, only 40 percent of the world's companies reside in the U.S. market. That means that by investing only in the U.S., you shut yourself off from more than half the investing opportunities worldwide. And if you look at an international index weighted according to where dividends are paid, 70 percent of those investments reside outside the U.S.

Investigating the advantages

In addition to keeping your portfolio from being tied to only one country's economy, investing in global dividend stocks offers several potential advantages in terms of expanding your opportunities and protecting your portfolio. The following sections describe the main benefits you can expect.

Expanding your investing universe

When you decide to invest globally, you open your portfolio to the many investment opportunities only accessible outside the U.S. Currently, a great deal of the economic growth in the world occurs outside the U.S., especially in emerging markets. With their educated populations looking for opportunities in a global market, Brazil, Russia, India, and China have seen astronomical growth in their economies. And they're just beginning their growth cycles.

Receiving higher yields

The sad fact for dividend investors is that the U.S. is one of the lowest-yielding stock markets in the world. The 4-percent average yield in the developed world outside the U.S. is twice the yield on the S&P 500. So expanding your universe of dividend paying stocks internationally really pays off. Not only do you get diversification into faster growing economies, which have potential for great capital gains, but you also get more income.

Collecting dividends from technology stocks

Very few U.S. technology companies pay dividends, and those that do pay tiny yields. Yet many technology companies outside the U.S. pay dividends, and most with a sizeable yield. So if you follow a dividend strategy in the U.S.

and want a minimum yield of 3 percent, you have to buy American deposi-tary receipts (see "Investing in American depositary receipts" later in this chapter) to avoid being severely underrepresented in the technology sector, which was the strongest sector in 2009.

Some mature U.S. technology stocks pay dividends, but they aren't high enough to satisfy an income-based strategy. Hewlett Packard pays 0.6 percent, Texas Instruments pays 1.9 percent and Microsoft pays 1.8 percent. Only Intel beats the S&P 500 with a yield of 2.9 percent. By going global, you can buy Taiwan Semiconductor Manufacturing, which not only services both the U.S. and Chinese market but also posts a yield nearly double the others: 3.5 per-cent. (Flip to Chapter 6 for more on the various investment strategies.)

Protecting your portfolio from weakness in the dollar

When you invest in foreign companies that pay dividends, they pay profits in other currencies that may be stronger against the dollar. As a result, you may see more profit in terms of dollar amount when your profits are converted. If U.S. companies do business in foreign countries, you may see a similar ben-efit when the company's foreign profits are converted to dollars.

Recognizing the disadvantages

Don't let talk of a struggling U.S. economy, a ballooning national debt, or a falling dollar lead you to immediately move all your money into foreign investments. Foreign investments carry their own unique risks, as I explain in the following sections.

Taking on higher risk

Investing in the U.S. may seem risky, but the risk levels in other countries may be nearly the same (such as in Western Europe and Japan) or even worse (like in emerging markets). The risks typically break down into the fol-lowing categories:

✔ **Currency risk:** Foreign currencies can rise and fall just like the dollar, and some can be even more erratic. If the currency falls against the dollar, an investment in even a good company can take a serious hit. Check out "Covering Currency Concerns" later in this chapter for details on this problem.

✔ **Regulation risk:** Companies in the European Union operate under even stricter regulatory controls than in the U.S. This wrinkle can add extra costs that cut into profits. Meanwhile, many young, emerging markets have little regulation to discourage shady business practices and cor-ruption. In such countries, the likelihood of managers stealing your money or companies folding is significantly higher.

✔ **Political risk:** When countries attempt to transition to a free-market economy, they often hit some speed bumps along the way. Developing nations are notorious for experimenting with capitalism and then doing an about-face when they run short of money, nationalizing large companies in major industries, such as oil. U.S. investors trying to capture some of the stunning growth in an emerging market can find their company nationalized at a moment's notice, typically resulting in a loss of their entire investment.

Paying a foreign withholding tax

Foreign countries tax dividends too, so you often end up in a double-taxation scenario, having to pay foreign taxes along with U.S. taxes on dividends. See "Addressing Potential Tax Issues" later in this chapter for more information.

Dealing with variations in dividend payments

In the U.S., companies typically pay dividends quarterly. When you invest in foreign countries, however, you can't count on companies following this same standard. Here are some of the variations you can expect:

✔ **Fewer payments:** Many European companies pay dividends annually or biannually.

✔ **Interim and final dividend payments:** Some British firms pay quarterly dividends, but most British, Irish, and Japanese companies make two yearly payments called *interim* and *final dividends.* (Final dividends are typically larger than the interim payouts.) These payments aren't true biannual dividends because they're not necessarily paid six months apart. Sometimes companies can make the payments as close as four months apart.

✔ **Erratic emerging dividends:** In developed nations, you can count on the regularity of two or four dividends payments a year. In emerging markets the payment schedule can be a complete mystery. Some companies pay dividends five times a year but with no set schedule.

✔ **Greater likelihood of dividend cuts:** U.S. and British companies tend to keep their dividend payouts steady, unless a company experiences major setbacks. Companies in other countries are less inhibited about cutting dividends when profits take a tumble.

Accepting less transparency

Many foreign markets have much less transparency than the U.S. market. This characteristic can mask conflicts of interest and sweetheart deals from the government. For many foreign companies, access to material information or even news stories can be difficult, making research a time-consuming chore. (Chapter 8 gives you more guidance on researching possible investments.)

Losing the international diversification advantage to globalization

Not all countries move in the same direction at the same time. Theoretically, when one country is down, others rise to fill the gap. With globalization, however, the world has gotten much smaller; this shift was apparent in 2008 when the U.S. markets tanked and nearly brought down the rest of the world's economy. With financial institutions and multinational corporations crossing borders, markets are much more connected than ever before. The days of using one country as a safe haven while the rest of the world crumbles are quickly fading.

Examining a Few Ways to Go Global

You're convinced. The U.S. economy seems shaky and you've decided to diversify. Now, you just need to know how to go about moving your investment capital to foreign countries. In the U.S., you have three options: getting into American depository receipts, investing in global dividend-based mutual funds or ETFs, or buying shares on a foreign exchange. The following sections explore these options.

Investing in American depository receipts

American depository receipts, better known as ADRs, are by far the easiest way to buy and directly own foreign stocks in the U.S. ADRs are dollar denominated and trade like equities on the U.S. stock market, but they aren't stocks. They're certificates issued by U.S. banks, which hold the underlying foreign shares in the local market and issue the certificates, or receipts, on the U.S. market to represent a specific number of the underlying security. Some ADRs represent two or more shares of the underlying stock.

ADRs offer several advantages over other methods of investing in foreign markets. ADRs

- ✔ Are *dollar denominated.* Shares trade in dollars, and dividends are paid in dollars.
- ✔ Trade on the U.S. market.
- ✔ Avoid currency issues (which I discuss in "Covering Currency Concerns" later in the chapter).
- ✔ Reduce the huge administration and transaction costs involved with buying shares directly on a foreign exchange.

✔ Are regulated by the United States Companies that trade as ADRs must file financial statements with the SEC.

✔ Pay dividends that qualify for lower tax rates, if you hold them the necessary holding period. For more about holding period requirements, check out Chapter 20.

Investing in ADRs comes with some potential disadvantages, including the following:

✔ The underwriter of an ADR charges a fee for its services. This cost is typically modest and transparent, but it comes directly out of your dividend.

✔ Usually only companies with a large capitalization become ADRs.

✔ Very few ADRs represent stocks in emerging economies.

✔ ADR performance can be difficult to predict due to currency exchange issues. Even though you receive dividends in dollars, they're paid in local currency and converted by the receipt issuer. A radical change in exchange rates can mean more or less money in dividends year over year. This swing makes predicting the actual dividend difficult even if it remains consistent in its home market.

Investing through a mutual fund or ETF

To buy foreign equities not available as ADRs, the best route is to buy an international mutual fund or ETF (exchange-traded fund). (For more about investing in mutual funds, check out Chapter 15. For more about ETFs, see Chapter 16.) Many mutual fund and ETF companies offer funds that track stocks abroad. You can buy a fund that tracks the whole world, including or excluding U.S. stocks. You can buy funds that invest in just one country or specific area of the market, such as only Europe or only Asia.

Mutual funds and ETFs take all the hassle, much of the cost, and some of the risk out of investing in foreign stocks by offering the following advantages:

✔ All the advantages of mutual funds and ETFs listed in Chapters 15 and 16, such as building a diversified portfolio in which you can buy shares with a minimal investment

✔ Convenience

✔ Dollar denominated (see the preceding section for more on dollar denomination)

✔ Purchased in the U.S.

- Managed by professional U.S. asset managers with expertise in these markets who have researched and visited these foreign companies to gain firsthand insights and hard-to-access local information

- Financial institutions that can manage currency risk

- Management fees much less than the cost of buying many foreign stocks on your own

Whether you're using mutual funds or ETFs to invest in U.S. or foreign stocks, the same disadvantages apply, as explained in Chapters 15 and Chapter 16.

Buying directly on foreign exchanges

Many full-service brokers and even some discount brokers let you buy and sell equities directly on a foreign stock exchange. For stocks that don't trade as ADRs, buying directly offers one advantage and several potential disadvantages. The one sole advantage of direct trading on foreign exchanges is that you gain access to markets and stocks not represented by ADRs.

The potential disadvantages of direct trading on foreign exchanges abound. The main drawbacks are

- Higher transaction costs as the *bid-ask spread* widens. The *bid* is the highest price a buyer is willing to pay for a security, and the *ask* is the lowest price acceptable to the seller. The difference between them is the *spread*. The party that needs the trade done more quickly pays the spread.

- High administration costs because the broker charges for currency conversion.

- Greater currency risk. These stocks trade in the local currency.

- No protections provided by U.S. laws and regulation. The corporate governance structures of most foreign countries are much looser than the U.S.

- Less respect for shareholders' rights.

- Harder-to-find material information. These firms aren't required to file financial data with the SEC. Look to the company's Web site for information. Of course, many of these sites aren't in English.

- Smaller and riskier companies than those that trade as ADRs.

Covering Currency Concerns

Currency issues in foreign shares arise because, well, they trade on foreign markets in foreign currencies. Because you're buying stocks with U.S. dollars, every buy and sell transaction or dividend payment needs to be converted from dollars to the local currency. If you've ever traveled to a foreign country, you know that exchanging currencies is not only a hassle but also often costly and confusing. You trade in 100 dollars at the bank and get 55 euros. Head to the ATM five minutes later, and you get 66 euros. This same phenomenon can occur when you're buying and selling foreign stocks and collecting dividends. As a result, even a stock that experiences no movement on the market can see its price move because of the exchange rate.

Although several factors can affect the actual exchange rate you receive, including fees charged to process the exchange, the biggest changes occur due to the relative strength or weakness of the dollar.

- ✔ **A depreciating dollar** helps foreign equities because the value of the foreign currency, and hence the foreign profits, are worth more compared to the dollar. Since 2002, the dollar has been in a sharp decline against the euro, yen, and British pound. This weak dollar has been good for owning foreign equities and receiving their profits.

- ✔ **An appreciating dollar** hurts foreign investments. A stronger dollar suddenly makes foreign investments less valuable. If a foreign company sees earnings growth but its currency falls versus the dollar, the profits aren't worth as much in the U.S.

Addressing Potential Tax Issues

Dividend investors are accustomed to issues relating to double-taxation, but these issues deal with double-taxation within the U.S. — taxing profits that corporations earn and then taxing them again when investors receive the profits as dividends.

When investing in foreign stocks, you also face a type of double-taxation — having your dividends taxed by the foreign country and then having to pay taxes in the U.S. In the following sections, I explore these tax issues in greater depth.

To calculate your foreign withholding taxes and credits, fill out IRS Form 1116.

Taxing qualified dividends

As I discuss in Chapter 20, certain U.S. dividends qualify for the lower tax rate of 15 percent rather than the stockholder's ordinary tax rate. What qualifies for the lower tax rate in the U.S. can change when those dividends come from companies in foreign lands.

- ✔ **U.S. possession:** Dividends from a foreign corporation can qualify for the lower tax rate if the company is incorporated in a U.S. possession, including American Samoa, Guam, and Puerto Rico.

- ✔ **ADRs that trade on an established U.S. securities exchange:** If the company's shares or ADRs trade on an established U.S. securities exchange, such as the New York Stock Exchange or the NASDAQ Stock Market, the dividends can qualify for the lower tax rate. (Flip to the earlier section "Investing in American depository receipts" for more on ADRs.)

- ✔ **Income tax treaty:** Dividends from a company may be eligible if the country has a comprehensive income tax treaty with the U.S. The following countries don't have satisfactory treaties:

  - Bermuda

  - Netherlands Antilles

  - The former Soviet republics of Armenia, Azerbaijan, Belarus, Georgia, Kyrgyzstan, Moldova, Tajikistan, Turkmenistan, and Uzbekistan

Accounting for withholdings

Governments are always very good about grabbing money wherever they can, and dividends have always been a ripe target. Just because you own a foreign stock in the U.S. and collect dividends here doesn't mean you escape dividend taxes in the company's country.

For tax purposes, when U.S. investors own ADRs they're treated as owning underlying stock in the foreign company. Hence, they're subject to taxes in a foreign country. The foreign company, the bank making the ADR, or even your stockbroker withholds the taxes you owe on the dividends and sends them to the local taxman. You receive the difference.

The United Kingdom doesn't withhold taxes on dividends to U.S. investors. You receive the same amount as a local shareholder.

Foreign equities held in U.S. mutual funds and ETFs experience the same tax withholding as an individual. The fund's custodian receives a dividend after the tax is paid. Like regular taxes, mutual funds and ETFs pass through the dividend, tax withholding deduction, and the tax credit to the shareholders paying the taxes.

Remembering tax credits for withholdings

If you pay a tax withholding to a foreign country, the Internal Revenue Service typically gives you some sort of credit on the taxes you paid to the other government. Yes, mighty big of them.

For instance, say you buy an ADR. Your dividend is $100 and the foreign country withholds 10 percent or $10. You receive the remaining $90. On your U.S. tax form, you must report your earnings of $100 in taxable income, but if your U.S. tax liability is 15 percent, you get a credit for the 10 percent you paid to the foreign country and pay the remaining 5 percent to the IRS. You still pay a 15 percent tax, but this credit carves it up between two jurisdictions.

Of course, if the foreign tax rates are higher, you don't get any money back. If the foreign withholding tax is 20 percent, for example, but you qualify for the 15 percent tax rate in the U.S., the IRS isn't going to issue you a refund for the extra 5 percent. But you have satisfied your obligation to the IRS.

If you directly purchase a foreign stock outside the U.S., you're responsible for determining the correct foreign withholding tax so you can claim your tax credit. Failure to do so may result in a double-taxation scenario in which you lose your tax credit.

Part V
Managing Your Portfolio

The 5th Wave   By Rich Tennant

PHIL HARRISON VISITS HIS TAX ATTORNEY

©RICHTENNANT

The new tax law goes on to say that "...all taxpayers shall be exempt from these extra charges except...", and this is the part that bothers me, Phil, "...except for Phillip Harrison of 120 Colby Ave., Patterson, New Jersey."

In this part . . .

Although other parts of this book don't exactly
encourage you to micromanage your investments,
they do tend to focus your attention on the intricacies
of finding and choosing dividend stocks. In this part,
you take a step back to get a better view of the entire
landscape.

Here, I guide you through the process of developing an
effective investment strategy, show you where and how to
buy shares, and show you how to adapt your strategy to
favorable and unfavorable changes in tax legislation that
may affect your after-tax profit.

Chapter 18

Choosing an Effective Stock-Picking Strategy

. . . .

In This Chapter

▶ Reducing your exposure to risk with dollar cost averaging

▶ Spotting value through the dividend connection approach

▶ Investing against the grain with the relative dividend yield approach

▶ Buying good stocks that have temporarily fallen out of favor

▶ Going for gold with proven Dividend Achievers

. . . .

*Y*ou've mastered the basics. You can size up promising dividend stocks, sift out real losers, and manage a dividend stock portfolio as well as any investor on Wall Street. Now you want an edge — a system you can rely on to pick the best of the best almost every time.

Everyone has a favorite stock-picking strategy, and you can find loads of information about various strategies on the Web or through books. In this chapter, I highlight dividend stock-picking strategies that I deem the most fundamentally sound. You can pick one of these strategies or use any or all of them as a point of reference for developing your own, unique approach.

Minimizing Risk through Dollar Cost Averaging

Regardless of what your dividend investment strategy is, consider combining it with a dollar cost averaging approach. Dollar cost averaging isn't so much a stock-picking strategy as it is a method of systematically investing in anything over a long period. Here's how it works:

1. **Choose a dollar amount to invest on a regular basis.**

2. **Choose a regular time interval during which you can consistently invest the chosen dollar amount; for example, $100 per month or $250 every quarter.**

   For example, perhaps you choose to invest $100 on the 15th of each month.

3. **Invest the chosen dollar amount on the predetermined schedule no matter what — buy shares whether the market is up or down.**

The primary idea behind dollar cost averaging is that over time, you pay a reasonable average price for the shares you own. You don't get stuck investing a huge amount of money all at once when the share price is high and then suffer a huge loss if the price drops significantly below what you paid. Of course, you don't benefit by purchasing a large number of shares when the price is low, but that's the trade-off.

Dollar cost averaging offers several additional advantages:

- ✔ It takes the emotion out of investing, so you're less likely to make costly impulsive decisions.

- ✔ You can put a small amount of money to work in the market immediately instead of having that money sit in a relatively low-yielding bank or money market account until you've saved enough to buy shares.

- ✔ It keeps you saving and investing on a regular basis even when you may not want to, such as when the market is falling.

- ✔ It works to your advantage in bear markets. As share prices fall, you can buy more shares for the same amount of money.

Dollar cost averaging works best with mutual funds, dividend reinvestment plans (DRIPs), and direct purchase plans (DPPs) because you can purchase fractional shares to maximize every dollar. (For more about DPPs and DRIPs, see Chapter 14.) In addition, no-load funds, and many DRIPs and DPPS don't charge commissions, so all your capital is invested. (Check out Chapter 15 for the lowdown on mutual funds.)

If you're buying ETFs (exchange traded funds, covered in Chapter 16) or individual stocks, you can't buy fractional shares, so you may need to adjust your dollar amount accordingly. For example, if you set aside $100 a month to buy shares, but they're selling for $52 a pop, you can invest $104.

Reinvesting dividends is a classic way to implement the dollar cost averaging strategy.

Dollar cost averaging does have one potential drawback: Unless you're buying shares directly from a no-load mutual fund or investing directly with one company, you pay a broker commission every time you make a purchase. Commissions on ETFs and stocks can take a bite out of the capital you're actually investing. For example, if the commission is $12 per trade and your $100 per month buys ten shares, you either pony up another $12 out of your wallet or take it out of your capital, leaving you with only $88 to invest. Over the course of the year, you're paying $1,440 to buy 120 shares, whereas purchasing all those shares at once costs you $12 for the one trade and saves you $132.

In addition to all the dividend-centric books in this chapter, a very good book that appreciates dividends without focusing on them is Benjamin Graham's *The Intelligent Investor* (Harper & Row). This book gives much more detail on dollar cost averaging, the value strategy I explain in Chapter 6, and the concepts in Chapter 8. Known as the "father of value investing," Graham was a renowned investor who later taught finance at Columbia University. His most famous student was Warren Buffett, whom many consider the best investor in the world.

Embracing the Dividend Connection

The *dividend connection,* also known as the dividend-yield total return approach, is a strategy presented in Geraldine Weiss's book *The Dividend Connection: How Dividends Create Value in the Stock Market* (Dearborn Financial Publishing). According to this approach, you buy blue-chip stocks that have dropped in price and attained a historically high yield. You sell when the price is high and the yield is low. The following sections help you find blue-chip stocks and apply this strategy to investing in them.

Identifying blue-chip stocks

The first order of business in this strategy is to identify blue-chip stocks. According to Weiss, stocks must meet or exceed *all* of the following six criteria to be considered blue-chips:

- ✔ The dividend increased at least five times over the past 12 years.
- ✔ The stock carries a Standard & Poor's quality rating of A- or greater.
- ✔ The company has at least 5 million common shares outstanding.
- ✔ At least 80 institutions hold the stock.
- ✔ The company paid dividends for at least 25 years without interruption.
- ✔ Corporate profits have grown in at least 7 of the last 12 years.

Finding the connection

The connection in dividend connection refers to the link between a stock's yield and its underlying value. For a stock to be a good value it must post a high yield at a low price. So what constitutes a high yield and a low price?

- ✔ **High yield:** A dividend yield comparable to a past high yield that occurred at the end of a big price decline for this particular stock.

- ✔ **Low price:** A price comparable to a past low price that coincided with a high dividend yield.

Because each stock and each sector has its own price and yield range, nobody can tell you specifically what's a high yield or a low price. You must research each stock's history and examine its peaks and valleys to understand whether today's price is high or low. One of the main benefits of Weiss's book is that she lists the historic yield ranges for 75 blue chips from 1982 through 1994. It's a great historical record for data that's very hard to find on the Internet. Most free stock data on the Web only goes back 10 or 15 years, and that's mostly share prices, not dividend yields. The biggest downside to the strategy is you need this data to follow it. The trend's pattern can take years to appear on a graph, so you have to plot out 5 to 10 years worth of data. Combining Weiss's book and the Web charts, you can get a graph measuring a company's price versus yield over 27 years.

A low price and a high yield don't necessarily signal a good opportunity. They usually mean the company is having problems, such as falling profits, that may result from rising expenses, a poor economy, or poor management. Find out why the price is low and the yield is high before you buy. Weiss's approach of sticking with blue-chips increases the odds that the company and its share price will recover, but it offers no money-back guarantee.

I like this approach a lot; it pretty much provides a foundation for all the other approaches in this chapter. By plotting out price versus yield, this approach gives you clear signals for when to buy and sell a stock. And if you put a few charts together, they provide data that can help determine when the broad market is nearing the top of a bull run or the bottom of a bear market. But as I mention earlier, you have to chart out these graphs over a few years to find the highs and lows. Plus, you still have to do some fundamental analysis (as I explain in Chapter 8) to find out why the stocks have such low prices.

Going Against the Flow with Relative Dividend Yield

The relative dividend yield (RDY) strategy takes the dividend connection strategy I discuss in the preceding section one step further. To determine whether a stock is underpriced or expensive, this strategy compares a stock's yield to the dividend yield of the broader market. The full strategy is explained in the book *Relative Dividend Yield: Common Stock Investing for Income and Appreciation* by Anthony E. Spare with Paul Ciotti (Wiley).

RDY isn't a good strategy for those seeking instant gratification. It's a long-term strategy of three to five years that doesn't rely on past earnings, forecasted earnings, or P/E ratios to determine valuations. Flip to Chapter 8 for more on valuing stocks.

The RDY approach encourages investors to be patient, disciplined, independent, contrarian investors who move against the crowd by focusing on large companies that have experienced trouble but are familiar, well-known businesses stable enough to eventually recover. According to Spare, using absolute yield to identify undervalued stocks (as in the dividend connection approach) can leave you in a lot of mature, slow-growth industries.

RDY investors want capital appreciation as well as income. Because the yield on a RDY stock doesn't need to be very high (just higher than the market), it helps identify good values in both weak and strong markets. According to Spare, using RDY over the long term provides a portfolio with a higher stream of income, a 1.5 to 2 percent better total return, and a lower risk than the S&P 500 index does.

Sizing up a stock

The RDY reflects investor sentiment. According to Spare, a high RDY indicates despair in the market, whereas a low RDY signals investor enthusiasm. Following the relative dividend yield strategy, you buy when other investors are selling and sell when other investors are buying. This strategy's followers expect the following:

✔ **High yield:** All RDY stocks have higher than average yields. RDY investors don't buy a stock until its yield is typically at least 50 percent higher than the market. By looking at yield, RDY identifies undervalued stocks, which are expected to eventually see capital gains in terms of price. Still, the high yield likely represents a significant amount of the investor's returns.

✔ **Low risk:** RDY stocks have lower risk than the rest of the market because they're neglected stocks. When RDY identifies a potential candidate, the stock has already been beaten down and underperformed the market for some time. Because the stock's share price has already seen a significant drop, it's less likely to fall farther.

✔ **Long holding periods:** The typical holding period for an RDY stock is three to five years. When the stock's share price recovers and moves higher, it causes the stock's relative yield to drop below the market's yield, creating the sell signal.

✔ **Low turnover:** Holding stocks for longer periods means you sell only about a quarter to a third of the portfolio in a given year, compared to a 100 percent turnover at most mutual funds. Low turnover leads to lower transaction costs, leaving more money to be invested and generating better returns. In addition, fewer sales means fewer capital gains realized in any given year, which leads to a lower tax bill. Chapter 20 delves further into tax issues.

✔ **Less volatility:** Because RDY portfolios hold mostly large, mature companies with a reputation for paying consistent dividends, these stocks don't fall as much as the broader market in bear markets or stay down as long.

Much like the dividend connection (see "Embracing the Dividend Connection" earlier in this chapter), RDY gives you buy and sell signals based on yield. This strategy seems a bit more complicated than the dividend connection, which uses absolute yield. *Absolute yield* looks at a company's yield alone, independent of other variables, for buy signals. Spare says comparing yield to the market gives you buy signals in both weak and strong markets, while the dividend connection doesn't. Again, you need charts to help determine where your stock is in terms of its historic price and yield.

Calculating the market index dividend yield and a stock's relative dividend yield

The first step in determining a stock's relative dividend yield is to determine the dividend yield for the broader market — the *market index dividend yield.* Add up the annual dividends from all the stocks in the S&P 500 index and then divide by the index's current value (market capitalization):

Market Index Dividend Yield = S&P 500 Indicated Dividend ÷ S&P 500 Market Capitalization

If the idea of adding up the annual dividends from all the stocks in the S&P 500 doesn't thrill you, you can find the total S&P 500 indicated dividend and the total market capitalization on the S&P 500 Web site. Head to `www.standardandpoors.com/indices/market-attributes/en/us` and under Latest Standard & Poor's 500 Market Attributes click S&P 500 Earnings and Estimates, which opens a Microsoft Excel worksheet. The numbers you need are below "Data as of the close of." The S&P 500 started the year 2010 with a yield of 2 percent.

To calculate the relative dividend yield (RDY), divide the stock's yield by the market index dividend yield:

Relative Dividend Yield (RDY) = Stock's Yield ÷ Market Index Dividend Yield

Taming the Dogs of the Dow

The Dogs of the Dow strategy takes the relative dividend yield strategy in the preceding section to its extreme. Instead of going to the pound and taking a chance that some mangy mutt will make a good pet, this simple yet effective strategy uses dividends to find out-of-favor stocks that can beat the market. The strategy is detailed in the 1991 book *Beating the Dow: A High-Return, Low-Risk Method for Investing in the Dow Industrial Stocks with as Little as $5,000* by Michael B. O'Higgins with John Downes (HarperCollins).

O'Higgins doesn't look at the broad market or even the 500-stock universe of the S&P 500. Instead, he limits himself to just the 30 stocks that constitute the Dow Jones Industrial Average (DJIA) — the oldest measure of the U.S. stock market. He then whittles down his list to the ten most beaten-down stocks of the Dow (the Dogs of the Dow). The following section reveals the strategy in full.

Mastering the strategy

The Dogs of the Dow strategy is deliriously simple:

1. **List the yields of all 30 Dow stocks.**

   You can find a list of the 30 Dow stocks at most financial Web sites, as well as `TheWallStreetJournal.com` and `www.Djaverages.com`.

2. **Buy the ten highest yielding stocks in the Dow in equal dollar amounts.**

3. **Hold your shares for a year.**

4. **Repeat Steps 1 through 3, selling any shares that don't make the cut.**

   On average, four stocks fall off the list each year.

Dow or S&P 500?

Although the S&P 500 is a broader index covering about 70 percent of the market's total capitalization and is the prime benchmark for asset managers, the Dow is still *the* market benchmark for the rest of the country. That's because the Dow is widely accepted by the public, and all of its 30 constituents are solid blue-chip companies of huge economic importance. Even if they're dogs, they're still big dogs.

The editors of the *Wall Street Journal,* which is published by Dow Jones, choose the 30 stocks in the average. Though the specific criteria to become a Dow stock remains unknown, essentially these large, widely-held, stable, conservatively-run businesses are considered the most economically important in their industries. As of publication, rumor has it that News Corp., which owns Dow Jones, may sell the index division. Check out Chapter 2 for more on the indexes.

If you don't have enough money to buy ten stocks or want a more concentrated, less diversified portfolio, buy five stocks. After making a list of the ten highest-yielding Dow stocks, identify the five on that list with the lowest share prices. This approach gives you the five high-yielding/lowest-priced stocks, known as the *Small Dogs* or *Puppies of the Dow.*

Comparing the results

According to O'Higgins, a Dogs of the Dow portfolio annually outperforms the Industrial Average. He compared the total cumulative return of the Dogs and Puppies of the Dow strategies versus the index (excluding commissions and taxes) from 1973 through 1998.

O'Higgins determined the portfolio with the ten Dogs earned three times as much as the Dow, while the Puppy portfolio earned more than five times the index. However, the returns have recently been much less consistent. The strategy took a big hit in 2008 during the financial crisis, especially with Dow component General Motors sliding toward bankruptcy. According to the Web site www.DogsoftheDow.com, over the five years ending December 31, 2008, the DJIA outperformed the Dogs and the Puppies three out of five years. The average annual total return for the five years was 0.6 percent for the Dow, –1.3 percent for the Dogs, and 2.0 percent for the Puppies. Over the 15-year period, the index posted an average total return of 9.8 percent compared to the Dogs' average of 8.1 percent and the Puppies' 8.4 percent.

In terms of simplicity, this strategy is my favorite. No math, just make a list and follow the recipe. However, the results from the Dogs of the Dow Web site leave a lot of doubt about whether this approach remains a consistent strategy or a fad. I recommend you do more research before adopting this method.

Investing in the Dogs through mutual funds

Because of SEC restrictions, no mutual fund is allowed to own only 10 stocks. However, a few mutual funds use the Dogs of the Dow as a basis for their portfolios, including the following:

- ✔ Hennessy Total Return (HDOGX)

- ✔ Hennessy Balanced (HBFBX)

- ✔ Payden Growth & Income Fund (PDOGX)

- ✔ Elements Dogs of the Dow (DOD), an exchange-traded note that tracks the index

Exchange-traded notes (ETNs) aren't the same as ETFs. They don't hold any stocks, but are *subordinated debt* (debt with less of claim on assets) issued by an investment bank. These notes have credit risk, which means the investor receives nothing if the issuer goes bankrupt.

Checking Out the Dividend Achievers

The *Dividend Achievers* strategy focuses on companies with a proven track record of increasing their dividend payments. The approach is outlined in *Beating the S&P with Dividends: How to Build a Superior Portfolio of Dividend Yielding Stocks* by Peter O'Shea and Jonathan Worrall (Wiley). To join the list, a company must increase its dividend at least ten years in a row. Miss one dividend increase, and the company falls off (or fails to get on) the list.

The ten-year rule is tough, but it removes the uncertainty of inconsistent dividend payments. A company that can increase dividends over a ten-year period shows it can sustain dividend growth through both up and down economic cycles. It also implies less risk and volatility than the general market. (Want even more stability? Check out the list of S&P 500 Dividend Aristocrats in the appendix.)

In January 2010, the Broad Dividend Achievers Index removed 89 companies and added 18 new companies for a total of 210. About 75 percent of the deletions came from the financial, real estate, and insurance industries. You can find the complete list at `http://www.indxis.com/USBroad.html`.

As of November 30, 2009, the Broad Dividend Achievers Index had a yield of 2.90 percent and a five-year dividend growth rate of 10.52 percent. According to Dividend Achiever Index managing firm Indxis, the Broad Dividend Achievers beat the S&P 500 Index for the 10-, 15-, and 20-year periods through December 31, 2009. A $10,000 investment in the index on November 30, 1999, would be worth $11,183 ten years later, for a 1.06 percent annualized return, compared with $9,443 in the S&P 500, for a –0.57 percent annualized return.

As an investor, you can pick and choose stocks from any of the 12 indexes that follow the Dividend Achievers methodology (listed at www.indxis.com/ DividendAchievers.html). For greater diversification, you may want to consider investing through a mutual fund or ETF. One mutual fund that follows the Dividend Achievers methodology is Vanguard Dividend Appreciation Index Fund (VDAIX). Several ETFs also focus on the Dividend Achievers:

- ✔ PowerShares Buyback Achievers Portfolio (PKW)
- ✔ PowerShares Dividend Achievers Portfolio (PFM)
- ✔ PowerShares High Yield Equity Dividend Achievers Portfolio (PEY)
- ✔ PowerShares International Dividend Achievers Portfolio (PID)
- ✔ Vanguard Dividend Appreciation ETF (VIG)

History of Dividend Achievers

The Dividend Achievers began in 1979 when the credit rating agency Moody's compiled a list of companies that had increased their annual dividend payments for ten or more consecutive years. The *Handbook of Dividend Achievers* was first published four years later and is still published annually. A financial information firm named Mergent bought the division called Moody's Investor Service in 1998 and rebranded the handbooks under the Mergent name.

The first index based on the dividend achiever methodology launched in 2004. By the end of 2008, more than $3 billion was invested in products based on the methodology. Mergent acquired Kinetic Information System in 2006 and turned that into a new company for index creation and licensing called Indxis. Indxis currently manages all 12 Dividend Achievers indexes.

Chapter 19

Buying and Selling Dividend Stocks: Where and How

*R*egardless of how much you know about investing, you can set up an account with any online discount brokerage and start buying and selling dividend (or any other) stocks this afternoon — assuming, of course, the stock market is open and you can transfer some money into your account.

Before forging ahead with that plan, however, you may want to consider your options. If you're not fully confident in what you're doing or want a professional opinion before you issue a buy or sell order, you may benefit from the expertise of a full-service broker, who doubles as a financial advisor. If you opt to go it alone and process your transactions through a discount broker, you also need to consider the various types of buy and sell orders and how to place orders.

In this chapter, I provide information and guidance to help you choose between teaming up with a full-service broker and flying solo with a discount broker. If you choose the discount broker option, I bring you up to speed on how to issue buy and sell orders on dividend stocks.

 The only way you can buy shares yourself is by enrolling in a Direct Purchase Plan (DPP), which I explain in Chapter 14. Otherwise, you must go through a broker — someone who has passed the exams and background check necessary to receive broker certification.

Deciding Between a Full-Service and Discount Broker

In the stock market, you find two species of brokers — full-service and discount:

- **Full-service broker:** A *full-service broker* does everything a discount broker does and then some. She can help you develop an investment strategy that's suitable for your situation and goals, suggest particular stocks, issue the necessary buy and sell orders on your behalf, and help you make the necessary adjustments to your portfolio as your situation and goals change. Typically, you develop a personal relationship with one stockbroker and/or financial advisor at a brokerage house.

- **Discount broker:** A *discount broker* simply follows orders. You tell him to buy 200 shares of XYZ for $20 a share, and that's what he does. If you want to be the master of your own destiny, a discount broker is the choice for you. You do your own research, take full credit for your gains, and take full responsibility for your losses.

Whether you decide to work with a full-service or discount broker, consider costs, minimum balance, products, services, and reputation. Which option is best depends entirely on your preferences. In the following sections, I lay out the pros and cons of each option so that you can make a well-informed choice.

Debating the benefits and drawbacks of a full-service broker

Having an expert around to watch your back and call your attention to potentially incredible investment opportunities may sound like an ideal arrangement, but before you take the plunge, consider the following pros and cons of hiring a full-service broker.

Full-service advantages

Hiring a full-service broker to manage your portfolio is like hiring a mechanic to fix your car. If you find car engines as confusing as a foreign language, a highly qualified mechanic committed to providing top-notch service and not ripping off his customers is likely to do a better job servicing your car than you can do yourself. In addition to providing superior service and maintenance suggestions to keep your car trouble-free, the mechanic frees you to do your thing so that you can focus on your day job, spend more time with your family and friends, enjoy your life, and not have to worry about playing the role of grease monkey on your weekends off.

A trained, skilled, and experienced full-service broker who's committed to serving your best interests can save you loads of time, energy, and worry while potentially boosting your portfolio's earnings more than enough to cover his fees and commissions. A great broker eats, sleeps, and breathes Wall Street. His job is to research companies, keep his finger on the pulse of the stock market, and earn his clients money — something you may not have the time, skill, or interest to do yourself.

Depending on your broker and the relationship you develop, you may receive some additional perks. A good full-service broker examines your financial situation and helps you develop a custom plan. Such a plan is likely to go beyond investing in the stock market and may include developing a budget or savings plan, obtaining sufficient life insurance, offering tax-saving strategies, and planning your estate.

Regardless of whether you fly solo or hire an expert, stay on top of your finances. No one cares as much about your money and how fast it grows as you do. That's because no one else depends on it for their retirement or other goals.

Full-service disadvantages

Enlisting the assistance of an expert always comes with a price tag. In the case of a full-service broker, that price tag may represent a combination of commissions and fees called *transaction costs* and may come in much higher than it would at a discount brokerage. In addition, a good full-service broker may be reluctant to work with investors with small nest eggs and screen them out by requiring higher minimum investments. This bias isn't automatically a bad thing as long as you have the money, but if you don't, it may prevent you from gaining access to some of the most qualified full-service brokers.

Whether you go full-service or discount, focus on keeping costs down. Your total return, or *net profit,* is determined after portfolio costs. If your portfolio earned a profit of $600 one year, but it took $700 worth of expenses to build and maintain it, you actually end up with a $100 loss. To paraphrase Forrest Gump, Wall Street is like a box of chocolates; you never know what you'll get in terms of returns from year to year. So although you can't control how big of a profit you earn, you have complete control over the expenses you pay.

When dealing with full-service brokers, be aware of the possibility of conflicts of interest. If the broker is more concerned with padding her pockets than optimizing your portfolio, she may sell you investment products that are more profitable for her or her investment firm than for you. Brokers have also been known to engage in a shady activity called *churning,* in which they encourage clients to buy and sell more often than necessary so the brokerage can earn a commission with each transaction.

Always ask your advisor the rationale behind each recommendation. If the advisor can't explain why a particular investment is a good one or you don't like the reason, don't buy the investment. Also keep tabs on the turnover rate of stocks in your portfolio. If your broker is constantly buying and selling (and raking in commissions with each transaction), express your concern and put a stop to it if all the activity isn't clearly in your best interest.

Examining the pros and cons of discount brokers

Discount brokers are best for the do-it-yourselfer. If you like to do your own research, understand how to trade, and don't want investment products pushed on you, you'd probably prefer a discount broker.

The difference between discount brokers and full-service brokers is the same as the difference between a cashier and a top-notch salesperson. Like a cashier, a discount broker simply processes the transaction after you already decided, on your own, what to buy (as opposed to the full-service broker — discussed in the preceding section — who, like a salesperson, helps you choose the right products and services to meet your needs and then processes the transaction). A shady salesperson, however, may try to sell you products and services that put more money in his pocket rather than the products and services that are truly best for you.

In the following sections, I describe the advantages and disadvantages of discount brokers in greater detail so that you have a clearer idea of the tradeoffs.

Discount broker advantages

When you see the title *discount broker,* you pretty much know the one big advantage that discount brokers have over their full-service counterparts – they charge less to process buy and sell orders. Some charge as little as $3 to process a transaction, regardless of the number of shares you buy or sell.

Another big advantage is that except for the relatively small transaction fee, the broker doesn't have any vested interest in what you're buying or selling. Though that may seem like a disadvantage, it prevents any conflict of interest. The broker has nothing to gain through the sale of a particular investment product, so she has no reason to try to influence your choices.

Discount broker disadvantages

With discount brokers, however, you pay less and you get less. You voluntarily give up any expert advice a broker may have to offer. As a result, you're flying solo. However, that doesn't mean you're flying blind. Most discount brokers provide plenty of educational materials and research tools to help you screen for stocks and track market conditions. Some may even provide access to analyst reports from top Wall Street firms.

Another drawback you can expect from some discount brokers is that although the transaction fees are low, the broker may charge other fees to make up the difference, including inactivity fees, fees for closing an account, paperwork fees, IRA custodial fees, and maintenance fees. You can mitigate any losses from these fees by researching brokers carefully, comparing fees, and avoiding brokers who are clearly set up to take their clients to the cleaners.

For details on selecting a discount broker, head to "Finding and Choosing a Discount Broker" later in this chapter.

Choosing a Full-Service Broker

Many people have neither the interest, ability, nor time to manage their finances. After a hard day's work, most people just want to relax with their friends and family. They don't want to come home to a bunch of homework.

A full-service broker can take the hassles and headaches of dividend investing off your plate. However, a lot of shady characters play the role of full-service broker, so be careful. In the following sections, I show you how to choose a reliable and reputable broker.

Deciding between the fiduciary and suitability standards

Full-service brokers don't like to be called stockbrokers these days. They prefer more glamorous names such as investment advisor, account executive, financial consultant, financial planner, or retirement specialist. This list can also include analysts, insurance agents, accountants, and attorneys. What the broker calls himself, however, doesn't matter as much as the standard of business he follows: *suitability* or *fiduciary.* The following sections delve into these standards.

Fiduciary

If at all possible, get a full-service broker who follows the fiduciary standard. *Fiduciaries* are responsible for doing the right thing for their clients' investments at all times. The fiduciary is required to work for your best interests and your financial goals first rather than for himself or his firm.

Fiduciaries must also register with the SEC or their state to receive the designation of *Registered Investment Advisor* (RIA). The SEC is in charge of regulating RIAs managing more than $25 million. RIAs with less under management typically register with their states. To determine whether a particular firm is an RIA, perform a search at www.adviserinfo.sec.gov.

Fiduciaries typically pursue further studies to receive advanced accreditation, such as the following:

- ✔ Certified Financial Planner (CFP)
- ✔ Chartered Financial Analyst (CFA)
- ✔ Chartered Financial Consultant (ChFC)
- ✔ Certified Public Accountant/Personal Financial Specialist (CPA/PFS)

Neither the federal nor any state government requires a person to hold any of these designations or have any kind of degree in order to work as a "financial planner." If your advisor is a registered investment advisor (RIA), a CPA, or an attorney, you can be sure they're acting as a fiduciary. If you see CFP, CFA, or ChFC after an advisor's name, that person has been professionally certified to have met certain education and ethical requirements, but none of these designations guarantees the person is a fiduciary. Always ask.

Suitability

Most stockbrokers follow the suitability standard — the less rigorous of the two. Unlike fiduciary, *suitability* essentially says the broker doesn't have to put your interests first. As long as the product is suitable to your goals and risk tolerance, the broker isn't required to sell the best or cheapest product. He can sell you the product that pays him the highest commissions and fees.

For example, although many mutual funds track the S&P 500 Index, your broker can stick you with a fund that charges an expense ratio of 1 percent and pays him a front load of 5 percent instead of putting you in a comparable no-load fund with an expense ratio of 0.18 percent. (Chapters 15 and 16 give you more info on expense ratios and loads, respectively.)

Stockbrokers who follow the suitability model only need to register with the National Association of Securities Dealers, a nongovernmental industry regulating body.

Checking out investment preferences

Like individual investors, brokers have preferences in terms of strategy. Some brokers prefer high-growth stocks, and others focus more on value. Some tend to prefer mutual funds over investing in individual stocks. Though you want someone who knows all the available investment vehicles, you also want someone who's as committed as you are to dividend investing. If the broker is more bullish on growth stocks, his focus may wander from the types of companies you're interested in investing in.

Before hiring a broker, ask a few questions about the strategy he recommends without letting him know your preferences. Ask what percentage of your portfolio he would recommend investing in growth stocks, dividend stocks, and bonds. Ask whether growth or dividend stocks are a better choice right now. Ask about the tradeoffs between growth and dividend investing. The answers the broker provides should paint a pretty good picture of his preferences.

Asking about fee structure

No financial advisor works for free. They all have some way of receiving compensation for their services. This compensation typically comes in one of the following forms:

- **Fee-only compensation:** The financial advisor charges a fee for her advice and for managing your portfolio. The fee is usually an hourly rate, flat fee, retainer, or a percentage of the profits your portfolio earns. Paying a percentage of your profits is usually best because it minimizes potential conflicts of interest and aligns your advisor's interests with yours. If your portfolio gains, she makes more money. If it declines, she makes less (or no) money.

- **Fee-based compensation:** The financial advisor can charge fees and collect commissions from any third-party products she sells. The idea here is that the commissions can offset some of the costs you're required to pay. The commissions, however, have the potential of creating a conflict of interest.

- **Commissions:** Brokers compensated with commissions are mainly salespeople working for commissions rather than for their clients. Even well-intentioned advisors are likely to be swayed into selling products that put more money in their pockets.

In Chapters 4 and 18, I recommend implementing a dollar cost averaging approach to diminish risk. And throughout the book I recommend a dividend reinvestment strategy. Each of these strategies requires investing relatively small amounts of money over time. Some full-service brokers may let you reinvest your dividends with no additional fee, but some don't. When shopping for a full-service broker, ask about the cost of implementing these strategies. Small fees can add up quickly when they're charged to you on a monthly or even a quarterly basis.

Ask your financial advisor how she gets paid and whether she's getting paid to make certain recommendations. Don't be afraid. It's your money, and you're the client. You wouldn't buy a car without asking the price, so why would you buy stock without asking? Consider it comparison shopping. Ask whether you can get something similar for less. Get a few quotes. You may be able to negotiate a lower fee. Tell the financial advisor you want a signed document outlining her fee structure and fiduciary status before becoming a client.

While you're asking about the cost, ask about how risky the investment is as well. Sometimes the upside isn't worth the risk of losing money.

Conducting your own background check

When you're in the market for a financial advisor or full-service broker, ask friends, family members, and colleagues for recommendations. Choosing someone who's provided satisfactory service to at least one person you know is usually a good place to start. You can then do your own research to double-check the person's or the firm's credentials. Or, if you still have no leads, you can start poking around online to find some promising candidates.

To find reputable full-service brokers or investment advisors, check out the following sources:

- ✔ National Association of Personal Financial Advisors (NAPFA) is an organization of fee-only financial planners. NAPFA members agree to follow certain standards and must achieve a certain level of competence. Visit www.napfa.org.

- ✔ SmartMoney at www.smartmoney.com publishes an annual survey of discount and full-service brokers.

- ✔ Barron's online.barrons.com publishes an annual survey of discount and full-service brokers.

- ✔ Financial Industry Regulatory Authority (FINRA) at www.finra.org provides free broker reports. Each report lists any complaints or penalties filed against the broker or his firm.

Finding and Selecting a Discount Broker

If you want to make your own investment decisions and don't need the premium services offered by a full-service broker, you may prefer to use a discount broker. Most of them allow you to trade online for a very low commission.

First, decide on your main criteria for a discount broker. Is it the cheapest trade, the best trading system, the best research tools and information, or something else? After deciding what's most important, head online and comparison shop. Following is a list of the top discount brokers in alphabetical order. All have solid reputations, but I'm not recommending one over any other:

- Charles Schwab: www.schwab.com or 866-232-9890
- E*Trade: us.etrade.com or 800-387-2331
- Fidelity: www.fidelity.com or 800-Fidelity
- Firstrade: www.firstrade.com or 800-869-8800
- Interactive Brokers: www.interactivebrokers.com or 877-442-2757
- Muriel Siebert: www.siebertnet.com or 800-872-0711
- Options Xpress: www.optionsxpress.com or 888-280-8020
- Scottrade: www.scottrade.com or 800-619-7283
- Sharebuilder: www.sharebuilder.com or 800-747-2537
- SogoTrade: www.sogotrade.com or 212-668-8686
- TD Ameritrade: www.tdameritrade.com or 800-454-9272
- TradeKing: www.tradeking.com or 877-495-5464
- Vanguard: www.vanguard.com or 877-662-7447
- Wells Fargo: www.wellsfargo.com or 866-243-0931

When comparing discount brokers, consider the cost of implementing a dollar cost averaging strategy and dividend reinvestment strategy with each broker. Some online brokers offer automatic investing with lower commissions and fees per trade, which is perfect for a dollar cost averaging strategy. If you plan on reinvesting dividends, you also want to make sure that your reinvestment transactions are free or at least reasonable. (To determine what's "reasonable," comparison shop.)

Buying and Selling Shares

Everyone knows you can buy and sell shares of stock on the stock market. Some investors, however, don't realize the nuances of the different buy and sell orders — market orders, time orders, limit orders, stop-loss orders, and so on. By understanding these different types of orders and using them correctly, you can maximize your dividend profits and minimize your potential losses. This knowledge is especially helpful if you're working with a discount broker, who doesn't provide the same guidance as a full-service broker. (See the rest of this chapter for more on choosing a broker.)

In the following sections, you get to brush up on the different types of orders before you make your first (or next) trade. For more about the various types of orders, check out *Stock Investing For Dummies,* 3rd Edition, by Paul Mladjenovic (Wiley).

Market orders

The *market order* is the simplest, most straightforward way to buy or sell stock. You place an order to buy or sell shares, and it gets filled as quickly as possible at the best possible price. Market orders carry no time or price limitations. Stocks with high trading volume process the trade immediately. Stocks with a low trading volume may take longer to trade and experience a wide *bid-ask spread* — the difference between the seller's asking price and the buyer's bid amount.

Market orders are the only trades that always go through on the day they're placed. The downside of the market order is you never know what price you've paid until after the trade is completed. If the market is very volatile on the day you place the order, you can end up paying a price very different from the one you were expecting.

Limit orders

Limit orders are the flip side of market orders. With a market order, you want the trade to go through immediately and aren't price sensitive. With a *limit order,* you want a specific price for a purchase or sale regardless of how long getting that price takes. You're willing to wait to get what you want — just remember that you may wait forever if the stock never reaches your limit. Limit orders also allow you to trade without having to pay close attention to the market.

Say you want to buy shares of Carrel Industries. You've done your homework and think that the price is currently overvalued at $25. You can put in a limit order for 100 shares at $20. If the share price drops to that threshold, you get the stock at your price. Otherwise, your order remains unfilled.

You can also use a limit order on the sell side. If you bought shares at $20 and the stock is moving higher, you can put a limit order in to sell the shares at $25.

Limit orders (among other kinds of trades) often don't go through on the day you place them, so you need to place a time order (which I explain in the following section) with a limit order.

Time orders

Two kinds of *time orders* determine how long an order (such as a limit order — see the preceding section) remains in effect:

- ✔ **Day orders:** *Day orders* expire at the end of the trading day on which you place them. If the stock you want is at $42 and you place a day order to buy shares at $40, the order expires unfilled if the stock doesn't fall to $40 during the trading session.
- ✔ **Good-till-canceled:** Just like it sounds, the *good-till-canceled order* stays in effect until one of two things happen: Either the stock hits the price you want and the trade goes through, or you call your broker and actively cancel the order (although note that some brokers put a 30 or 60 day limit on good-till-canceled orders).

Stop-loss orders

Stop-loss orders work similarly to limit orders but with a different strategy. With a limit order, you know how much profit you want to earn, so you place a limit to sell your shares at the specific price that locks in that profit. With the stop-loss order, your stock is rising and you want to let it ride to see how far the stock goes while protecting the capital gains already in the share price if the shares fall.

The stop-loss order puts in a sell order to sell your shares if they fall to a specific price below where the shares are today, usually 10 percent below the current share price. For instance, if you bought Carrel Industries at $20 and it's now trading at $30, you put the stop-loss order in at $27. If the stock falls to $27, your shares are sold. That order gives the dividend stock enough room to bounce around in a day-to-day trading range yet protects 70 percent of your profit.

Trailing stop orders

Trailing stops are a technique that uses the stop-loss orders from the preceding section to preserve your dividend stock's profits. *Trailing stops* are stop-loss orders that trail the movement of the stock's price. As the stock moves higher, you keep moving the stop-loss order higher to protect more profits.

In the preceding section's example, shares of Carrel Industries are selling for $30 and you have a stop-loss at $27, or a 10-percent drop in price. If the stock rises to $36, you move the stop-loss order to $32.40 to maintain that 10-percent floor. If the stock moves to $40, you cancel that stop-loss and replace it with a new one at $36. By trailing the stock by the same amount as the price increases, the stop-loss progressively protects more and more of your profits than if you had left it at $27.

Brokers rarely institute trailing stops, so you can't just set it and forget it. You have to actively manage your trailing stops.

Short sales

Wall Street calls buyers *long on stocks.* You expect your stock to move higher, and you have unlimited profit potential. However, you can also profit from a falling market or declines in individual stocks. Selling a stock first with the expectation of buying it back later at a lower price is known as *selling short* or *shorting a stock.* This strategy is one of the main ways to make money in a bear market. Instead of buying low and selling high, you first sell high with the hope of later buying low.

Selling short is a three step process.

1. **You borrow shares.**

   Your broker borrows the shares you want to sell from either his own inventory or one of his clients. If the broker doesn't have easy access, he may need to go into the market to buy the shares for you to borrow.

2. **You sell the shares.**

   You tell your broker to sell the shares with either a market order or a limit order. Then your account is credited with the proceeds from the sale.

3. **You buy new shares and return them to the lender.**

   To close the trade, you buy shares and give them back to the client or broker you borrowed them from. If the system works in your favor, the stock falls and you buy the shares at a lower price than you sold them for, garnering a profit for yourself (because you paid less than you received for them). If you sell 100 shares at $30 and buy them back at $20, you earn $1,000 (100 shares times $10).

You can put a stop-loss order on a short sale too, to limit the potential losses. See the nearby sidebar "Going short can leave you short" for more on the potential dangers of shorting.

Going short can leave you short

Going short is much riskier than going long. When you buy shares of stock, the worst that can happen is that the share price falls to $0 and you lose your entire investment. However, the sky's the limit on your profit potential.

The situation is the exact opposite with short selling. The most you can earn is what you sold it for, and that's if the stock falls to $0. The potential losses, however, are unlimited. Although you can only lose 100 percent of your investment on a long trade, you can lose much more than 100 percent on a short trade.

For instance, if you expect a stock price to fall and sell short 100 shares at $30, you receive $3,000. If the stock keeps rising instead of falling and you, conceding it was a bad trade, buy the shares back at $70, you have to pay $7,000. You lose both your initial profit and an additional $4,000.

Chapter 20

Tuning In to Changes in Tax Laws

In This Chapter

▶ Knowing how Uncle Sam taxes dividends

▶ Differentiating between qualifying and nonqualifying dividends

▶ Unraveling the complexities of taxing dividends in mutual funds

▶ Grasping the dividend tax ramifications when investing in ETFs, MLPs, and REITs

▶ Staying on top of changes in the tax code

Successful investing isn't only about earning handsome returns but also about how much of that money you walk away with at the end. If your investment earns an 8 percent return that's taxed at 30 percent, your net return is actually only 5.6 percent (.08 return × .7 untaxed percentage = .056 after-tax return). Instead of earning $80 on a $1,000 investment, you pocket only $56. Tax that same investment at only 15 percent, and your net return climbs to 6.8 percent (.08 return × .85 untaxed percentage = .068 after-tax return). Instead of netting only $56 per $1,000 invested, you keep $68.

For a clear explanation on how to calculate after-tax returns, check out the section "Calculating your after-tax return" later in this chapter.

If you're reinvesting your returns, taxes take an even bigger bite out of your net profit, because each dollar the taxman takes is one fewer dollar you can put back into the stock market. As a result, your compounding dividends compound less dramatically.

To maximize your net return on investments, brush up on and stay current with the tax code. This chapter highlights key areas of interest to dividend investors and shows you how to stay on top of any changes in how the government taxes earnings.

Consult a tax specialist for specific advice. Although this chapter provides plenty of valuable information on how to lighten the tax burden on your investment returns, I'm not a tax specialist. Plus, tax laws do change. The information in this chapter is intended to help you gain a better understanding of investment-related tax issues and identify tax issues you may want to discuss with your accountant when developing your investment strategy.

Brushing Up on Dividend Taxation

The government often uses tax policy to encourage certain economic and consumer activity. To stimulate the economy in the early 1980s, for example, the government slashed tax rates on long-term capital gains. Up to that point, capital gains were taxed as ordinary income at a rate as high as 70 percent. The tax cut lowered the rate on long-term capital gains to 20 percent, helping to fuel one of the largest economic expansions in history.

After the tech bubble burst in 2000, the economy slowed once again. To pull the country out of another recession, in 2003 President George W. Bush signed into law the Jobs and Growth Tax Relief Reconciliation Act (JGTRRA), which cut taxes again, this time on ordinary income, capital gains, *and* dividends.

In the following sections, I explain some of the tax issues that affect investors, particularly investors who focus on dividend stocks. I reveal the negative effects of double taxation on corporate profits and dividend returns, the positive effects of the JGTRRA, and how you (as a dividend investor) benefit from the tax changes provided for in the JGTRRA. I explain how to tell the difference between a qualifying and nonqualifying dividend and how to make sure you hold shares long enough to take advantage of any available tax breaks.

Dividends are taxed in the year they're received. The time the payment arrives, not the *date of declaration* (date the board of directors announces the dividend payment), determines when the dividend is taxed. Head to Chapter 2 for more on the date of declaration and other important dividend-related dates.

Recognizing the drawbacks of double taxation

In taxing dividends, the government engages in a form of double dipping, more commonly referred to as *double taxation*. With double taxation, the government collects taxes on the same money twice — it taxes the company's profits (typically at a rate of 35 percent) and then taxes the dividends investors receive, which come out of the company's after-tax profits. Prior to JGTRRA, this arrangement meant the government could receive 35 percent of a company's profits and then up to another 38.6 percent of each investor's cut!

Double taxation has several effects on how companies do business and where investors choose to put their money:

✔ To dodge the double-taxation bullet, many corporations choose to invest all of their profits in research, development, and other ventures rather than distribute a portion of the profits to investors.

✔ Investors also are motivated to dodge the double-taxation bullet by investing in companies that *don't* pay dividends. Instead of relying on dividends for their returns, investors tend to shift their focus to growth and rely on share price appreciation for their returns when they sell their stock.

✔ The threat of double taxation may drive management to invest in projects with less potential merely to avoid the double tax, which may be bad for the company and investors.

Getting a break with the JGTRRA

The JGTRRA reduced the dividend tax rate from the investor's ordinary income tax rate to a maximum of 15 percent for most taxpayers or 5 percent for taxpayers in the 10- to 15-percent tax brackets. This tax cut represented a huge savings for dividend investors, as shown in Table 20-1, which compares the old and new rates, their pieces of your dividend per $1,000, and how much the new rates save you.

Table 20-1	JGTRRA's Effect on Dividend Tax Rates			
Old Tax Rate/ Bracket	*New Tax Rate*	*Old Tax*	*New Tax*	*Savings*
10%	5%	$100	$50	$50
15%	5%	$150	$50	$100
27%	15%	$270	$150	$120
30%	15%	$300	$150	$150
35%	15%	$350	$150	$200
38.6%	15%	$386	$150	$236

These new, lower tax rates triggered three major changes in the market:

✔ **They leveled the playing field for growth and income investors.** Prior to this act, growth stocks were more attractive from a tax perspective because capital gains were taxed at a significantly lower rate than dividends.

✔ **The tax cuts put more money in taxpayers' pockets, fueling the economy.** Dividend-paying companies could afford to pay higher dividends, and as demand for stock rose, so did share prices.

✔ **More companies started paying dividends.** The reduction of the long-term capital gains tax in the early 1980s triggered a trend of decreasing dividend payments. To avoid the high taxes on dividends, more companies invested more of their profits in growth, and investors preferred reaping their rewards in capital gains, which were taxed at a lower rate. The JGTRRA reversed this trend.

JGTRRA provisions

The Jobs and Growth Tax Relief Reconciliation Act of 2003 called for more than simply lowering the tax rate on dividends. It includes many important provisions for taxpayers. Here are the four most important to investors:

✔ Reduction in the tax rate on net capital gains (net long-term capital gain minus any net short-term capital losses) to 15 percent from 20 percent and to 5 percent from 10 percent for taxpayers in the 10- and 15-percent tax brackets. However, from 2008 through 2010, the 10- and 15-percent tax brackets actually pay no capital gains taxes, a 0-percent rate.

✔ Reduction in the tax rate on qualifying dividends to match the rate for long-term capital gains, resulting in a new maximum tax rate of 15 percent and 5 percent for taxpayers in the 10- to 15-percent tax bracket.

✔ Reduction in federal income tax rates for taxpayers in the higher tax brackets. Rates were reduced to 25, 28, 33, and 35 percent from 27, 30, 35, and 38.6 percent, respectively.

✔ Expansion of the tax brackets so that more taxpayers qualify for lower tax rates. Under the old law, for example, couples earning between $47,450 and $114,650 were in the 27-percent tax bracket. Under the new law, earnings between $56,800 and $114,650 fall in the 25-percent tax bracket, and those earning $14,000 to $56,800 are taxed at a rate of 15 percent.

Identifying qualifying dividends

All dividends aren't created equal. Some qualify for JGTRRA tax breaks, and some don't. Almost all dividends paid by U.S. corporations qualify for the lower tax rate. Notable exceptions included REITs (real estate investment trusts, covered in Chapter 13) and master limited partnerships (MLP, which I discuss in Chapter 10). If the dividends qualify for the lower tax rate, the investor needs to meet the holding period requirements I spell out in the following section. Dividends paid by foreign corporations may qualify if the corporation's stock or American Depository Receipts (ADRs) are traded on well-established U.S. securities markets or the corporation is eligible under a tax treaty with the United States.

Determining which stocks don't qualify is a little easier than determining which stocks do qualify. Any item in the following list can *disqualify* a dividend from preferred tax treatment under the JGTRRA:

✔ Dividends from preferred stock that's treated more as an interest-bearing debt instrument than a true dividend-paying stock.

✔ Dividends paid into tax-deferred retirement accounts, including IRAs, 401(k) plans, and deferred annuities. The tax is levied as ordinary income when you withdraw money.

✔ Dividends from money market accounts.

- ✔ Dividends from insurance policies.

- ✔ Dividends from mutual funds attributable to interest and short-term capital gains.

- ✔ Majority of dividends from S-Corporations.

- ✔ Dividends paid to investors named as nominees.

- ✔ Dividends paid by tax-exempt organizations, including some mutual savings banks and savings institutions such as credit unions, mutual insurance companies, farmers' cooperatives, nonprofit voluntary employee benefit associations (VEBAs), and building and loan associations.

- ✔ Stocks, including MLPs and REITs, that have built-in tax preferences. See "Understanding MLP and REIT Taxation" later in this chapter for details.

Meeting the holding period requirement

Even if the dividends come from a qualified company, another factor that can disqualify dividends from the JGTRRA-preferred taxed rate is a failure on your part to hold the shares for long enough. You can't just buy a dividend stock a day before the *ex-dividend date* (point after which the dividend is removed from the share price), sell your shares the day after you collect the next dividend, and expect to receive preferential tax treatment under the JGTRRA. You have to hold your shares for a reasonable amount of time. What's reasonable? That depends on whether you're holding common or preferred stock:

- ✔ **Common stock:** You must hold your shares for more than 60 days during the 121-day period beginning 60 days prior to the ex-dividend date. In other words, you have to buy your shares at least one day (up to 60 days) before the ex-dividend date and then hold them for at least 61 days.

- ✔ **Preferred stock:** You must hold your shares for more than 90 days during the 181-day period beginning 90 days prior to the ex-dividend date. In other words, you have to buy your shares at least one day (up to 90 days) before the ex-dividend date and then hold them for at least 91 days.

The day you purchase your shares doesn't count, but the day you sell your shares does. Chapter 2 gives you more info on common and preferred stock.

When the company issues you a federal tax form 1099-DIV, it lists the monetary value of the dividends that potentially qualify for the lower tax rate. Whether they do qualify depends on how long you held the shares. It's up to you to determine whether they qualify or not. Check the ex-dividend date and the date you bought and sold the shares to determine whether your dividends qualify for the lower tax rate. Better yet, check the ex-dividend date and your purchase date prior to selling shares and make sure you've met the holding requirement *before* you sell.

Wondering whether the tax break will survive

The JGTRRA's original sunset provision stated that any and all tax benefits were to expire after the 2008 tax year. The Tax Increase Prevention and Reconciliation Act of 2005 extended the expiration date to December 31, 2010. Unless Congress extends the deadline again, the dividend tax break ends on that date, and dividends go back to being taxed as ordinary income at rates up to 35 percent. The tax on capital gains increases to a maximum rate of 20 percent.

In March 2009, Senator Max Baucus proposed making a selection of tax breaks permanent, including the reduced tax rates on long-term capital gains and dividends for taxpayers in the 10-, 15-, 25-, and 28-percent tax brackets. Dividends would be taxed at 20 percent in higher tax brackets. As of this book's publication, no decision has been made. In light of the federal government's fiscal deficit, many political observers believe that President Barack Obama won't extend tax provisions for capital gains. As for dividends, some relief is expected for taxpayers in the lower tax brackets. However, taxpayers in the higher income brackets should prepare to pay a higher tax rate on their dividends in 2011.

Delaying taxes with tax-deferred accounts

If you're holding your dividend stocks in an IRA, KEOGH, SEP, or other tax-deferred retirement account, you can forget all this business about holding-period requirements. Any dividends you receive are added to the pot tax-free (for now, anyway). You pay taxes only when you withdraw money from the account.

Being able to reinvest tax-free for decades provides a great benefit, in that you have more money to invest. With tax-deferred accounts, you reinvest 100 percent of your income. The big trade-off for being allowed to reinvest your dividends and grow your capital gains for years without paying taxes is that you may not receive the lower tax rate. When you begin withdrawing your money, it may be taxed at the same rate as ordinary income.

Most tax-deferred accounts are prohibited from owning master limited partnerships. The tax accounting on these companies is too complicated to handle in a tax-deferred fund.

Taxing Dividends from Mutual Funds

Mutual funds are pass-through investment vehicles, as explained in Chapter 15. If the funds pass at least 90 percent of the portfolio's profits to the shareholders, the fund's tax obligation gets passed through to the shareholders as well. If the fund holds any income, it must pay taxes on that, so most funds pass through 100 percent of their profits. The profits that mutual funds distribute can take many forms, each with its own tax rules:

- ✔ **Capital gains:** From the sale of assets

- ✔ **Ordinary dividends:** Mostly from stocks, but can include all kinds of taxable income

- ✔ **Interest distributions exempt from taxation:** Such as municipal bonds or other obligations from state and local governments

- ✔ **Interest:** From bonds and other debt obligations

- ✔ **Non-dividend distributions:** A portion of your initial investment returned to you, which isn't considered income

To further complicate the determination of tax rates on profits is the fact that holding requirements for lower tax rates apply to both how long the fund holds certain stocks and how long you hold your shares in the fund. At the end of the tax year, your mutual fund issues you a 1099-DIV indicating which dividends and capital gains qualify for the lower tax rates and which don't *inside the fund.* To determine whether these dividends and capital gains actually qualify for you, you must account for the length of time you held your shares in the fund. In the following sections, I explain how these two levels of criteria contribute in determining the tax rates for profits on dividend stocks held in a mutual fund.

Don't assume because the fund says this amount of dividends are qualified that they actually receive the lower tax rate. The fund doesn't take into consideration *your* holding period when it declares qualified dividends. It just lets you know that the fund has done its part to make them "potentially" qualified by holding them for the 61-day period. Both you and the fund need to hold the appropriate shares for 61 days of the 121-day period surrounding the ex-dividend date. But they don't have to be the exact same 61 days.

Inspecting your 1099-DIV

Each year, typically in January or February, but sometimes as late as early April, you can expect to receive a late Christmas present from each of your dividend stocks and mutual funds — a 1099-DIV (shown in Figure 20-1).

The 1099-DIV reports all your taxable income distributions from the fund so you can account for them appropriately on your tax return. If your present doesn't arrive, contact the fund company for the information.

As you can see, this form breaks the distributions out into little boxes (although some forms present the information in columns). In the following sections, I describe the contents of certain boxes so that you can decipher the amounts and gain a clearer understanding of how these amounts are taxed.

Figure 20-1:
Form 1099-
DIV reports
dividends
and capital
gains you
earned
inside your
fund.

PAYER'S name, street address, city, state, ZIP code, and telephone no.		1a Total ordinary dividends $	OMB No. 1545-0110	**Dividends and Distributions**
		1b Qualified dividends $	20**09** Form **1099-DIV**	
		2a Total capital gain distr. $	2b Unrecap. Sec. 1250 gain $	**Copy A** **For Internal Revenue Service Center** File with Form 1096.
PAYER'S federal identification number	RECIPIENT'S identification number			
RECIPIENT'S name		2c Section 1202 gain $	2d Collectibles (28%) gain $	For Privacy Act and Paperwork Reduction Act Notice, see the **2009 General Instructions for Forms 1099, 1098, 3921, 3922, 5498, and W-2G.**
		3 Nondividend distributions $	4 Federal income tax withheld $	
Street address (including apt. no.)			5 Investment expenses $	
City, state, and ZIP code		6 Foreign tax paid $	7 Foreign country or U.S. possession	
Account number (see instructions)	2nd TIN not. ☐	8 Cash liquidation distributions $	9 Noncash liquidation distributions $	

Form **1099-DIV**   Cat. No. 14415N   Department of the Treasury - Internal Revenue Service

Box 1a. Total ordinary dividends

The amount in this box represents all dividends (both qualified and unqualified) paid by the fund.

Box 1b. Qualified dividends

If your mutual fund owns stock in companies that pay qualified dividends, a portion or all of the total ordinary dividends reported in box 1a may appear in box 1b, depending on how long the fund held its shares. Remember that these figures represent the dividends that qualify for the mutual fund; to determine whether they qualify for you, head to "Meeting the holding-period requirement" earlier in this chapter to check on the holding periods for common and preferred stock.

Box 2a. Total capital gain distribution

Box 2a is guilty of a misnomer. Instead of being called "total capital gain distribution," it should be labeled "total long-term capital gain distribution" because the fund's short-term capital gains are reported as unqualified dividends.

Capital gains inside mutual funds are just like capital gains in individual stocks. If a fund sells a stock for more than it paid for its shares, the profit is a capital gain. If the fund held the sold asset for more than one year, the profit is treated as a long-term capital gain.

Even though you haven't cashed out your fund shares and regardless of whether those long-term capital gains were reinvested or distributed to shareholders, you need to pay taxes on them. During the writing of this book, the tax rate on long-term capital gains was 15 percent.

Don't get stuck paying taxes on gains you never received. Mutual funds may earn capital gains throughout the year, but they distribute their long-term capital gains only at the end of the year. Although this setup may seem like a positive to the guy who buys late in the year, it's not. Any capital gain distribution lowers the mutual fund's net asset value (NAV). If you buy near the end of the year and receive the distribution, but the fund's share price drops, you end up even. However, you may still get stuck paying taxes on these gains that left you cash neutral. Before buying a mutual fund late in the year, check its capital gains distribution date.

Remembering other important dividend taxation considerations

Although the 1099-DIV so considerately does some computing for you (see the preceding section), it doesn't give you everything you need to know. The following sections point out a couple of other numbers to be aware of as well as a situation that may affect your dividends' taxation.

Nonqualified dividends

Nonqualified dividends are all dividends paid to the fund that fail to qualify for the lower tax rates, as I describe in "Identifying qualifying dividends" earlier in this chapter. For these dividends, you pay taxes at your rate for ordinary income. Surprisingly, the 1099-DIV doesn't include a box for this number. You have to figure it out yourself:

Total Ordinary Dividends – Qualified Dividends = Nonqualified Dividends

For example, if the fund reports $280 in total ordinary dividends and $200 in qualified dividends, it earned $80 in nonqualified dividends:

$280 – $200 = $80

Because the fund reports everything that's not a capital gain as a dividend, nonqualified dividends may not actually be dividends. The mutual fund reports income that falls into any or all of the following distribution categories as nonqualified dividends.:

✔ **Nonqualified dividends:** These are dividends from stocks not held long enough to qualify for the lower tax rate. If it's a nonqualified dividend for the fund, it's not qualified for you.

✔ **Taxable interest:** Any interest the fund earned from Treasury bills or other debt in which the fund held cash is taxable interest.

✔ **Short-term capital gains:** Profits on assets held for less than a year are short-term capital gains, paid to fund shareholders as dividends.

Short-term capital gains you receive from the fund refer to how long the fund held the stock in the portfolio, not how long you held the fund shares.

Because short-term capital gain distributions are taxed at the shareholder's maximum tax rate along with nonqualified dividends, treating short-term capital gains as taxable income may seem harmless, but it's not. For instance, if you earn a short-term capital gain in any other (non-mutual fund) investment you sell and suffer any kind of capital loss in a separate investment, you can use the loss to offset the tax liability on the gain. However, because short-term capital gain distributions aren't broken out in mutual funds, you have to pay taxes on them at the full rate no matter what. Even if the fund lists the short-term capital gains on the 1099-DIV, they're still considered ordinary, nonqualified dividends. You can't lower the tax liability with a capital loss.

Reinvested dividends

When mutual funds reinvest dividends, additional tax issues arise:

✔ Even though the fund reinvests the dividends, you must pay taxes on them, just as if you had received a cash distribution.

✔ The new shares have their own cost basis, different from your initial investment. The *cost basis* is the price used to determine capital gains or losses; typically, it's the price paid for an asset, but not always. Keep track of the cost basis of these new shares bought with dividends because when you sell these shares, you use that number to calculate your capital gain or loss on the sale.

✔ The new shares have a new purchase date. Keep track of this date to determine whether any distributions or capital gains related to these shares meet the holding period requirements for lower tax rates.

Checking your holding period for capital gains

Just like a stock, you earn a capital gain if you sell your fund shares for more than you paid. If you sell for less than you paid you get a capital loss. If you held your fund shares for more than a year, you pay the lower long-term capital gains rate. Less than a year, and you pay your ordinary tax rate.

Accounting for January dividends

If the fund receives dividends in the last quarter of the year but distributes the dividend in January, the fund can treat the distribution as if it were paid on December 31 the prior year. It may look like a mistake, but it's not. This situation means these dividends also get taxed as part of the prior year's income. Tax rates again depend on the holding period; I discuss holding period requirements earlier in the chapter.

Gaining a tax break of sorts

Although mutual funds contain some tax "penalties," such as not allowing you to offset short-term capital gains in mutual funds with short-term capital losses in other investments, they do provide a backhanded tax break. Mutual funds lower taxable income by using the portfolio's earnings to pay off the fund's expense ratio. For example, if the fund yields a dividend 3 percent of fund assets but the expense ratio is 1 percent of fund assets, it uses the first 1 percent of income to pay all the management costs, leaving the investor with a net yield of 2 percent.

Although you end up with less cash in your pocket, this strategy lessens your dividend tax liability and keeps the fund from having to sell assets to cover expenses, which would incur additional costs.

Taxing Dividends from ETFs

Like mutual funds, EFTs (exchange traded funds) are investment companies and share many of the same traits. Dividend-related tax issues are similar between the two as well. When investing in dividend-focused ETFs, keep the following tax issues in mind:

- ✔ ETFs must distribute all dividends to their shareholders.
- ✔ ETFs must hold stocks that pay qualified dividends the required 61-day holding period to receive the preferred tax rate.
- ✔ To receive qualified dividends from an ETF, hold the ETF shares in your personal account for the required holding period as well.
- ✔ Interest, short-term capital gains, and nonqualified dividends are taxed as ordinary income.

✔ Most ETFs don't pay long-term capital gains. Some do, but it's very rare. If yours does, go to the ETF company's Web site or give the company a call to see what it says about long-term capital gains.

ETFs can hold many kinds of assets, each with exotic tax structures. If you're investing for dividends, be sure your ETF holds equities. Consult a tax professional for specific advice related to your investments. For more about ETFs, check out Chapter 16.

Looking at MLP and REIT Taxation

Some of the most attractive dividend stocks play by entirely different tax rules than those that apply to the majority of dividends. In the following sections, I describe the unique tax advantages (and some drawbacks) of real estate investment trusts (REITs) and master limited partnerships (MLPs).

For more about MLPs, check out Chapter 10. For more about investing in REITs, see Chapter 13.

REIT taxation

Real estate investment trusts (REITs) are similar to mutual funds. They allow investors to share in profits from a pool of real estate investments without having to actually purchase individual properties. When the real estate market is cruising along, REITs generally perform very well as dividend stocks, delivering yields of between 6 and 9 percent. In addition, the dividends usually keep flowing even when share prices take a dip because to preserve their tax advantages, they must pay out at least 90 percent of their income to shareholders in the form of dividends.

By agreeing to pay out nearly all their income and only invest in certain types or real estate assets, the tax code gives REITs a unique advantage over other dividend-paying corporations. REITs avoid paying any corporate taxes and pass through the tax obligation to their shareholders. At the end of the year, shareholders receive a Form 1099, which reports cash distributions in three forms: dividends, long-term capital gains, and return on capital, which I discuss in the following sections.

Dividends for REITs

Unfortunately for investors, these dividends don't qualify for preferential treatment under JGTRRA. They're taxed as ordinary income. ("Brushing Up on Dividend Taxation," earlier in the chapter gives you more information on how the JGTRRA legislation changed dividend taxation.)

Long-term capital gains for REITs

Capital gains can be included in your dividend payment. If the REIT sold assets at a profit and they qualify as long-term capital gains, you pay the lower tax rate on this portion of the dividends.

Return on capital for REITs

REIT dividends also contain a component called *return on capital* — the portion of a REIT's dividend over and above its taxable income, primarily due to depreciation of assets. In essence, the firm returns some of your investment to you based on the fact that the value of the real estate holdings depreciates over time. Although this move puts some tax-deferred cash in your pocket now, it lowers the cost basis of your shares, increasing the capital gains you must report when you sell your shares:

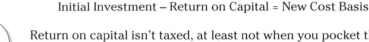

Initial Investment – Return on Capital = New Cost Basis

Return on capital isn't taxed, at least not when you pocket the money. The tax liability is deferred until you sell your shares in the REIT.

Suppose you buy 100 shares of a REIT at $50 a share, for a total of $5,000. The company pays a 9-percent yield of $450. Of that, $150 qualifies as ordinary dividends, and $300 is a return of capital. Even though you paid $5,000 for your shares, the IRS now lists your cost basis as $4,700:

$5,000 – $300 = $4,700

A year later you sell the shares for $60 each, or $6,000 for a profit of $1,000 (not counting the $300 you received in return on capital):

$6,000 – $1,000 = $5,000

With the long-term capital gains rate of 15 percent, you may expect to pay $150 in taxes:

$1,000 × 0.15 = $150

However, the return on capital lowered your cost basis to $4,700, so you have to report capital gains of $1,300:

$6,000 – $4,700 = $1,300

You tax bill rises to $195 rather than the $150 on your original cost basis:

$1,300 × 0.15 = $195

The one shining light here is that you pay the 15-percent tax rate rather than the higher rate for ordinary dividends.

REITs may require you to pay a bigger chunk of the tax bill, but don't let that scare you off. The important number to look at is your return *after taxes.* You may walk away with more money in your pocket by investing in a REIT with a 7-percent yield, even after paying taxes, than you would by investing in a non-REIT with a 2- or 3-percent yield.

MLP taxation

Master Limited Partnerships (MLPs), discussed in Chapter 10, dodge the double-taxation bullet because they aren't corporations. They're true partnerships in which every investor is a partner. Investors aren't even called shareholders (they're *unitholders*), and partnerships don't pay taxes. The profits and expenses are divided proportionally among the partners. Profits pass tax-free through the partnership to the unitholders, who must report their profits on their individual tax returns. Unfortunately for investors, this arrangement can severely complicate tax calculations and significantly add to the paperwork.

Before investing in an MLP, consult a tax specialist and get answers to the following questions (I discuss these issues in more detail later in this section):

- ✔ In how many different states does the MLP do business?
- ✔ How many units can I purchase in a specific MLP before I have to file a tax return in each state in which the partnership does business?

Unlike REITs and mutual funds, MLPs don't have to pay a cash distribution to investors. You can owe tax on MLP earnings without actually receiving any cash. However, most MLPs have internal governing agreements that require them to pay out all their available cash flow.

Rather than a 1099-DIV, the MLP issues a Schedule K-1 with your cash distributions broken out into various sources of income, each of which may be taxed at a different rate, as explained in the following sections.

Dividends for MLPs

Like the REIT, the MLP's taxable income in the form of dividends is taxed at your ordinary income tax rate. It isn't eligible for the preferred lower tax rate. Flip to "Brushing Up on Dividend Taxation" earlier in the chapter for more on the varying tax rates for investment income.

Long-term capital gains for MLPs

Capital gains can be included in your dividend payment and are taxed at the preferred rate.

State taxes

You also have to pay taxes to each state the MLP does business in, which can be a paperwork nightmare. Your tax adviser can help you figure out which forms you need to fill out for whom.

The reason investors agree to deal with the tax headache is because MLPs pay a much higher yield than most dividend stocks. For most people, the extra income is worth the aggravation.

Return on capital for MLPs

All cash distributions that don't fall under taxable income are considered a return on capital. This recapture of depreciation isn't taxed now, but it lowers the taxable cost basis of your shares. (See "Return on capital for REITs" earlier in the chapter to get a handle on this calculation.) When you sell your shares later, only the part that represents a true capital gain from your initial cost basis is eligible for the lower capital gains tax rate. All the return on capital that lowered your tax basis is taxed at the rate of your ordinary income.

The taxable cost basis continues to fall as long as you hold the MLP, so, the longer you hold the shares, the more tax you pay when you sell.

Most tax computer programs tell you where to input the numbers. However, with MLPs, you're usually better off hiring a tax professional.

Tax-deferred accounts

MLPs pass the entire tax burden to investors. In an attempt to avoid this burden, you may consider putting your MLP in a tax-deferred account, but it doesn't do you much good. The IRS wants its cut, so it has set a $1,000 limit for taxable income from partnerships held in tax-deferred accounts. If you go over, the account gets hit with a big tax bill. That's right. The tax-deferred account has to pay a significant amount of taxes. Sorta defeats the purpose.

Don't put MLPs into tax-deferred accounts.

Remaining Vigilant of Possible Tax Code Changes

The government is constantly fiddling with the tax code in an attempt to collect taxes without choking the life out of the economy. As a result, those tax incentives can go poof any time Congress decides to pull the plug or simply fails to renew the incentives before they expire. Some changes in the way returns are taxed can even tip the scales when you're trying to decide which investment is a better deal. Start taxing dividends as ordinary income, for example, and the number of companies paying dividends and the number of investors buying dividend stocks soon slump.

As the government fiddles with the tax code, be prepared to adjust your strategy accordingly. Crunch the numbers to determine your real (after-tax) return on a particular investment and see whether you can improve your real return by moving you money to a different investment type.

Calculating your after-tax return

Here's a formula for calculating the after-tax return on an investment:

> After-Tax Return = Percent Return × (1.00 – Percent Tax)

For example, if a particular investment earns you a 7.5 percent return and is taxed at 20 percent:

> .075 × (1.00 – .20) = .06 or 6 percent

Suppose you own a dividend stock that's generating a total return of about 7 percent. Approximately 4 percent of that is from capital gains, and the other 3 percent is from dividends. Further, suppose you're paying 15-percent tax on both capital gains and dividends:

> .07 × (1.00 – .15) = .0595 or 5.95 percent

Now, imagine you can purchase a bond that earns a 9-percent return but that's taxed as ordinary income at 35 percent:

> .09 × (1.00 – .35) = .0585 or 5.85 percent

The two returns after taxes are pretty much a tossup. You may favor the bond because it's the same return with less risk, or you may favor the dividend stock because it has the potential of share price appreciation and dividend growth.

Now suppose the tax benefits of the JGTRRA (discussed earlier in the chapter) expire and you have the misfortune of having your income place you in the top income tax bracket. The after-tax return on your dividend stock suddenly looks a little less comparable. Your capital gains are now subject to a 20-percent tax, and your dividends are taxed as ordinary income at a rate of 38.6 percent:

$$.04 \times (1.00 - .20) = .032 \text{ or } 3.2 \text{ percent}$$

$$.03 \times (1.00 - .386) = .01842 \text{ or } 1.842 \text{ percent}$$

Adding those two figures together, your after-tax return is now slightly more than 5 percent, causing you to lean a little closer to investing in bonds.

Bankrate.com has an ROI (return on investment) calculator that takes into account taxes and inflation. Go to www.bankrate.com, click Calculators, scroll down to Retirement Calculators and click View more retirement calculators, and click Return on investment calculator. The ROI calculator appears, and you can enter the number of years you plan to have the money invested, rate of return, initial investment, annual additional investments, inflation rate, and tax rate.

Staying tuned in to tax news

Short of rubbing elbows with senators and members of Congress, you can never really count on the government keeping you in the loop on upcoming or pending changes to the tax code. You can add yourself to the IRS mailing list to receive timely updates, but you'll probably end up with a lot more junk mail than you know what to do with.

A better solution is to head to Chapter 7 and subscribe to one or more of the financial publications I recommend or regularly visit one of the Web sites I highlight in that chapter. Chances are pretty good that if the government is considering any tax changes that may affect investors, it'll stir up plenty of buzz in the media.

Part VI
The Part of Tens

"Choosing the right dividend stock is like choosing the right hat. You find one that fits you best and then you stick with it."

In this part . . .

The Part of Tens is full of easily digestible tips, tricks, and insights designed to improve your success and enhance your life (or at least keep you mildly entertained). In this part, I cover the ten most common myths and misconceptions about dividends and ten common dividend investing mistakes (plus info on how to avoid them). And check out the appendix, which offers a list of Dividend Achievers.

Chapter 21

Setting the Record Straight: Ten Common Misconceptions about Dividends

Stock market investors and analysts often take sides on the issue of investing in dividend stocks. On one side are the cheerleaders who believe dividend stocks are the next best thing to free money. On the other are the naysayers who believe that dividend stocks are the next worst thing to a government takeover.

As is usually the case when people start taking sides, their radical beliefs are based on myths or misconceptions implanted in them by misinformation or someone else's misdirected advice. Truth tends to lie somewhere in between, and only by stripping away some of the most common and influential myths is the truth revealed. In this chapter, I bust the ten most common myths and misconceptions about investing in dividend stocks to provide you with a more balanced view.

Dividend Investing Is Only for Old, Retired Folks

Dividend investing is admittedly attractive for seniors, whose goals are typically capital preservation and income. Younger investors, however, can also benefit from a dividend investing model, even if it comprises only a portion of their portfolios.

Although seniors may want to stick with large, well-established corporations, younger investors may want to aim more toward the middle to lower end of the dividend spectrum. Younger investors wanting growth stocks should buy up-and-coming companies that are established enough to pay small dividends but demonstrate that they still have plenty of growth potential (in both capital appreciation and dividend payments).

Dividend investing isn't a get-rich-quick strategy. It's a great way to build wealth over the long term (which means you want to start when you're young) to secure a steady cash flow for your retirement years. All affluent older investors were young once, and many of them followed a relatively conservative dividend investment strategy even then to build their wealth.

I Can Get Better Returns with Growth Stocks

Although growth stocks may offer more in terms of share price appreciation, dividend stocks often make up the difference in dividend payments. Dividend stocks can see returns grow in three ways:

- Share prices can rise.
- Dividend payments can increase.
- Reinvested dividends can purchase more stock. More shares pay out more dollars in dividends, which you can then reinvest again, and increase the profits from capital appreciation.

When comparing growth and dividend stocks, compare their potential in terms of *total* return on investment. For the dividend stock, this means share price appreciation *plus* dividends.

Sometimes, slow and steady really does win the race. Growth stocks may carry a higher potential for bigger returns, but they also carry a higher risk for bigger losses. If you do experience a loss, your other holdings need to perform that much better to make up the difference.

Dividend Stocks Are Safe Investments

Investing is risky no matter how you slice it; the risk of losing money is always present. However, some investments, including dividend stocks, tend to be safer than others. I say "tend to be" because even traditionally safer investment vehicles can take a hit. In 2009, for example, financials and real estate, which had paid reliable dividends for some time, went into a tailspin.

Don't put all your investment eggs in one basket. Even when investing in safer options, diversify to spread the risk among several sectors and among companies in the various industries you choose to invest in.

Companies Limit Their Growth by Paying Dividends

Growth investors often argue that companies paying dividends would be better off reinvesting that money to fuel their growth. Although this suggestion may be the case with some companies in certain situations, the reasoning is only valid if that money is well spent.

Companies that don't pay dividends give managers unrestricted use of the profits. Corporate executives often make acquisitions or start projects more to boost their personal worth (through bonuses and reputation) than to boost shareholder value. Risky acquisitions outside the company's main business often promise big results and just as often turn into money pits. Meanwhile, a commitment to paying dividends keeps management honest. Knowing the company must generate a certain amount of cash flow per quarter to pay the dividends shareholders expect tends to motivate management to manage effectively. In addition, paying dividends leaves management with less capital to squander on risky business ventures. As a result, management must evaluate prospective business ventures more carefully.

Some of the largest companies in the world pay dividends, and they didn't start out big. They began from scratch and grew; many continue to post significant growth despite paying dividends.

Companies Should Always Pay Down Debt before Cutting Dividend Checks

Debt isn't necessarily a bad thing, although excessive debt certainly is. Whether a company should pay down debt before cutting dividend checks depends on the circumstances. If the company is buried in debt and struggling in a tough economy, paying down debt before paying dividends is not only a good idea but also an essential move to protect the company's survival. If, on the other hand, the company carries a reasonable debt load and its other fundamentals are solid, continuing or even raising dividend payments sends a positive message to the market.

Before purchasing a dividend stock, carefully inspect the company's quarterly reports and take a close look at the quick ratio, which I explain in Chapter 8. The *quick ratio* indicates whether the company's current assets are sufficient to cover its liabilities. The break-even point is a quick ratio of one, which usually means the company can afford to cover its liabilities, including its declared dividend payout. Anything less than one may mean that the company needs to borrow money to pay dividends, which is a bad sign.

Companies Must Maintain a Stable Dividend Payout

Companies are not obligated to pay dividends or to keep the payment stable after they start. However, dividend cuts tend to reflect poorly on a company and its share price, so companies tend to be conservative in establishing a dividend policy. Companies protect themselves by choosing a dividend payment method that allows them to manage shareholder expectations:

- **Residual:** With the *residual approach,* the company funds any new projects out of equity it generates internally and pays dividends only after meeting the capital requirements of these projects. In other words, investors receive a cut of the profits only if money is left over at the end of the quarter. Knowing this, investors are less likely to sell their shares if they don't receive a dividend payment for a particular quarter because they know next quarter may still bring a dividend.

- **Stability:** A *stability approach* sets the dividend at a fixed number, typically a fraction of quarterly or annual earnings, called a payout ratio. This gives investors a greater level of certainty that they'll receive a dividend and how much it's likely to be. Companies that implement a stable dividend payment approach tend to make conservative projections so that they don't disappoint shareholders.

- **Hybrid:** The *hybrid approach* is a combination of the residual and stability approaches. Companies that follow this approach tend to set a low, fixed dividend that they feel is easy to sustain and then distribute additional dividends when they can afford to do so.

My Dividend Increases Won't Even Keep Up with Inflation

Some companies' dividend increases do in fact fail to keep pace with inflation. Your goal as a dividend investor is to ensure that the dividend payments from companies you invest in at least keep up with inflation and hopefully exceed the inflation rate. If you're a growth investor looking for income, don't dump a stock just because dividend payments aren't keeping pace with inflation. Look at the stock's total return, including share price appreciation, and continue to monitor the company's fundamentals and the market at large. If the company is doing well, especially in a tough market, it may have the potential to raise dividend payments sometime in the future and perform well for you

All Dividends Are Taxed at the Same Rate

As I discuss in Chapter 3, dividend investing fell out of favor in the 20th century because of unfavorable dividend taxation. A major reason for the resurgence of dividend investing was the lowering of the tax rate on dividends (15 percent or less during the writing of this book). The catch is that not all stocks qualify for the lower tax rate. To qualify, you have to hold the stock in your portfolio for at least 61 consecutive days during the 121-day period that begins 60 days before the ex-dividend date. Dividends that fail to qualify get taxed at the investor's regular tax rate. (One exception is master limited partnerships, which pass all their tax liabilities back to investors; check out Chapter 10 for more info.) For a full explanation about the tax issues regarding dividend stocks, visit Chapter 20.

The day on which you buy the stock doesn't count toward the 60-day holding requirement. Flip to Chapter 2 for more on important stock-purchasing dates.

You Should Always Invest in High-Yield Stocks

Don't judge a stock by yield alone. Yield is a valuable measure of how much bang you're getting for each of your investment bucks, but it alone doesn't determine a stock's true value; you also need to look at the share price, as I discuss in Chapter 8. You can use a minimum yield to screen out stocks that don't meet your income requirements, but carefully evaluate a company's fundamentals before investing in it.

A high yield can mean many things — some positive, some negative. High yield may be a sign that the company's share price is sinking and that the company may be in trouble. If the high yield is out of whack with its sector, that may be a sign of an impending dividend cut. By the same token, don't immediately write off low-yield stocks. Chapter 6 gives you some questions to ask about a down stock before you make any decisions.

REITs and Bank Stocks Are No Longer Good for Dividends

Two major factors that contributed to the fiscal crisis of 2008–2009 were a housing bubble that pushed the prices of real estate properties to astronomical heights and banks that approved mortgage loans for borrowers who couldn't afford the payments. Not surprisingly, real estate investment trusts (REITS) and bank stocks, traditionally big dividend payers, were some of the hardest hit in the stock market crash of 2008–2009. With little cash to pay their obligations, many REITs and banks were forced to cut or eliminate their dividends. However, a few strong companies continue to pay out dividends and even raise payments because they took less risk and managed their debt well. As many investors write off all these companies in one fell swoop, now is the time to look for bargains among the healthy survivors.

Chapter 22

Ten Dividend Investing Mistakes and How to Avoid Them

In This Chapter

▶ Sidestepping buying pitfalls

▶ Relying on your own due diligence

▶ Managing your portfolio

*I*n the world of investing, you can never completely eliminate risk, but you can reduce it by making more good decisions and fewer bad ones. In this chapter, I highlight some of the most common and serious dividend investing mistakes you can possibly make so that you can avoid them and improve your odds.

Buying a Stock Solely on a Hot Tip

Your uncle's neighbor's friend's wife works for a tech company that's about to score a huge government contract. The stock's been flatlining for the past two years, but after news breaks about this development, share prices will skyrocket. Anyone with the cash and foresight to invest in it now will be retiring on their own private islands by the end of the year, but those who pass up the chance will be kicking themselves well into the following year. You gotta buy, right?

Not so fast.

A hot tip is just that — a tip, an idea to follow up on. You still need to do your research — pull up the company's quarterly statements over the past year or so, crunch the numbers, see whether any insiders are buying shares, and perhaps even speak with one of the company's representatives (or at least your broker) to check on the company's prospects moving forward.

Don't rely solely on the word of a friend, relative, colleague, or even broker to choose which stocks to buy. Verify anything you hear with the kind of thorough personal research I describe in Chapter 8.

Skipping Your Homework

Fear and greed often prevail on Wall Street, primarily because people tend to invest with their hearts rather than with their heads. They chase hot stocks when they should be avoiding them and then dump everything — good stocks and bad — when the sell-off starts. Those who win the day are the investors who do their homework and keep a cool head when everyone else is losing theirs.

The best way to keep a cool head is to know what you own, what you're buying, what you're selling, and why. If you know you own well-managed companies that have a solid track record for growing sales, profits, and dividend payments, you're less likely to get spooked when the market takes a dive. You can look for deals instead of looking for the exits.

Expecting to Buy and Sell Shares Just for the Dividend

Wouldn't it be great if you could buy a stock the day before the company is due to pay dividends, collect your dividend payment, and then sell the stock? On the surface, this strategy seems like a good way to beat the market, especially if the company has announced a big one-time dividend payout. Unfortunately, this clever trick doesn't work.

Sure, you may be able to collect the dividend payment, but when you try to sell the stock the next day, you'll be sorely disappointed. Share prices are reduced to reflect that dividend payout, and if you sell immediately after the dividend payment date, you pretty much break even. (Check out Chapter 2 for more on important dates related to dividends.)

Focusing Solely on Yield

When people start investing in dividend stocks, they automatically gravitate to the high-yield stocks. But depending on the industry, a high-yield stock can just as often be a sign of trouble as a sign of big profits. Don't let yield blind you to a company's growth prospects. Often, a company with a lower-than-average dividend that's experiencing solid growth and consistently increasing its dividend may be a better choice than a company with a larger yield that's currently in stagnation mode.

If you own a $10 stock paying a 2.5-percent yield, you receive 25 cents a year. If the share price and dividend payout both increase 10 percent each year, after ten years the stock would be worth $23.57, and the dividend payout would be 59 cents a year. Compared to current share price of $23.57, the yield remains 2.5 percent. But based on your original cost of $10 a share, the yield has more than doubled to 5.9 percent. Every time the dividend payout grows, not only does the yield on your initial investment grow, but your investment continues to beat inflation.

Don't buy a stock simply because it has a high yield. Find out whether the yield is high because of high dividend payments, low share price, or both. Examine the company's fundamentals as well as the broad market and economic environment. Perform additional research to ensure that the company is sound before you invest in it.

Focusing on Current Rather than Future Dividends

When you look up a stock's dividend, you're looking at its current dividend, which is like looking at yesterday's news. It's relevant, because that's what you get paid this year. But as an investor, you're less interested in what the dividend's paying now and more interested in its potential to grow in the future. Unfortunately, nobody has a crystal ball to reveal how much a company will pay in dividends in the future, but you can make an educated prediction by examining the following:

✔ The company's recent and long-term trend in raising dividends

✔ Management's income projections

✔ Any significant developments that may alter the company's past trend of free cash flow

You may be better off buying shares in a company that pays a lower dividend if the company shows a lot of potential for raising its dividend moving forward, rather than a high dividend that remains static.

Failing to Monitor Stocks and the Market

Assuming you purchase stock in large, well-managed companies with a solid track record of paying dividends, you can sleep a little more soundly than most growth investors or Wall Street speculators. However, you shouldn't fall asleep at the wheel. Even big companies can fail — just look at Bear Stearns, Lehman Brothers, and Chrysler.

Always keep tabs on your money, the stocks you've purchased, and the news. If you're open to hearing bad news, you can usually pick up on the warning signs before a massive sell-off. When you start hearing people in the know talking about impending bubbles, that's usually a good sign that you need to perk up your ears and make exit plans. Focus your plans not only on reducing risk but also on taking advantage of new opportunities.

For example, the market gave plenty of signs that trouble was afoot. The mortgage meltdown in the real estate industry started about a year before the 2008–2009 stock market crash and the failure of many financial institutions. Investors who closely monitored the market and recognized the red flags got out while the gettin' out was good. Those who assumed that these large institutions couldn't possibly go belly-up lost their shirts.

Buying a Stock Just Because It's Cheap

Knowing the difference between a low share price and a good value is the difference between making and losing money; just because a stock is cheap doesn't mean it's a bargain. Admittedly, buying a cheap stock is tempting. If shares are selling for 50 cents, you can scoop up 200 shares for a hundred bucks. In addition, you can more easily imagine 50-cent shares doubling in price than you can imagine shares selling for $100 a pop doubling in price. However, buying a stock just because it's cheap isn't investing — it's speculating or betting. Those 50-cent shares can just as easily lose half or all of their value, which is usually what happens.

To steer clear of this trap, carefully research a cheap stock's company fundamentals. Unlike large and higher-priced stocks, you usually find very little other information about these low-priced companies. In Chapter 8, I explain how you can determine a stock's intrinsic value and get a clearer idea of what you're buying and the company's prospects. Fortunately, companies that have a history of paying dividends are rarely cheap, but when they are, that's a screaming buy. As long as you stick with the dividend investing model, you should be free of any temptation to buy a stock solely because it has a low share price.

Holding a Poor-Performing Stock for Too Long

Letting go is tough, especially if you own stock in a company that's performed well for you in the past or even one that experiences only short-lived highs. Waiting to sell until you get even is a loser's strategy. You don't keep fishing at a once-fertile fishing hole after the fish leave. You move on to a new spot. On Wall Street, emotional attachments can be brutal, and hope can be your true enemy. If a company has experienced a serious setback and is losing market share, don't let your emotions get in the way. Cut your losses, dump your shares, and find another place to invest your money.

How do you know when to get out? Here are a few guidelines:

- ✔ **If the company eliminates the dividend, get out immediately.** The company is in crisis mode.

- ✔ **If the company cuts the dividend, take a close look to get an idea of the company's growth prospects in light of this cut.** Selling this stock is a judgment call. A dividend cut shows the company needs to conserve cash, typically to manage its debt. This move typically shows that management hasn't been on top of finances and risk management. If the cut comes because of broader economic conditions, you have to determine whether you believe this management team can steer the company through dangerous waters. If the cut is because of the company's internal problems, sell immediately.

- ✔ **If the company's share price drops more than 10 percent but the company maintains the dividend, do a little more investigation.** This situation is another judgment call. First, look at the rest of the market. Is the price down because of a sharp decline in the sector or broad market? Is this company part of the sector causing all the trouble?

  For instance, if in early 2009 you held bank or real estate stocks that hadn't cut their dividends, you may have expected them to soon follow their peers with a dividend cut. In that case, sell. If the yield is way out of whack with the rest of the sector (off by, say, 4 percentage points), that may be another warning sign to get out. On the other hand, if during a market downturn your stock is part of a stronger, more defensive industry that continues to do business and should rally with the economy, hold on for the ride and consider buying more.

- ✔ **If the share price drops and the company boosts the dividend payout, buy more shares.**

Failing to Account for Taxes

Too many investors focus on the amount they stand to gain and don't stop to think about how big a bite taxes can take out of that figure. Financial success isn't necessarily based on how much money you earn — how much money you keep is what matters.

Regardless of where you put your money — stocks, bonds, real estate, CDs, money market funds, and so on — always consider the tax ramifications of your investment decisions. Investors pay only 15 percent taxes on dividends and long-term capital gains (as opposed to paying their regular tax rate, which could be as high as 35 percent at publication, on short-term gains and interest). If you earn $200,000 and lose 35 percent in taxes, you walk away with $130,000. Pay only 15 percent in taxes, and you keep $170,000, or about 31 percent more. If you need to, talk to an accountant to develop a strategy that maximizes your after-tax returns. If the government decides to raise taxes on dividends to 30 percent, be prepared to adjust your strategy to take advantage of other investments with lower tax rates (if available, of course). Chapter 20 delves further into tax considerations.

Giving Too Much Credence to Media Reports and Analysis

Financial newspapers and magazines, Web sites, and investment TV and radio shows are all excellent sources of information, but they're not always right. That's because they rely on information from company insiders. If investors learned anything from the meltdown in the financial sector in 2008, it's that people lie and management isn't always forthcoming about what's going on in a company. Here a few points to remember about media sources:

- Monthly magazine articles on investing are written about two months before publication. Conditions may radically change in an industry, the economy, or the market to make this information out of date before it even hits the newsstand.

- Television financial personalities are entertainers first and analysts or commentators second. Television commentators tend to be big cheerleaders for the stock market, even in the face of all evidence to the contrary, because that's what keeps viewers.

- Web sites and blogs may have a personal agenda to promote and may not follow strict journalistic standards for accuracy.

Don't assume any single source is 100 percent reliable. A company's financial documents are always the best source. Financial newspapers and their Web sites come second. But newspapers can make mistakes, too. Always verify the information by comparing it to other sources and your own instincts and insight.

Appendix

The Dividend Aristocrats

*T*hroughout this book, I recommend that you build a stock portfolio of well-managed companies with solid fundamentals, strong profit growth, and a history of consistently raising dividend payments. Standard & Poor's has created just such a list. Called the *S&P 500 Dividend Aristocrats Index,* it measures the market performance of S&P 500 constituents that who have followed a policy of consistently increasing dividends every year for at least 25 years.

It's a pretty select group of companies, and a great place to start looking. In normal times, these are among the most stable companies in the United States. Yet even aristocrats can sometimes run into trouble, so be sure to check the S&P 500 Market Attributes for the latest list (it's updated every December). Go to www.standardandpoors.com/indices/market-attributes/en/us and click to expand Latest S&P 500 Market Attributes, where you find a link to a Microsoft Excel spreadsheet of the current Dividend Aristocrats.

Table A-1 includes the most consistent dividend producers in America as of December 2009 — the Dividend Aristocrats.

Another, longer list to be aware of is the Dividend Achievers list, which I discuss in Chapter 18. It also focuses on companies with a proven track record of increasing their dividend payments. However, to join the Achievers list, a company must increase its dividends only ten years in a row.

Table A-1	Dividend Aristocrats as of December 2009			
Name	*Ticker Symbol*	*Sector*	*Annual Dividend*	*Yield as of 12/31/09*
3M Co.	MMM	Industrials	$2.04	2.5%
Abbott Laboratories	ABT	Healthcare	$1.60	3.0%
AFLAC Inc.	AFL	Financials	$1.12	2.4%

(continued)

Table A-1 *(continued)*

Name	Ticker Symbol	Sector	Annual Dividend	Yield as of 12/31/09
Air Products & Chemicals Inc.	APD	Materials	$1.80	2.2%
Archer Daniels Midland Co.	ADM	Consumer Staples	$0.56	1.8%
Automatic Data Processing, Inc.	ADP	Information Technology	$1.36	3.2%
Bard (C.R.) Inc.	BCR	Healthcare	$0.68	0.9%
Becton, Dickinson and Co.	BDX	Healthcare	$1.48	1.9%
Bemis Co. Inc.	BMS	Materials	$0.90	3.0%
Brown-Forman 'B' Corp.	BF.B	Consumer Staples	$1.20	2.2%
CenturyTel, Inc.	CTL	Telecommunication Services	$2.80	7.7%
The Chubb Corp	CB	Financials	$1.40	2.8%
Cincinnati Financial Corp.	CINF	Financials	$1.58	6.0%
Cintas Corp.	CTAS	Industrials	$0.47	1.8%
Clorox Co.	CLX	Consumer Staples	$2.00	3.3%
The Coca-Cola Co.	KO	Consumer Staples	$1.64	2.9%
Consolidated Edison Inc.	ED	Utilities	$2.36	5.2%
Dover Corp.	DOV	Industrials	$1.04	2.5%
Emerson Electric Co.	EMR	Industrials	$1.34	3.1%

Name	Ticker Symbol	Sector	Annual Dividend	Yield as of 12/31/09
Exxon Mobil Corp.	XOM	Energy	$1.68	2.5%
Family Dollar Stores Inc.	FDO	Consumer Discretionary	$0.54	1.9%
Grainger (W.W.), Inc.	GWW	Industrials	$1.84	1.9%
Integrys Energy Group, Inc.	TEG	Utilities	$2.72	6.5%
Johnson & Johnson	JNJ	Healthcare	$1.96	3.0%
Kimberly-Clark Corp.	KMB	Consumer Staples	$2.40	3.8%
Leggett & Platt, Inc.	LEG	Consumer Discretionary	$1.04	5.1%
Lilly (Eli) & Co.	LLY	Healthcare	$1.96	5.5%
Lowe's Cos, Inc.	LOW	Consumer Discretionary	$0.36	1.5%
McDonald's Corp.	MCD	Consumer Discretionary	$2.20	3.5%
The McGraw-Hill Companies, Inc.	MHP	Consumer Discretionary	$0.90	2.7%
PepsiCo, Inc.	PEP	Consumer Staples	$1.80	3.0%
Pitney Bowes Inc.	PBI	Industrials	$1.44	6.3%
PPG Industries Inc.	PPG	Materials	$2.16	3.7%
Procter & Gamble Co.	PG	Consumer Staples	$1.76	2.9%
Questar Corp.	STR	Utilities	$0.52	1.3%
Sherwin-Williams Co.	SHW	Consumer Discretionary	$1.42	2.3%

(continued)

Table A-1 *(continued)*

Name	Ticker Symbol	Sector	Annual Dividend	Yield as of 12/31/09
Sigma-Aldrich Corp.	SIAL	Materials	$0.58	1.1%
The Stanley Works	SWK	Consumer Discretionary	$1.32	2.6%
SUPERVALU Inc.	SVU	Consumer Staples	$0.35	2.8%
Target Corp.	TGT	Consumer Discretionary	$0.68	1.4%
VF Corp	VFC	Consumer Discretionary	$2.40	3.3%
Walgreen Co.	WAG	Consumer Staples	$0.55	1.5%
Wal-Mart Stores Inc.	WMT	Consumer Staples	$1.09	2.0%
S&P 500 Index		Index		2.0%

Index

• C •

• F •

• Q •

• R •

Business/Accounting & Bookkeeping

Bookkeeping For Dummies
978-0-7645-9848-7

eBay Business
All-in-One For Dummies,
2nd Edition
978-0-470-38536-4

Job Interviews
For Dummies,
3rd Edition
978-0-470-17748-8

Resumes For Dummies,
5th Edition
978-0-470-08037-5

Stock Investing
For Dummies,
3rd Edition
978-0-470-40114-9

Successful Time
Management
For Dummies
978-0-470-29034-7

Computer Hardware

BlackBerry For Dummies,
3rd Edition
978-0-470-45762-7

Computers For Seniors
For Dummies
978-0-470-24055-7

iPhone For Dummies,
2nd Edition
978-0-470-42342-4

Laptops For Dummies,
3rd Edition
978-0-470-27759-1

Macs For Dummies,
10th Edition
978-0-470-27817-8

Cooking & Entertaining

Cooking Basics
For Dummies,
3rd Edition
978-0-7645-7206-7

Wine For Dummies,
4th Edition
978-0-470-04579-4

Diet & Nutrition

Dieting For Dummies,
2nd Edition
978-0-7645-4149-0

Nutrition For Dummies,
4th Edition
978-0-471-79868-2

Weight Training
For Dummies,
3rd Edition
978-0-471-76845-6

Digital Photography

Digital Photography
For Dummies,
6th Edition
978-0-470-25074-7

Photoshop Elements 7
For Dummies
978-0-470-39700-8

Gardening

Gardening Basics
For Dummies
978-0-470-03749-2

Organic Gardening
For Dummies,
2nd Edition
978-0-470-43067-5

Green/Sustainable

Green Building
& Remodeling
For Dummies
978-0-470-17559-0

Green Cleaning
For Dummies
978-0-470-39106-8

Green IT For Dummies
978-0-470-38688-0

Health

Diabetes For Dummies,
3rd Edition
978-0-470-27086-8

Food Allergies
For Dummies
978-0-470-09584-3

Living Gluten-Free
For Dummies
978-0-471-77383-2

Hobbies/General

Chess For Dummies,
2nd Edition
978-0-7645-8404-6

Drawing For Dummies
978-0-7645-5476-6

Knitting For Dummies,
2nd Edition
978-0-470-28747-7

Organizing For Dummies
978-0-7645-5300-4

SuDoku For Dummies
978-0-470-01892-7

Home Improvement

Energy Efficient Homes
For Dummies
978-0-470-37602-7

Home Theater
For Dummies,
3rd Edition
978-0-470-41189-6

Living the Country Lifestyle
All-in-One For Dummies
978-0-470-43061-3

Solar Power Your Home
For Dummies
978-0-470-17569-9

Internet

Blogging For Dummies,
2nd Edition
978-0-470-23017-6

eBay For Dummies,
6th Edition
978-0-470-49741-8

Facebook For Dummies
978-0-470-26273-3

Google Blogger
For Dummies
978-0-470-40742-4

Web Marketing
For Dummies,
2nd Edition
978-0-470-37181-7

WordPress For Dummies,
2nd Edition
978-0-470-40296-2

Language & Foreign Language

French For Dummies
978-0-7645-5193-2

Italian Phrases
For Dummies
978-0-7645-7203-6

Spanish For Dummies
978-0-7645-5194-9

Spanish For Dummies,
Audio Set
978-0-470-09585-0

Macintosh

Mac OS X Snow Leopard
For Dummies
978-0-470-43543-4

Math & Science

Algebra I For Dummies,
2nd Edition
978-0-470-55964-2

Biology For Dummies
978-0-7645-5326-4

Calculus For Dummies
978-0-7645-2498-1

Chemistry For Dummies
978-0-7645-5430-8

Microsoft Office

Excel 2007 For Dummies
978-0-470-03737-9

Office 2007 All-in-One
Desk Reference
For Dummies
978-0-471-78279-7

Music

Guitar For Dummies,
2nd Edition
978-0-7645-9904-0

iPod & iTunes
For Dummies,
6th Edition
978-0-470-39062-7

Piano Exercises
For Dummies
978-0-470-38765-8

Parenting & Education

Parenting For Dummies,
2nd Edition
978-0-7645-5418-6

Type 1 Diabetes
For Dummies
978-0-470-17811-9

Pets

Cats For Dummies,
2nd Edition
978-0-7645-5275-5

Dog Training For Dummies,
2nd Edition
978-0-7645-8418-3

Puppies For Dummies,
2nd Edition
978-0-470-03717-1

Religion & Inspiration

The Bible For Dummies
978-0-7645-5296-0

Catholicism For Dummies
978-0-7645-5391-2

Women in the Bible
For Dummies
978-0-7645-8475-6

Self-Help & Relationship

Anger Management
For Dummies
978-0-470-03715-7

Overcoming Anxiety
For Dummies
978-0-7645-5447-6

Sports

Baseball For Dummies,
3rd Edition
978-0-7645-7537-2

Basketball For Dummies,
2nd Edition
978-0-7645-5248-9

Golf For Dummies,
3rd Edition
978-0-471-76871-5

Web Development

Web Design All-in-One
For Dummies
978-0-470-41796-6

Windows Vista

Windows Vista
For Dummies
978-0-471-75421-3